Franco-British relations and Europe, from EEC membership to Brexit

Georges Pompidou – Études

Edited by Christine Manigand

Vol. 15

Olivier Sibre (ed.)

Franco-British relations and Europe, from EEC membership to Brexit

Georges Pompidou and Edward Heath

PETER LANG
Bruxelles · Berlin · Chennai · Lausanne · New York · Oxford

Bibliographic Information published by the Deutsche Nationalbibliothek
The Deutsche Nationalbibliothek lists this publication in the Deutsche Nationalbibliografie; detailed bibliographic data is available online at http://dnb.d-nb.de.

Library of Congress Control Number: 2025921398

Cover image: Bridgeman Images – Georges Pompidou and Edward Heath at Northolt Airport, March 20, 1972.

ISSN 1782-4931
ISBN 978-3-0343-6240-5 (Print)
ISBN 978-3-0343-6241-2 (ePDF)
ISBN 978-3-0343-6242-9 (ePUB)
DOI 10.3726/ b23411
Dépôt legal D/2025/5678/51

Published by P.I.E. PETER LANG s.a., Bruxelles (Belgium)

info@peterlang.com

This publication has been peer reviewed.

www.peterlang.com

Contact for General Product Safety Regulation (GPSR): gpsr@peterlang.com

Il y a une nation britannique, il y a une nation française, il y a une nation allemande, il y a une nation italienne, etc. Et, par conséquent, je ne crois pas qu'un pouvoir purement technocratique et administratif puisse s'imposer aux différents États et aux différentes nations, ou il ne pourrait le faire que s'il représentait une domination extérieure à l'Europe, ce que je ne veux pas non plus. Alors, que reste-t-il ? Il reste ce que j'ai appelé une confédération, qu'on peut appeler comme on veut, cela m'est égal, qui consiste à mettre ensemble un certain nombre d'États et à faire que les gouvernements de ces États s'entendent pour organiser entre eux un système de décision valable pour eux tous. Au fond, le Conseil des Ministres de la Communauté est déjà un embryon de gouvernement confédéral. Eh bien, c'est dans ce sens qu'il faut progresser et je serais bien étonné que le gouvernement britannique ne soit pas, sur ce point, de mon avis, car je n'imagine pas la nation britannique telle que je la connais et telle que je l'admire d'ailleurs, vouloir renoncer brusquement à sa personnalité nationale. Pour toutes ces raisons, je crois qu'il faut donner à l'Europe comme son objectif principal d'être elle-même, et c'est après qu'on verra le rôle qu'elle joue ou qu'elle pourra jouer par rapport aux autres.

—GEORGES POMPIDOU, INTERVIEW GRANTED TO THE BBC, 17 MAY 1971

In all we do, we must show that the Community exists above all for the people of Europe. They will judge us by our vision and our determination in meeting their need, their hopes, and their aspirations. Let us show that the Europe we build is no empty monument, no bureaucratic blueprint, but a living democratic society, concerned with the welfare of Europe's citizens and with Europe's contribution to the world. For this purpose, we must recapture our European voice, the voice which we all of us instinctively recognize: a voice of reason, of humanity and moderation, which can be heard throughout the world.

—SPEECH BY EDWARD HEATH, PARIS, 19 OCTOBER 1972

A Europe alive to its great responsibilities in the common struggle of humanity for a better life. Thus, this ceremony marks an end and a beginning. An end to divisions which have stricken Europe for centuries. A beginning of another stage in the construction of a new and greater Europe. This is the task for our generation in Europe.

—SPEECH BY EDWARD HEATH, BRUSSELS, 22 JANUARY 1972

Table of Contents

List of Figures

Introduction

Olivier Sibre

Franco-British relations are centuries-old, part of a perpetual dialectic of conflict, alliance, and sometimes even disdain and attraction. Cliches surrounding the neighbour across the Channel are tenacious in France as in the United Kingdom, and are connected to an ever-expanding terminology, often driven by English humour.

With the Franco-British relation, we typically enter a historical constant, one that has lasted for almost a millennium. The two countries were the first to build a modern state in the thirteenth and fourteenth centuries, with the Hundred Years' War being the reflection of this unique emergence right in the middle of the feudal period. Since then, a definitive union of the two states was almost concluded in June 1940, with Jean Monnet's proposal for a French-British Union, which was submitted to Paul Reynaud and Winston Churchill in the context of the continental debacle. The fundamentals of the Franco-British relation, with the exception of the Vichy government, have essentially stopped shifting since at least 1904, with international crises on the continent almost always strengthening the strategic partnership between the two former European powers.

It is nevertheless true that the early 1970s were a much more important period that any other, with the UK's entry in the EEC. This meant, at least for the Europeans, the docking of Britannia in a European port, in powerful and almost definitive fashion, or at least we believed. The debates at the time in the British Parliament nevertheless reveal a strategy marked more by a specific domestic and international context – in addition to economic opportunism – rather than wholly positive support for the European project. It was these opportunistic arguments that Edward Heath, who was personally convinced of the historical dimension of European integration, used to convince British MPs and citizens. As for Georges Pompidou, after the refusals by de Gaulle, he probably had less difficulty, despite the mixed results from the 1972 referendum, explaining to the French the opportunity presented by this change, namely the 'natural' enlargement of the EEC, within a booming economic context, to include one of Europe's major economies. In both cases, it is certain that the crisis of Britain's industry and economy, as well as French prosperity and the success of the Common Market, gave each government arguments to support rapprochement, beyond cultural, historical, geopolitical, and even identity-based considerations. On the geopolitical and international levels, Pompidou closely monitored Willy Brandt's Ostpolitik. On the other side of the Channel, they imagined leading Western Europe within the EEC, notably with France and the FRG. The American factor nevertheless remained important, with Washington pressuring the UK to join the Common Market, and France feeling it was drifting away from the American partner by anchoring itself within European projects.

For all that, despite Labour's wishes, upon its return to power in February 1974, to renegotiate the accession conditions secured by Conservatives, and the uncompromising positions of Margaret Thatcher, Brexit was not so 'foreseeable' after 40 years of integration. It proved an arduous journey even for the negotiators from 2016 to 2020, including for Michel Barnier, who published a long account entitled *My Secret Brexit Diary: A Glorious Illusion.*

On 17 May 2024, the Institut Georges Pompidou organised its first conference abroad in the United Kingdom, in Oxford, with French and British academics. The IGP is using this book to explore the 'Pompidou-Heath couple', recent history, and key issues in Franco-British relations, all within a post-Brexit context that is not particularly favourable. This context changed entirely just a few weeks later with the British political pendulum swinging back during the July elections, which brought Labour back to power, and the government led by the new Prime Minister, Sir Keir Starmer. This publication is now situated amid a more 'positive' state of affairs for Franco-British rapprochement, bolstered by the state visit to the United Kingdom by French President Emmanuel Macron in July 2025.

The Institut Georges Pompidou does not pretend that this modest conference provided any inspiration for the two partners in recent months. At the very least, it is certain that the UK's entry into the Common Market proves that at certain moments of history, Continental tropism – and French tropism in particular – can be as powerful if not more powerful than 'Global Britain'.

As a leitmotif, as a continuous basis for history, the Franco-British relation represents an essential structural given in European history, as long as Europe remains a centre for the construction and evolution of history, and does not resign itself to becoming a periphery of the world, a simple peninsula of the Eurasian continent. This publication examines almost all sectors of Franco-British rapprochement within a European context since President Georges Pompidou and Prime Minister Edward Heath, including political, diplomatic, strategic, economic, and cultural aspects. It is based on recent research, as well as the opening of archives at the Archives nationales and the Bodleian Libraries, some of them recent. We hope it sustains the work of young researchers, and sparks an interest in revisiting history, with a view to reflecting on the contemporary relation between France and the UK, and the key issues it involves.

I would like to extend my warmest thanks to my French and British colleagues, the Maison Française d'Oxford, and the Embassy of France in London.

Preliminary Remarks

Guillaume Lacroix, First Counsellor of the French Embassy in London

Ladies and gentlemen,
It is an honour for me to say a few words on behalf of Ambassador Duchêne.

I would like to thank the Institut Georges Pompidou, which organised the conference; our host, the Maison Française d'Oxford; and all of the speakers and participants.

The Ambassador is proud to be associated with this event, which takes its place as part of the commemorations for the 120th anniversary of the Entente Cordiale, and just a few days ahead of the 80th anniversary of the Normandy Landings.

Times really have changed since the 1970s, as we will discuss today. But some factors of stability have proven unchanging in the Franco-British relationship: firstly our geography, which links us together; secondly security – both now and in the past, for we have been allies in protecting our borders and our values; and third, relations between our civil societies and our young people. All of these areas, which are central to our relationship, featured prominently on the agenda of the Franco-British summit of 10 March 2023, the first in five years.

I'd like to end on a personal note. I was born in 1971 when Georges Pompidou was president of France. Montboudif, Cajarc and Orvilliers are all familiar names to me. I can clearly picture them in my mind, even if the picture is in black and white. But when I think of President Pompidou, I also think of the speech he delivered on 28 February 1970 at Palmer House in Chicago, where I served before taking up my post in London. I encourage you to read, again and again, this tremendous, visionary speech about the environment and humankind's relationship with nature.

Thank you for your invitation. I hope you have a successful conference.

The Anglo-French Sibling Rivalry: From a Family Affair to the Pompidou-Heath Cooperation

Beatrice Heuser

Relations between the British Isles and the European Continent go back thousands of years. A wide-spread megalith culture spanned Western Europe from Hispania in the South and Britannia and Hibernia in the West (to use their later Roman names) to Scandinavia, and included much of France, the Netherlands, and northwest Germany. Skeletal finds, such as the Amesbury Archer, suggest that people moved backwards and forwards from Britain to the Continent.

Then in the Iron Age, Celts from the Continent arrived in Britain and later Ireland. Again, both islands were part of a huge culture, one that spread horizontally across the entire Continent, from the Black Sea to the Atlantic[1]. The Roman conquest of Britain in the first century A.D. added another layer in Britain's integration within a larger European whole, excluding only Ireland and northern Scotland[2].

The Middle Ages: Family Affairs

In the Middle Ages, Anglo-French relations were marked by kinship. After the fall of the Roman Empire in the West, Francia (modern France), in addition to the southern and eastern shores of the British Isles, were simultaneously invaded by Germanic tribes. Those invading France came across the Rhine from modern Belgium, the Netherlands, and western Germany, while those invading Britain came across the North Sea from the Jutland peninsula (the Angles) and Saxony, an area north and south-west of Hamburg[3].

---

1 Barry Cunliffe, *The Ancient Celts* (Oxford: Oxford University Press, 2018).

2 Michael Fulford, 'Coasting Britannia: Roman Trade and Traffic around the Shores of Britain', in Chris Gosden, Helena Hamerow, Philip de Jersey, and Gary Lock, eds., *Communities and Connections: Essays in Honour of Barry Cunliffe* (Oxford: Oxford University Press, 2007), 54–74.

3 Today's Lower Saxony, not to be confused with the eastern *land* Saxony, which acquired this name by quirks of dynastic succession.

The Germanic invaders integrated differently: in France, the Francs' German language gave way to the local Latin vernacular, while in central and eastern Britain, the Germanic dialect replaced earlier Celtic languages. (These survived only in the west: in Northern Scotland, Ireland, Wales, and until the early twentieth century in Cornwall.) The Germanic language of Anglo-Saxon was in turn challenged by French. In 1066, a Viking tribe that had settled around the Seine estuary in France, and that had become thoroughly frenchified in language and customs, invaded England and became the ruling elite, replacing the previous Germanic (Anglo-Saxon) elite. Ironically, this invasion of England from the south – from the shores of France – was the last in a long series of Viking invasions originating from Scandinavia starting in 793.

These Northmen or Normans – who also gave their name to the Seine estuary, and who under one Vilhelm or William defeated the last Anglo-Saxon king at Hastings in 1066 – are in a narrower sense at the beginning of our story of Anglo-French rivalry[4]. The Norman monarchs of England continued to hold lands both in France and on the British Isles, while extending their conquests to Ireland, Wales, and Scotland. The fact that their heart beat mainly for their French lands at least until the end of the twelfth century is illustrated by their burials in Normandy.

Anglo-French relations turned into a family affair in the twelfth century when Eleanor (Alienor) of Aquitaine, the heiress to the south-western portion of modern France, successively wed French King Louis VII, the scion of the Capetian dynasty, and after divorcing him, Plantagenet King Henry II of England. Between Eleanor and Henry, they owned almost all of western France, excluding only Brittanny, but formally owed homage for these holdings to the King of France. This created predictable tensions and led to a first Hundred Years' War (c.1152–1259), in which the Plantagenets prevailed first but the Capetians after, culminating with a Capetian prince having himself proclaimed King of England in London in 1216, supported by English barons who had risen up against their Plantagenet King[5].

4 Richard Huscroft, *The Norman Conquest: A New Introduction* (Abingdon: Routledge, 2013).

5 Robert Gibson, *Best of Enemies: Anglo-French Relations since the Norman Conquest* (London: Sinclair-Stevenson, 1995).

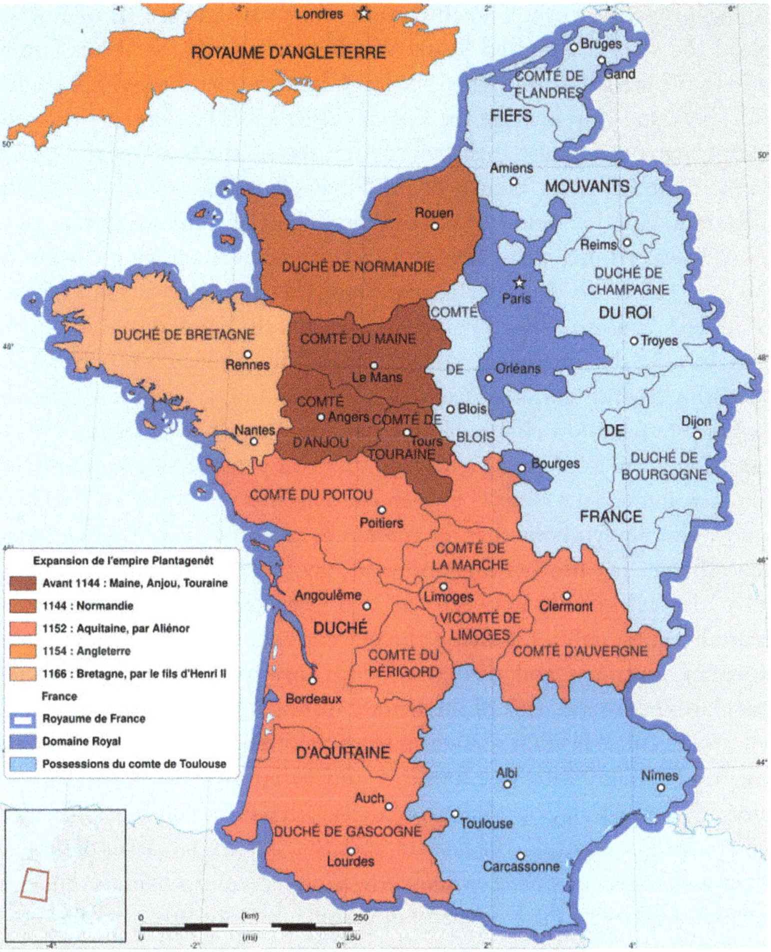

Figure 1.1. French map of the growth of the Plantagenet Empire, from 1144 to 1166

Source: By © Sémhur / Wikimedia Commons, CC BY-SA 4.0, https://commons.wikimedia.org/wiki/File:France_1154-fr.svg

Eventually the Plantagenets won this round, but a new conflict loomed when another dynastic marriage between the Capetian princess Isabella and the Plantagenet King Edward II provided an excuse, one generation later, for a

Plantagenet claim to the French throne. Their son Edward III of England started the second Hundred Years' War by challenging the Valois family's claim to the French throne when the last Capetian ruler died without a male heir. The Valois claimed that the French (or Salic) succession laws ruled out not only females, but also their heirs[6]. After several spells of war and periods of peace, the Lancaster branch of the Plantagenet line seemed to triumph when, following his victory over the French host at Agincourt (Azincourt), Henry V was named as his heir and successor by French King Charles VI, who gave Henry his daughter in marriage. Their son Henry VI of England was indeed crowned King of France in 1431, but the wheel of fortune turned again. In 1453, the forces of his uncle Charles VII won the decisive battle that ended this second Hundred Years' War at Castillon, curiously a battle that few Englishmen know about. Almost all of the English royal family's French possessions were lost, ending a four-century competition for the domination of France, but not the rivalry between the dynasties.

It was highly symbolic that the monarchs of the two countries addressed each other as 'my Brother England' and 'my Brother France'. The cultural and biological kinship between the two dynasties also took the form of cultural commonalities. During the eleventh century, 'Romanesque' and 'Norman' churches and cathedrals, arguably inspired by the previous Ottonian Renaissance east of the Rhine, sprung up in Normandy, with the new architectural fashion spreading from there across France and England, and into Scotland with Dunfermline and Jedburgh Abbeys, as well as St Andrew's Cathedral. Court literature was written in French in both England and France. For example, the famous epos that became a marker of national identity in France, the *Song of Roland*, was preserved in a manuscript in the Bodleian Library of the University of Oxford. Eleanor brought *trouvères* or troubadours from her court in Aquitaine to enliven the Plantagenet courts on both sides of the Channel. Castles greatly resembled each other, and most of the housing for peasants and townsfolk was similarly half-timbered. The high and low in England drank wines imported from Aquitaine (especially

6 On the Hundred Years' War, see Anne Curry: 'War, Peace and National Identity in the Hundred Years' War', in Anja Victorine Harmann and Beatrice Heuser, eds, *War, Peace and World Orders in European History* (Abingdon: Routledge, 2002), 157–70; Desmond Seward: *A Brief History of the Hundred Years War: The English in France, 1337–1453* (London: Hachette UK, 2013).

Bordeaux and Bayonne). English clerics studied at the Sorbonne and other Continental universities, although some form of teaching also existed at Oxford from the end of the eleventh century onward.

Antagonism marked Anglo-French relations despite all these similarities and bonds. Well over two centuries of on-and-off war had taken generations of Englishmen onto battlefields in France and had in the process crystallised an early French and English nationalism. Judging by their portraits, neither Henry V of England nor his brother-in-law and rival, King Charles VII of France, were great beauties, but both seem to have inspired the loyalty of their soldiers as few before them. The respective battle cries of 'England and Saint George' and 'Montjoie Saint Denis' transformed this personal vassal-loyalty into something that would stick to a larger polity, surviving the reigns of individual monarchs[7].

The ensuing *proto-national* rivalry was captured in the allegorical dispute between the heralds of England and France, written shortly after the expulsion of the English forces from most of France after Castillon. In it the two heralds claim superiority for their respective countries. Having compared the beauty of French and English women, their forests for hunting, and their histories, the English herald claims that the English:

> Are more richly and amply provided at sea with fine and powerful ships than any other nation of Christendom, so that they are kings of the sea, since none can resist them; and they who are strongest on the sea may call themselves kings[8].

The Herald of France disputes this, saying:

> It is very true that he who is strongest on the sea may call himself king of the sea while his strength lasts. [Y]our kingdom is an island, and therefore everything which is taken there or brought away must be conveyed in ships. You may have seaports all around your kingdom, and in each of these ports there is shipping: therefore ... there must of necessity be a great number and force of ships. But ...

---

7 Maurice Keen, 'The Angevin Legacy, Dynastic Rivalry and the Aftermath of the Hundred Years War, 1453–1491', in H. Skoda, P. Lantschner and R. L. J Shaw, eds., *Contact and Exchange in Later Medieval Europe, Essays in Honour of Malcolm Vale* (Martlesham, Suffolk: Boydell Press, 2012), 145–158.

8 Henry Pyne, ed., *England and France in the Fifteenth Century: The Contemporary French Tract Entitles 'The Debate between the Heralds of France and England Presumed to Have Been Written by Charles, Duke of Orleans, Translated for the First Time into English...* (London: Longmans, Green & Co., 1870), 17.

> notwithstanding [these], you do not employ it in such a manner as to entitle you on that account to be advanced to honour.

For the English kings did not use them to fight the infidel, in order to win back what was once Christian territory: they had never 'made magnificent war at sea'. Consequently 'the King of France, when he pleases, will be king of the sea above you', as having many more resources, he is better suited to bearing this title[9]. In this fictional dispute, the person of the king is still the point of reference, but it is two countries, neatly divided geographically – as the French herald notes gleefully, England was limited to its island, having lost its French possessions – that are vying for pre-eminence. The heralds speak for France and England respectively, not just for their kings.

The elite of England could still have read and understood this work, but by the late fifteenth century, an evolved form of Anglo-Saxon, English, was the main language, and spoken even at court. Following the Romanesque/Norman, Gothic church architecture united all of Europe, even though vernacular architecture gradually took on distinctive patterns in different parts of Europe beginning with the end of the second Hundred Years' War. French *châteaux* began to change their functions from the previous emphasis on fortification to that of palaces, a transition that can clearly be observed in the *châteaux* along the Loire.

The Tudor kings – the first of whom had ironically been an exile in France, from where he returned to England to seize the crown from the horseless Richard III at the Battle of Bosworth in 1485 – still laid claim to the crown of France, as demonstrated in their coat of arms, even though only Calais and a bit of its hinterland remained after 1453. The second Tudor monarch, Henry VIII, saw himself very much as the sporting rival of King Francis I, to the point of oscillating between actual warfare and knightly tournaments in their famous encounter in 1520 on the Field of the Cloth of Gold. Calais was lost in 1558 during the reign of Mary I Tudor, who, married to Philip II of Spain, had brought England back into the Catholic fold. But she was succeeded by her Protestant half-sister Elizabeth,

---

9 Pyne, ed., *England and France*, 47–50.

and henceforth flirtations of English monarchs with Catholicism were dangerous, costing one his head and another his throne.

From Family Affairs to Confessional Divergence

The dynastic rivalry had turned into religious strife with Henry VIII's embrace of the Protestant Reformation. England/Britain and France would henceforth combine family problems with religious opposition. As most of Europe was torn apart by civil wars between Protestants and Catholics, the dividing lines cut through individual kingdoms. English monarchs began to interfere forcefully in the religious strife on the Continent, which just happened to give them special rights as protectors of Protestantism in the Channel port of Flushing (Vlissingen) and the town of Brill (Brielle).

When the Scot James VI Stuart assumed the English crown as James I, he largely kept religion out of politics in the British Isles and refused to become involved in the civil war of the Holy Roman Empire, which would last 30 years, and was confessional in nature. Yet his son Charles I, married to the sister of French King Louis XIII – who after the confessional wars put France back on the path to absolutism – wanted to emulate his brother-in-law's constitutional example and devout Catholicism. This would unleash civil war in his realm and cost him his head. When the ensuing Protestant Commonwealth under Oliver Cromwell ended with the restoration to the throne of Charles' eponymous son, the second of that name, both Scottish and English Protestants – by now the majority of the population – eyed with suspicion any sign of a rapprochement with France or Catholicism. Charles II died a king, and in his bed. But in the 1680s, the Catholic King Louis XIV of France ended the tolerance of the Edict of Nantes and expelled the Protestants from France. Upon his conversion to Catholicism and production of a (Catholic) son by a second marriage, Louis' cousin, Charles II's brother James Stuart (II of England and VII of Scotland), was deposed by his Protestant first child Mary (II), cementing the link between the crown and Protestantism. Here ended the family connections between the French and English crowns.

When, upon the extinction of the Stuart line, the Protestant Elector of Hanover claimed the henceforth united crown of England and Scotland, via inheritance through his grandmother, Louis XIV and then Louis XV feebly supported attempts by the Catholic supporters of the Catholic Stuart Jacobites. But both Louis had larger fish to fry in quarrels with their Continental neighbours. During the eighteenth century, confessional strife had ceased in most parts of Europe, and competition of an economic nature and for the acquisition of overseas territories began to dominate British-French relations. A religious nuance would nevertheless continue to influence French-British relations even until the twentieth century, as we shall see[10].

Britain and France also drifted apart culturally, as Protestant elements were eliminated from French society, and Catholicism was suppressed in the United Kingdom. Scotland, which before its union with England in 1707 had had a special relationship with France – mainly to jointly counterbalance England – was by now staunchly Protestant, and shared the same misgivings about Catholicism, marring Scottish views of France. This was in spite of the huge contributions that the (increasingly united) British and French cultures made to the Enlightenment. In very different ways, both cultures embraced a fascination with 'the Ancients', with Greek and Roman forms and style. France turned to classical lines in architecture even when fashion still dictated formally styled gardens, over-dimensional hoop skirts and mountains of powdered hair. In 1778, the escape of the French frigate *Belle Poule* from persecution by the Royal Navy, in the context of the American War of Independence supported by France, was famously celebrated with such a hair style. The British elite had abandoned hoop skirts early in the seventeenth century under the influence of the Dutch sobriety imported by Mary II and her Dutch husband in 1688. By the eighteenth century, it was well into modest exteriors in order to hide the embarrassment of riches within, such as classical columns decorating entrances and hallways, garden-parks with sheep, and well-disciplined 'naturalism'. While social tensions in France, especially between the middle classes and the nobility, led to the Revolution, the investments of English and Scottish entrepreneurs in the industrialisation of their country defused much of the social tension there, promising prosperity for greater parts of society.

---

[10] Jeremy Black, 'The Anglo-French Alliance 1716–1731. A Study in Eighteenth-Century International Relations', *Francia* 13 (1985), 295–310.

Figure 1.2. Example of ca. 1780 “big hair” themed hairstyle, with objects placed in the hair to make a statement

Source: <https://commons.wikimedia.org/wiki/File:Coiffure_Belle-Poule_2A.jpg>

Politically, France and the United Kingdom were of course torn apart by the Seven Years’ War, and subsequently by French support for the War of Independence for Britain’s North American colonies. There was a period of peace following the Peace of Paris in 1763, which ended the Seven Years’ War, but the settlement favoured Britain so much that it instilled lasting resentment in France. There was intensive trade, especially as the British textile industry took off towards the end of the century[11]. On the whole, France and Britain tended to align on adversarial sides in international politics[12].

---

[11] William O. Henderson, ‘The Anglo-French Commercial Treaty of 1786’, *The Economic History Review* 10/1 (1957), 104–12.

[12] Jeremy Black, ‘Anglo-French Relations 1763–1775’, *Francia* 18/2 (1991), 99–114.

Revolution vs Evolution, Republic vs Monarchy

Apart from the competition for colonies that would poison French-British relations in the long nineteenth and early twentieth centuries, the rivalry was recast in two ways with the French Revolution and the Napoleonic Wars[13]. First, in Britain the former created a lasting fear of lower-class insurrections against the upper-middle and upper-class establishment, one which would haunt governments that, until this day, are recruited mainly from an elite in terms of background, money and education. France was thus the scary model to be avoided through the gradual adaptation of demands from below if absolutely necessary[14]. The subsequent seesawing of France between monarchies and republics increased the suspicions that the British ruling class had toward French ways, which represented inconstancy and repeated upheavals.

Nevertheless, there was not only colonial rivalry between the two countries, but also a degree of cooperation, especially in and around Europe. Both countries abolished slavery and had liberal tendencies (relative to their times), and showed sympathy with national liberation movements, especially that of Greece, which appealed to the classical education shared by British and French elites. They also had a common interest in keeping a balance of powers favourable to their own situation in and around Europe, thereby checking a further increase in Russian power. Lord Palmerston for one, who dominated British foreign policy from 1830 to 1865, and twice served as prime minister, worked well with the French, especially during the Crimean War, in which the two countries fought side by side to deny Russia its push towards the Straits and into Ottoman-held territory[15]. There was some sympathy for Napoleon III, whose wife had a Scottish grandfather, and their hapless son, especially when the family sought exile after Napoleon's defeat at the hands of the Prussians in September 1870. All three are buried in Farnborough. There had been talk about the son marrying Queen Victoria's youngest daughter, but Louis-Napoleon, the 'Prince Imperial', died young before negotiations were much advanced.

---

13 Jeremy Black, 'Anglo-French Relations in the Age of the French Revolution 1787–1793', *Francia* 15 (1987), 407–33.

14 Alan Sked, 'Talleyrand and England, 1792–1838: A Reinterpretation', in Thomas Otte and Glyn Stone, eds., *Anglo-French Relations since the Late Eighteenth century* (Abingdon: Routledge, 2008), 13–30.

15 David Brown, 'Palmerston and Anglo-French Relations, 1846–1865', *Diplomacy and Statecraft* 17/4 (2006), 675–92.

Secondly, while the Revolution and the ensuing wars renewed the process, which had begun in the sixteenth century, of turning peasants into Frenchmen by replacing royalism with a Republican Nationalism[16], the Napoleonic Wars also served to turn soldiers serving on the Hanoverian side into Britons[17]. By serving together for many years in war, new generations of Scots, Welshmen and Englishmen got to know each other more intimately than their fathers and grandfathers had in living memory. This was a process similar to that of the Hundred Years' War, which created proto-nationalist identities in both France and England, but this time it lastingly affected the consciousness of a greater part of the population, spreading and being kept alive by print media in increasingly literate societies.

Natural Allies

In theory, by the late nineteenth century, newly Republican France and the slowly but steadily more democratic United Kingdom were two powers in Europe that might have been natural allies against the Continent's autocratic empires. This was – again in theory – recognised by their Entente Cordiale, a friendship treaty of 1904 that might have materialised much earlier had politicians on both sides of the Channel not been so influenced by the passions stoked by colonial competition[18]. The two countries' rivalry in other parts of the world had toxic influences on their relations in Europe, exacerbating the tide of nationalism that swept over the entire Continent[19]. It was more the traditional British preoccupation of ensuring that the closest part of the Continental mainland's coast – Belgium – would not fall under hostile domination than any commitment to France that pushed the British government to become a belligerent in the First World War. This brought British soldiers closer than ever to their French counterparts and population than any war since the first and second Hundred Years' Wars. The experience was so traumatic for the survivors, however, that the nostalgia for Hinky Dinky Parlay

16 Eugene Weber, *Peasants into Frenchmen* (Stanford, CA: Stanford University Press, 1976).

17 Linda Colley, *Britons: Forging the Nation 1707–1837* (New Haven, CT: Yale University Press, 1992).

18 John D. Hargreaves, 'Entente Manquée: Anglo-French Relations, 1895–1896', *Cambridge Historical Journal* 11/1 (1953), 65–92.

19 T. G. Otte, 'From "War-in-Sight" to Nearly War: Anglo-French Relations in the Age of High Imperialism, 1875–1898', *Diplomacy and Statecraft* 17/4 (2006), 693–714.

Voo[20], and hanky panky between British soldiers and French civilians, faded behind recollections of the horrors of the war. Nor did they expunge the older feelings of national rivalry.

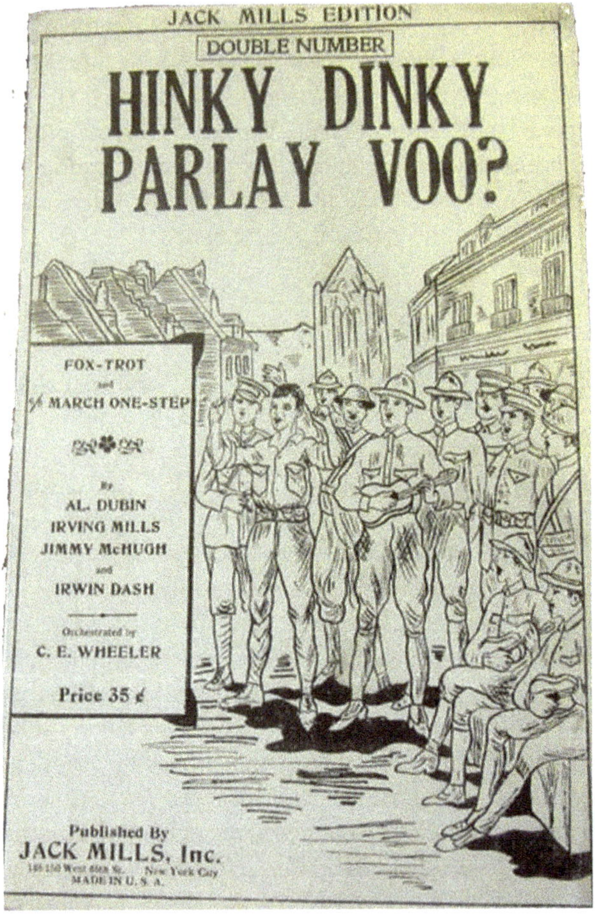

Figure 1.3. Sheet music cover

Source: By Unknown author – Pritzker Military Museum & Library, CC BY-SA 4.0, <https://commons.wikimedia.org/w/index.php?curid=59509001>

---

20 A popular British song of the 1920s referring to the amorous adventures of British soldiers in France during the First World War.

In what we now know proved to be an interwar period, Britain and France should again have been natural allies, as both were proper democracies at the time by most standards (although universal adult suffrage was fully established in Britain only in 1928, and France in 1945!). Yet imperial rivalry still marred their relations in the 1920s and 1930s. In the former decade, when Germany was a democracy (admittedly with a very rocky domestic political life), French governments were seen by their British counterparts as being excessively vindictive towards Germany, and alarmist about possibilities of a German resurgence and territorial revisionism[21]. After Hitler's rise to power, French fears were even more justified, but the British political elite was largely still caught in the 1920s, thinking that the French were 'hysterical', and that one should have understanding for German breaches of the Treaty of Versailles imposed on them in 1919. As a result, the two main pillars of the international order – the only two states that were permanent members of the Council of the League of Nations from its inception to its dissolution – singularly failed to coordinate their plans to use their military might, colonies, protectorates, and other allies to uphold an international order increasingly undermined and threatened by Japan, Italy, and Germany[22].

At least Britain and France stood together in finally drawing a line for Nazi German expansion, giving an unconditional guarantee of defence to Poland in the spring of 1939 in the event of a German invasion, which materialised on 1 September 1939. Both stood by their word with minimal hesitation and declared war on Germany within two days. They did not, however, have the slightest plan for implementing this, or indeed for helping Poland, which would fall under the concerted German and Soviet assault, and become a vassal state to the USSR for half a century.

The camaraderie of the First World War was not quite repeated in the Second World War. Instead of fighting alongside the French in France as the previous generation had done in the First World War, the British military and political leadership – deeply scarred by that experience – instead withdrew their expeditionary forces as quickly as possible from the beaches around

[21] Andrew Barros, 'Disarmament as a Weapon: Anglo-French Relations and the Problems of Enforcing German Disarmament, 1919–1928', *The Journal of Strategic Studies* 29/2 (2006), 301–21.

[22] Glyn Stone, 'From Entente to Alliance: Anglo-French relations, 1935–1939', in Alan Sharp and Glyn Stone, eds., *Anglo-French Relations in the Twentieth Century: Rivalry and Cooperation* (Abingdon: Routledge, 2000), 180–204.

Dunkirk. Many French saw this as a deep betrayal, however sensible or necessary the British withdrawal might have been at the time. A part of the French government seized power to surrender to Germany on 22 June 1940, taking France out of the war. To prevent the French navy from falling summarily into German hands, on 3 July 1940 the Royal Navy bombed and sank a concentration of the former's ships in Mers El Kebir, the chief naval base in French Algeria. This was also seen as a betrayal in France (no warning was given, and close to 1,300 French sailors were killed), one that was not forgotten by French mariners.

Only a fraction of French forces escaped from France with the ministers and military who had refused to surrender, to fight alongside the British thereafter. 'A beautiful friendship' might have resulted from the Free French, under one General Charles de Gaulle, creating a government in exile and setting up their headquarters in London. This is what the American romantic wartime film *Casablanca* (dir. Michael Curtiz) led its audiences to expect. Its script writers had not counted on the bitterness created in de Gaulle by the experience of being the *demandeur* in all relations with Britain – and from December 1941 the USA – alongside the memories of Dunkirk and Mers el Kebir.

There *was* something of a honeymoon in relations between the British and the French governments in the immediate postwar period (1946–1950), when Britain helped France secure a place among the five permanent leaders of the successor organisation to the League of Nations, the Security Council of the United Nations. This honeymoon was directly linked with de Gaulle's temporary absence from the French political scene, for after the war, the Third Republic was replaced by a Fourth Republic (1946–1958), with a much more collegial government structure. This, however, led to frequent changes in government in France; from 1950 onwards government initiatives favouring international cooperation, especially with the United Kingdom, repeatedly fizzled out with the fall of these governments.

Still, during the short period between 1946 and 1950, Britain and France crucially and jointly laid the foundations for European and later Atlantic defence cooperation. This began with making up for what should have happened during the interwar period, especially the late 1930s: Britain and France should have committed to each other's defence and coordinated their defence plans. The British-French mutual defence treaty of 1947 was the first step, signed with high symbolism at Dunkirk, as if to wipe out the memory of 1940. It was followed in 1948 by a treaty of mutual defence and other cooperation signed in Brussels by both countries together with the Netherlands, Belgium, and Luxembourg. The latter created the Western Union (renamed the Western European Union seven years later when Italy and West Germany were admitted), the first permanent defence alliance in peacetime since Antiquity. The application of its obligations was transferred later to the North Atlantic Treaty Organisation (NATO) established in 1950, after London and Paris jointly persuaded the US to sign a similar mutual defence treaty in Washington in April 1949, albeit one that had much more limited mutual commitments that left each member state free to decide how to react in case an ally is attacked. This might have been a new Entente Cordiale between the two countries, but one at the centre of a much larger alliance[23].

In 1951, however, the period of closest cooperation came to an end when, on the basis of Jean Monnet's brilliant plan, France, the Benelux countries, West Germany and Italy formed a Coal and Steel Community, thus integrating those parts of their national industries that were vital for waging war[24]. The point of this exercise was to make it impossible for these countries to go to war against each other. Britain kept out, with Deputy Prime Minister Herbert Morrison arguing that 'The Durham miners won't wear it'. Britain also kept out of the treaties of Rome. Deep-rooted cultural feelings about religion were one of the reasons why the United Kingdom refused to join the European Communities in 1957. Members of its Conservative government felt there was too much popery in signing the relevant treaties in Rome on an Easter Monday after a Catholic mass attended by the chief signatories.

Only four years after its signature, the British government had second thoughts, and in 1963 applied to join the European Communities, doing so again in 1967. But in 1958, Charles de Gaulle had become the President of a reformed French (by now the Vth) Republic. His mentality – incidentally much like Churchill's – was firmly anchored in the apotheosis

---

23 John Young, 'The Failure of the New Entente Cordiale: Anglo-French Relations, 1947–1950', in Sharp and Stone, eds., *Anglo-French Relations*, 264–79.

24 Kevin Ruane, 'Anthony Eden, the Foreign Office, and Anglo-French Relations, 1950–1954', in Sharp and Stone, eds., *Anglo-French Relations*, 280–300.

of the nation-state that had fully unfolded in nineteenth-century Europe. He believed there was an element of national and ideational rivalry for leadership of the Western world, in which France, Britain, and the US were vying for pre-eminence. He would have accepted a triumvirate in this leadership, but felt painfully excluded by the British-American special relationship for intelligence sharing and nuclear cooperation, which was built on a degree of wartime intimacy that the Free French, who were on the margins of the action, had not experienced. De Gaulle rightly feared that Britain was in it only for commercial interests, and willing to steer the Community in accordance with Washington's interests[25].

It was only after de Gaulle's resignation that his successor, Georges Pompidou, and his British counterpart Edward Heath, began negotiations for a third British application to join the European integration project, which is the main subject of this tome. Among the wider French and European populations, the new Britain was quite an attraction, with its rebellious lower-class culture, the Beatles and youth culture, Mary Quant's fashion revolution, and witty movies and iconoclastic TV series widely distributed in Europe. With the support of Pompidou, EC member states agreed to accept a third British application for membership, with a treaty to that effect being signed in 1972 and coming into force in 1973. There was much domestic opposition in the UK, however, headed by the Labour Party, leading to a referendum in 1975. With an electoral turnout of just under 65 %, 67.2 % of the voters favoured staying under the existing conditions, a comfortable majority.

With the benefit of hindsight half a century later, perhaps de Gaulle was right, and Pompidou wrong to support British membership. It is ironic to note that by the time of the 2016 referendum in the United Kingdom (with 52 % voting for Britain to leave the European Union, as the Communities have been known since 1993), Britain had indeed ensured that the Common Market was Europe's main feature. After the end of the Cold War, Britain had used its influence to open EU membership to many countries that had not shared the founding members' particular history of war and peace, and that joined mainly for EU money. At the same time, Britain blocked the deepening of institutions, the 'ever closer union' that might ultimately have

25 Joanne Wright, 'The Cold War, European Community and Anglo-French Relations, 1958–1998', in Sharp and Stone, eds., *Anglo-French Relations*, 324–43.

turned the EU into a federal state similar to the US. It is therefore ironic that Britain has had such a lasting influence on the shape and character of the EU we have today, despite having left it in January 2020.

Uniquely Comparable Allies

What remains, however, is that France and the United Kingdom are in many ways, as the French government has put it, 'uniquely comparable allies'. Both are democracies, albeit with quite different structures (presidential vs a Prime Minister and Cabinet system); both have a colonial past, territory of similar size, and post-colonial populations of similar size and composition, with all their tensions; a similar spectrum of political parties; and a comparable level of economic development. They both hold seats on the UN Security Council with the ensuing responsibilities, similar memberships in other international organisations, militaries with a tradition of expeditionary operations and wars, as well as nuclear weapons. Both share key democratic values, and a general analysis of the world situation.

In recognition of this, in 1995 French President Jacques Chirac noted, at a meeting at Chequers with the British Prime Minister, 'we cannot imagine a situation in which the vital interests of one our countries would be threatened without the vital interests of the other being similarly threatened'. In 2010, this recognition was taken further with the bilateral Lancaster House Treaties between the two countries, which formed the foundation for a series of joint defence-related endeavours, including a Combined Joint Expeditionary Force. There is thus a useful basis, and still much scope for further development in this special relationship between two nations and complex cultures that have done so much to shape Europe and the world.

Bibliography

Black, Jeremy, 'Anglo-French Relations 1763–1775', *Francia* 18/2 (1991), 99–114.
Black, Jeremy, 'Anglo-French Relations in the Age of the French Revolution 1787–1793', *Francia* 15 (1987), 407–33.
Black, Jeremy, 'The Anglo-French Alliance 1716–1731. A Study in Eighteenth-Century International Relations', *Francia* 13 (1985), pp. 295–310.

Brown, David, 'Palmerston and Anglo-French Relations, 1846–1865', *Diplomacy and Statecraft* 17/4 (2006), 675–92.
Colley, Linda, *Britons: Forging the Nation 1707–1837* (New Haven, CT: Yale University Press, 1992).
Cunliffe, Barry, *The Ancient Celts* (Oxford: Oxford University Press, 2018).
Curry, Anne, 'War, Peace and National Identity in the Hundred Years' War', in Anja Victorine Harmann and Beatrice Heuser, eds, *War, Peace and World Orders in European History* (Abingdon: Routledge, 2002), 157–70.
Fulford, Michael, 'Coasting Britannia: Roman Trade and Traffic around the Shores of Britain', in Chris Gosden, Helena Hamerow, Philip de Jersey, and Gary Lock, eds., *Communities and Connections: Essays in Honour of Barry Cunliffe* (Oxford: Oxford University Press, 2007), 54–74.
Gibson, Robert, *Best of Enemies: Anglo-French Relations since the Norman Conquest* (London: Sinclair-Stevenson, 1995).
Hargreaves, John D., 'Entente Manquée: Anglo-French Relations, 1895–1896', *Cambridge Historical Journal* 11/1 (1953), 65–92.
Henderson, William O., 'The Anglo-French Commercial Treaty of 1786', *The Economic History Review* 10/1 (1957), 104–12.
Huscroft, Richard, *The Norman Conquest: A New Introduction* (Abingdon: Routledge, 2013).
Keen, Maurice, 'The Angevin Legacy, Dynastic Rivalry and the Aftermath of the Hundred Years War, 1453–1491', in H. Skoda, P. Lantschner and R. L. J Shaw, eds., *Contact and Exchange in Later Medieval Europe, Essays in Honour of Malcolm Vale* (Martlesham, Suffolk: Boydell Press, 2012), pp. 145–158.
Otte, Thomas G., 'From "War-in-Sight" to Nearly War: Anglo-French Relations in the Age of High Imperialism, 1875–1898', *Diplomacy and Statecraft* 17/4 (2006), 693–714.
Seward, Desmond, *A Brief History of the Hundred Years War: The English in France, 1337–1453* (London: Hachette UK, 2013).
Sharp, Alan and Glyn Stone, eds., *Anglo-French Relations in the Twentieth Century: Rivalry and Cooperation* (Abingdon: Routledge, 2000).
Sked, Alan, 'Talleyrand and England, 1792–1838: A Reinterpretation', in Thomas Otte and Glyn Stone, eds., *Anglo-French Relations since the Late Eighteenth century* (Abingdon: Routledge, 2008), 13–30.
Weber, Eugene, *Peasants into Frenchmen* (Stanford, CA: Stanford University Press, 1976).

Into the European Community at Last: Reinventing Britain as a European Power?

Anne Deighton

Introduction

The achievement of the Heath-Pompidou duo in securing Britain's entry into the European Community (EC) in 1973 marked a sharp change in the British government's role as a European power[1]. Britain had, of course, had a long history as a European player, making alliances and engaging in military interventions on the continent, most recently and notably in the First and Second World Wars. Yet the cultural trope of being an independent, seafaring imperial power which could balance continental European power struggles still resonated, at least in elite circles[2].

However, in the United Kingdom (UK), the definition of Europe itself had always been as problematic as that of how 'European' Britain's Anglo-Saxon political culture really was. How far did 'Europe' and its European cultures stretch? How far to the east and south did its borders reach? This was never entirely clear, not least when national borders were shifting, and new nation-states were being formed in the twentieth century. Our focus is upon Britain's relationship with the six West European countries that created the European Economic Community (EEC) in 1958. The UK's perception of this institution was given greater emphasis than the relationship between Britain and 'Europe': the EC was to be the new setting for Britain's economy and

---

1 Nomenclature is important: since 1993, 'European Union' (EU); from the signing of the Merger Treaty of 1967 until 1993, 'European Communities' (EC); and from its founding in 1958 to 1967, the 'European Economic Community' (EEC) of France, West Germany, Italy, The Netherlands, Belgium, and Luxembourg.

2 This was elaborated by a Foreign Office official, Sir Eyre Crowe, as early as 1907, and retained a talismanic place in British elite thinking. For an overview of Crowe's life and career, Richard A Cosgrove, 'The Career of Sir Eyre Crowe: A Reassessment', *Albion* 4/4 (1972), 193–205.

still-ambitious international diplomacy in the face of its declining imperial reach[3].

We have rich personal archives, testimonials, and other non-state archives to supplement the official records of the period. However, a contemporary historian has always had a fearsome job, for many of the actors from the recent past are still alive, and indeed many are still politically active. Some may wish to 'edit' their own past actions in the light of contemporary events, so interviews given with the benefit of hindsight can carry their own dangers. Many British politicians now write their own memoirs and autobiographies. Yet, for balance, the official record for the recent past is often less than complete, not least given the time restrictions upon the release of some government papers. This is why enriching our knowledge of the earlier period under consideration with the help of new sets of private papers is an asset to the ever-developing interpretations of the past. In this way, historians can assess the past with greater accuracy and objective distance, all while accepting that our historical judgements are always provisional, coloured and informed by the present. This is particularly true for the post-Brexit period of European history.

Three sections follow. The first explores why joining the European Community was so problematic for the UK. The distinguished French historian Robert Frank has identified three chronological phases of British-European relations: 1713–1904, 1904–1961, and 1961–2016 ('Entrer, se faire une place et en sortir'). In contrast, this chapter gives greater importance to the significance of the immediate postwar years[4]. The second looks specifically at British diplomacy, especially towards France after Edward Heath became

---

3 The overriding importance of NATO was never forgotten in Britain, however. The Soviet Union was not generally considered a 'European' power as the Cold War developed, despite the clearly European origins of Marxist ideology, as the philosopher Isaiah Berlin pointed out to the Foreign Office in 1948. See Anne Deighton, 'Don and Diplomat: Isaiah Berlin and Britain's Early Cold War', *Cold War History* (2013), DOI:10.1080/14682745.2013.773213, and citations therein from the National UK Archives, FO/953/144, Berlin to FO, handwritten letter, 17 March 1948; FO/953/144, Rennie note, 19 March 1948.

4 Robert Frank, 'Introduction', in *Être ou ne pas être européen: Les Britanniques et l'Europe du XVIIe siècle au Brexit* (Paris: Belin, 2018). For a perceptive overview, see also Richard Davis, *Britain, France and the Battle for the Leadership of Europe, 1945–2007* (London: Routledge, 2023).

prime minister in 1970[5]. The third reinforces the observation that British membership of the Community was never without its difficulties. It concludes with remarks about the continuity of Britain's priorities over time and reflects briefly on the future of being 'European' after Britain's ill-conceived and badly managed exit from the EU from January 2020.

Joining? 1945–1967

The UK was not invaded or conquered in the Second World War, unlike its continental neighbours. Its hard-won victory left a legitimate pride in Britain's empire, military, governmental institutions, and resilient legal and constitutional system. British strategic thinking was dominated by a continual insistence on its own capacity to remain a 'leader' in international affairs in reshaping the international system, despite the costs this would involve given its own precarious financial position by the end of the war. This meant having a seat at the diplomatic 'top table' of peacemakers and new institution-builders, in addition to an 'independent' nuclear deterrent as the Cold War emerged, even as Britain was beginning to divest itself of its imperial possessions[6]. Britain could balance power on the postwar continent because of its occupied military zone in defeated Germany, and its place in the negotiations leading to the creation of West Germany in 1949. As the institutions of the new global order were being constructed, ideas about co-operation and supranational integration were also being explored, with the hope of creating a new regional order in Western Europe that might render yet another war impossible. This is the context in which Britain turned away from supranational integration efforts between 1950 and 1961. A fear of the Soviet Union and communism dominated British politics[7]. Early on, even

---

5 See, for example, Patrick Robert, *The Heath-Pompidou Summit: Franco-British European Honeymoon or Marriage of Convenience?*, PhD diss. (University of Reading, 2019).

6 From the mid-1940s onwards, the often violent dismantling of the vast British Empire was underway in India, Ceylon, post-mandate Palestine, Malaya, parts of Africa, and later the Gulf. The UK was eventually left with a national narrative based upon the image of a seafaring island with imperial outposts, and with close and special ties with the developing Commonwealth, and with the US via culture, language, sterling and economics.

7 British Anti-communism had been a major cultural phenomenon since the First World War.

the US looked to the UK for political leadership in Europe, while the British themselves were developing their different vision for the future, based upon intergovernmental structures and a 'vision' derived from the emerging Commonwealth model of informal cooperation. American efforts to create a quasi-federal decision-making system for Western Europe through the implementation of the Marshall Aid package were stalled by the British, who demanded consensus decision-making. At the same time, the effectiveness of the 1948 Council of Europe, a quasi-federal initiative, was stalled by Britain's insertion of an intergovernmental Committee of Ministers into the structure, thereby neutering the Council at birth. This led the Americans to think their wider quasi-federal strategy for Western Europe was failing, although the North Atlantic Treaty promised future military backing – via consensus – to West European countries. So by the autumn of 1949, the US started to turn instead to France for continental leadership, despite the volatility of French domestic politics in the Fourth Republic.

The turning point for both Britain and France came in May 1950, when the French-West German Schuman Plan for the joint control of coal and steel industries (the drivers of war) was proposed. This was spearheaded by the policy entrepreneur Jean Monnet and was to be called the European Coal and Steel Community. This was a key moment, the parting of the ways. Edmund Dell has argued that this was the moment when the British lost leadership of Europe[8]. It certainly marked the beginning of the West European supranational integration movement and dramatically opened the way to shaping the future EEC. There was pique in London about the Schuman Plan, not least because the Americans had been told about it before the British government. The personality mix really mattered in 1950 – then as now – and relations between the British and French became increasingly frosty and competitive. British reasoning at the time also reveals a raft of assumptions during this decision-making period marked by crisis. The plan did not fit with the Labour Party's vast domestic programme of nationalisation – and domestic politics were the priority of the Labour government. The Schuman Plan required a commitment to a joint, supranational management structure for coal and steel

[8] Edmund Dell, *The Schuman Plan and the British Abdication of Leadership in Europe* (Oxford: Oxford University Press, 1995); Anne Deighton, 'Brave New World – Brave Old World', *Contemporary European History* 28/1 (2019), 31–4.

even before any detailed procedures were fleshed out – a *loi cadre* approach. After unsuccessfully trying to propose an association with the founding members of the Coal and Steel Community, or even advisory, intergovernmental ways forward for coal and steel production, Britain rejected the Schuman Plan package. The persuasive Winston Churchill, no longer prime minister but leader of the Conservative Party in opposition, was also happy to stir up dissent. It is noteworthy that after this point, no major British political party was an unequivocal supporter of European supranational integration.

In the same year, even as the Pleven Plan for French-German integrated armed forces was also rejected out of hand by Britain, the Foreign Office began to synthesise Britain's attitude to continental integration. Supranationality, which was viewed as a far-sighted but potentially dangerous strategy developed by France to control a recovering West Germany, was acceptable to London, although British membership in any such scheme was out of the question. If France-led integration succeeded, the challenge would simply be to keep the new institutions firmly nested within the all-important NATO/ Atlantic Community, supported by notional intergovernmental European defence agreements (Brussels Treaty, 1948; Western European Union, 1955). The UK could subsequently still pursue its global role.

'Association' was the favoured British response that reflected the cultural and strategic doubts that the British held about integration, instead preferring the 'with, but not of' route that was taken from 1954, and then from 1956–9, with British proposals for free trade area solutions that would include the Commonwealth and dilute the EEC. A key 1951 Foreign Office document is worth citing here. Its superior tone is perhaps of a different era, but it resonates today.

> Apart from ... Commonwealth ties and the ... sterling area, we cannot consider submitting our political and economic system to supra-national institutions... Nor is there, in fact, any evidence that there is real support in this country for any institutional connexion with the continent. Moreover... it is not in the true interests of the continent that we should sacrifice our present unattached position which enables us, together with the United States, to give a lead to the free world.[9]

9 *Documents on British Policy Overseas*, Series 2/1, (London: Her Majesty's Stationery Office, 1986), PUSC (51)12.

This extraordinary planning document was in essence an implementation of Winston Churchill's famous 'Three Circles' party conference speech of 1948, which set the framework for strategic thinking about the place of Britain in the world, and has had enormous persistence over time as one of the most important strategic statements about Britain in the post-war era[10]. Britain, Churchill had argued, was the only country at the centre of the three great interlocking strategic circles of Western Europe, the US, and the Empire-Commonwealth. A British commitment to one circle alone would destroy the whole structure of the free world, and thus its ability to fight communism. The argument was that Britain's international leadership – the top priority – could only be guaranteed by sustaining its pivotal balance between the three circles. As a result, Britain was the Community's first supranational integration refusenik[11].

Yet the UK had failed to grasp West Europe's game-changing diplomacy, in which France became the continental leader. By 1950, it had seized the initiative and ingeniously used the Schuman Plan, and after 1957 the EEC, as substitute loci in Europe for French power. France too was decolonising, but it was to commandeer the EEC as the basis for a French-dominated post-imperial 'Euro-Afrique'. By the late 1950s, French President Charles de Gaulle, who understood Britain's strategic and cultural doubts about continental European integration so well, as well as the bilateral power struggle this implied, had no compunctions. He unilaterally kept Britain out of its European project with three vetoes in 1959 (free trade association); 1963 (EEC membership) after Conservative Prime Minister Harold Macmillan's application in 1961; and again in 1967, when Labour's Harold Wilson was prime minister[12]. During those years, the other five EEC members largely supported Britain's application, but judged that the relationship with France

10 Winston S. Churchill, *Europe Unites: Speeches, 1947 and 1948* (Cassell, 1950), discussed in Anne Deighton, 'Britain and the Three Interlocking Circles', in Antonio Varsori, ed., *Europe 1945–1990s: The End of an Era?* (London: Macmillan, 1995), 155–70.

11 It should be noted that Ireland, Denmark and Norway also applied for membership in 1961, and in 1967, but their applications also lapsed when Britain was turned down. Norway rejected membership after a referendum in 1972, but Denmark, Ireland and the UK joined in 1973.

12 M. Pine, *Harold Wilson and Europe: Pursuing Britain's Membership of the European Communities* (London: Bloomsbury, 2008); Piers Ludlow, *Negotiating the Gaullist Challenge: The European Community, 1963–1969* (London: Routledge, 2006).

was now more important than that with the UK. This was particularly true of Chancellor Konrad Adenauer of West Germany.

Joining: 1970–1973, Pompidou and Heath

We must now ask why it was that Britain's two earlier attempts to join the Community in 1963 and 1967 failed, but the third set of negotiations after 1970 proved successful. Had French diplomacy simply been driven by de Gaulle? Or was the setting now different? How far was success in 1973 due to the leadership skills and personal chemistry of Prime Minister Heath and President Pompidou?

Pompidou had taken office in June 1969 with the formidable task of following de Gaulle's charismatic tenure of office. Heath then became the Conservative Party's Prime Minister in June 1970, after an election campaign in which the sitting Labour Party had been tipped by the pollsters to win once again. Heath had been a member of the House of Commons since 1950, and was a deeply committed politician, but not a leader who found easy sympathy from party or public[13]. His archives reveal a man who was methodical, an early Conservative supporter of supranational integration, even making his maiden speech on this topic. He had been a key player in the failed negotiations of 1961–3. Yet it is clear that by 1970, US pressure, the evaporation of Britain's empire, and its relative international economic decline all pushed Britain relentlessly towards the EEC, whichever party was in power. British elites were committed to membership (whatever the cost); what they had to do was persuade the French that membership would be mutually beneficial.

After de Gaulle's '*Non*' of 1967 to the Labour government's attempt to enter the Community, the British application was left on the table. At the

---

[13] See, generally, Edward Heath, *The Course of My Life* (London: Hodder & Stoughton, 1998); Heath, *Old World, New Horizons: Britain, the Common Market and the Atlantic Alliance* (Oxford: Oxford University Press, 1970); Heath, 'Realism in British Foreign Policy', *Foreign Affairs* 48/1 (1969), 39–50. John Campbell, *Edward Heath: A Biography* (London: Jonathan Cape, 1993); Peter Hennessy, *The Prime Minister: The Office and its Holders since 1945* (London: Allen Lane, 2000). Christopher Hill and Christopher Lord, 'The Foreign Policy of the Heath Government', in Stuart Ball and Anthony Seldon, eds, *The Heath Government 1970–1974: A Reappraisal* (New York: Longman, 1996).

very important Hague Community Summit of 1969, Pompidou confirmed to the British that the application could continue to proceed, allowing for enlargement negotiations to start. It was necessary for 'the applicant states [to] accept the treaties and their political finality, the decisions taken since the entry into force of the treaties and the options made in the sphere of development'[14].

This key moment gave the essential impetus to Britain's subsequent diplomacy. This is highly significant and shows that even before Heath became prime minister the following June, both Labour and Conservative leaders realised that British membership was essential to British interests.

Indeed, Heath had already conducted talks in Paris with Pompidou, Prime Minister Chaban-Delmas and Foreign Minister Maurice Schumann in May 1970, even before he became prime minister. It is very revealing that in these talks in Paris, Schumann quizzed Heath about the nature of the 1961–3 negotiations, and how any new ones could be managed better. The prospect of a third failure was not one to be taken lightly by either side. On detail, Heath was at pains to suggest that the talks on deepening the Community should not 'proceed either too fast [or] in such a way as to frighten the British people'. He went on to argue that as 'keepers of the Communities' conscience', the Commission's negotiating procedures could slow up application proceedings by putting forward 'the pure milk of doctrine', which might prove troublesome to practical problem solving. He preferred 'some form of honest broker arrangement', in which differences especially between the Community and the US could be sorted out by strong individual diplomacy[15]. Heath's personal ambition and his desire to make a mark on the international system are clear.

---

[14] The Hague Summit, text of the communique, official English text of the Common Market summit's communique, Bodleian Library archive, Heath papers, EH 4/2/14/E, Political Office. I am deeply grateful to Dr Jeremy McIlwaine of the Bodleian Library, University of Oxford, for his assistance regarding the Heath papers. For the Hague conference of December 1969 final communique: <http://www.cvce.eu/obj/final_communique_of_the_hague_summit_2_december_19 69-en-33078789-8030-49c8-b4e0-15d053834507.html>.

[15] Soames to PM, 'Mr Heath's call on M. Schumann, 5 May 1970, 8 May 1970, additional note by Soames, 12 May 1970, Bodleian Library archive, Heath papers, EH/4/2/14/E. By January 1971, the French negotiators in Brussels were also asking for more bilateral diplomacy and another summit to jump start their own torrid negotiations, 'Paris Chronology' for Soames, Bodleian Library archive, Heath papers, EH/4/2/14/E.

The long-term and instinctive enthusiasm of Heath himself was naturally tempered by Briain's earlier national diplomatic failures, and by the fact that it was not clear that public opinion was as firmly behind British membership as was French public opinion, hence his promise to report regularly to Parliament, and the Party's manifesto focusing upon rather vague economic and security benefits that could come from membership. The malign presence of Enoch Powell MP, who was, until 1974, still in the Conservative Party, meant that fears about migration and race were never far beneath the surface. Industrial tension and unrest at home were also destabilising factors. However, the Labour Party – now in opposition – was also split on the issue of membership, as the Labour government had itself applied in 1967.

The Conservative manifesto for the June 1970 general election was cautious about the Community. There was little in the manifesto, or the campaign about Britain's leadership role in European politics. The manifesto's tone is low-key, explaining that the Conservative Party commitment was only to opening a negotiation based upon Britain's national interest, which reflected the caution revealed by public opinion polling. It said that:

> If we can negotiate the right terms, we believe that it would be in the long-term interest of the British people for Britain to join… and that it would make a major contribution to both the prosperity and the security of our country. The opportunities are immense. Economic growth and a higher standard of living would result from having a larger market. But we must also recognise the obstacles…. Our sole commitment is to negotiate; no more, no less.

When he became Prime Minister, Heath was supported by experienced diplomats, including Sir Christopher Soames as Ambassador to France (1968–1972), and Foreign Office officials, many of whom knew the dossiers from the experience of the 1960s, in addition to others, such as Michael Palliser (the father-in-law of the daughter of Paul-Henri Spaak)[16]. This was a deeply personal mission by Heath.

16 Soames was clearly very exercised by the fact that Sir Patrick Riley had essentially been sacked, as he was considered to have moved too close to de Gaulle's own position on the EC in 1967. Soames' correspondence with Heath veers at times towards the sycophantic: Soames, British Embassy, Paris, handwritten letter to PM, Secret and Personal, 26 May 1971, Bodleian Libraries, University of Oxford, Heath papers, EH/4/2/14/E. See also Melissa Pine, 'British Personal Diplomacy and Public Policy: The Soames Affair', *Journal of European Integration History* 10/2 (2004), 59–76.

After Richard Nixon became the US President in 1969, there was considerable uncertainty in foreign affairs. Meanwhile, the ongoing exploration of Ostpolitik and détente in the late 1960s was affecting the more rigid Cold War order. Heath however remained determined that he could generate a successful enlargement and succeed where his two predecessors had failed. Pompidou, who visited Moscow and Washington early in his presidency, was also obviously aware of these international changes. The emergence of an Ostpolitik driven by Bonn could alter the continental balance of power if relations between West Germany and the Soviet Union and its allies became too friendly. It now seemed that Britain's presence in the Community could help build a firmer balance of power alongside France against any aspirations of a potentially revisionist West Germany[17].

However, the French remained tough negotiators: Britain could only enter if it agreed to the Community's own terms, and it had been made clear by Community leaders that Britain was now the *plaideur*, whatever the government might say at home. As the leading civil servant of the day, Con O'Neill, lamented, this time round Britain had to 'swallow the lot' – that is, all the rules and the *acquis* if it was to join the Community[18].

The Heath archive and the British National Archives also reveal that personal bilateral contacts between Britain and France were of great importance. Bilateral summits were held in May 1971, March 1972, and May 1972, and a wider EC Summit in October 1972, with applicant states present. Personal relations between the two heads of state were never instinctively warm, and the British, at least, were measured in their private assessments of Pompidou's priorities and political management[19]. This emerged strongly after the referendum in France in April 1972, when the French voting public

17 Heath had detailed briefings on the developing international position when he first took office. This was also largely the view from the US, see CIA report, Secret, CIA-RDP85T00875R001500040036-9, 20, Weekly Summary special report: Pompidou: The Presidential Tightrope, October 1972.

18 David Hannay, ed., *Britain's Entry into the European Community: Report on the Negotiations of 1970–1972 by Sir Con O'Neill* (London: Frank Cass, 2000), 40.

19 For revealing correspondence on personalities from the British Embassy in Paris in April 1972, see in particular, HE Christopher Soames to Greenhill, 21 April, 1971, Bodleian Library, University of Oxford, Heath Archive, EH/4/0/14E (Armstrong file), letter and detailed report in which doubts about personalities are linked to the absolute necessity that the negotiations must succeed, whatever the cost, although success

agreed to enlargement, but as the turnout was relatively low (68 %), Pompidou considered this a grave set-back to his popularity and authority.

A technical negotiating structure operated in parallel to the summits from June 1970. In Brussels the details were argued and then agreed, although progress was slow until April 1971. The personal meetings between Heath and Pompidou had a wider agenda, which was intended to allow for the pride and sensitivities of both sides to be addressed, and again reinforced the view that the route to Brussels had to be through Paris. For Pompidou, British membership could reinforce his continued leadership of a French-dominated Europe. Heath afterwards liked to say that personal, private diplomacy, including secret talks on some kind of nuclear deal with Pompidou, sealed the bid and secured France's agreement to British membership, but this conflicts with the tripartite nature of the Western nuclear arrangement, and the overwhelmingly important role of the US therein[20]. Rather, it seems that the aims of Heath and Pompidou had merged by 1970, with domestic, economic considerations (and personal ambition) driving both men, albeit for different reasons, in addition to their mutual appreciation of the declining importance of mid-ranking European powers if superpower détente succeeded.

The documents also show that these practical questions relating to the economy, sterling, regional development and specific issues important for domestic policies on both sides were as crucial as restating agreement on the broader issues of integration for peace. Underlying this, for both the British and French, was the realisation that these negotiations could not be allowed to fail for the third time – the humiliation for both men, their countries and diplomats would be too intense. Of course, while successful high-level bilateral diplomacy could enhance the profile and careers of both leaders, a failure would reflect badly on them personally. The stakes were consequently always very high for both men.

'comes down to an Anglo-French understanding', which comes with all the risks that Pompidou might misjudge 'how high he can set the hurdle' for the British.

20 See chapter by Beatrice Heuser in this volume. More generally, Beatrice Heuser, *NATO, Britain, France and the FRG: Nuclear Strategies and Forces for Europe, 1949–2000* (London: Macmillan, 1997); Richard Ullman, 'The Covert French Connection', *Foreign Policy* 75 (1989), 3–33; Helen Parr, 'The Nuclear Myth: Edward Heath, Europe, and the International Politics of Anglo-French Nuclear Co-operation 1970–1973', *The International History Review* 35/3 (2013).

One of the most intriguing aspects of the negotiations was the use of language. The records show that the language used by both men was carefully crafted, often ambiguous, and frequently shrouded in generalities. For example, Heath, who knew the importance to Pompidou of the Community's economic and monetary union debates since the Werner report, stated that he 'fully supported the development of economic and monetary union…[but he was concerned that colleagues] should not be led to expect abrupt changes which might seem likely to affect their respective currencies'.[21] Likewise, the word 'political', with its slightly difference implications in French and English, became an enabler of progress for both sides. For the Community and Pompidou, it essentially meant a foreign policy stance which transcended national interests and eventually absorbed them into a union of Community interests. Pompidou used it cleverly to reset the negotiation away from supranationality, and more toward political convergence and agreement between states. As he said in January 1971:

> some people imagined that Europe could organise itself around a certain number of technical organisations and commissions which could in some fashion be the precursor of a European federation. But international life, whether it be federal or not, must be political … [but then] political power was elsewhere. It was in Washington [Marshall plan and NATO]. … .
>
> Thus European was anything but European … . [Now], it can only be a matter of building on what exists, a confederation of States resolved to harmonise their politics and integrate their economies … . But the government of Europe can only emerge from the uniting of national governments coming together to take decisions applying to all … . I therefore conclude that important decisions can only be taken on the basis of unanimous agreement and that what is at issue here is political reality rather than juridicial rule. … It is a question of making progress rather than in words, and of test[ing] change as one goes along.[22]

However, for British diplomats, a more 'political' EC meant greater focus on day-to-day cooperation in foreign policymaking and diplomacy, for eventual

---

21 The Prime Minister, 'Record of a conversation between the Prime Minister and the President of the French republic at the Élysee Palace', Paris, 21 May 1971, 1600 hours, Bodleian Libraries, University of Oxford, Heath Papers, EH4/2/14/E.

22 Pompidou press conference, 21 January 1971, classified, translated for FCO as Tel80. EH4/0/14E, Heath Archive, Bodleian Libraries, University of Oxford, Heath Papers, EH4/2/14/E.

European unity (but not union, not federation). This interpretation was very much in the minds and language of British diplomats, who had already participated in the early talks about the creation of the Conference on Security and Cooperation in Europe (CSCE) through an intergovernmental European Political Cooperation procedure for Community members even before Britain's membership was concluded. However, it was essential that collective foreign policymaking remained a mutual aim, without the implications for statehood that a totally integrated foreign and security policy would mean for all member states, with all its implications for national sovereignty, independence and national cultures. As Heath said at the May summit:

> I have long believed that Europe must grow steadily together in unity, and that Britain should be a part of that wider entity [...]. Only by working together can we play a full and worthy part in the outside world.[23]

Personal diplomacy thus eased the path, protected the dignity of all, and promoted a common ambition for deeper and enlarged Community via cooperation and 'distinctively European policies, in the first instance principally in economic matters and progressively on other fields'[24]. This evaded the eternally contested and difficult idea of the ultimate purpose of integration, especially monetary union involving the UK, and the maintenance of vital national interest clauses, thereby enabling both sides to move ahead to secure British membership, at least in the short term, although this continually presented British sceptics with fuel for their anxieties[25]. Ironically, Heath reverted to a more traditional British approach in, of all places, his speech marking the signing of the accession treaty, when he reverted to the image of Britain now leading the Community in new directions.

In sum, the relationship between Pompidou and Heath was not the principal reason for success in 1973, although both men did, this time, want

---

23 Statement by the Prime Minister at the Palais de L'Élysée, 21 May 1971, Bodleian Libraries, University of Oxford, Heath Papers, EH/4/2/14/E.

24 The extent of Heath's commitment to the long-term future and working of the Community was in many respects mirrored by Pompidou's own ambiguity on this issue, despite his being called the Master Builder of Europe, for example, at WPA/770/OPE, 'Annotated Agenda on textual agreements' n.d., Bodleian Libraries, University of Oxford, Heath Papers, EH/4/2/14/E.

25 Chief Conservative Party Whip to Douglas Hurd, Political Secretary, 24 May 1971, EH/4/2/13/E.

membership of the Community. International factors, including the developing détente, required France to balance its relations with Britain and the US, and to prevent the perceived competition from a rising West Germany. Likewise, the capacities of national diplomats in London and Paris were rightly supplemented by the technical-level diplomacy that was proceeding in parallel in Brussels, and which was to form the essential institutional and policy bedrock for enlargement. Yet if the relationship between the two leaders had ever broken down publicly and completely, it is possible that the diplomats could not have sustained the negotiating impetus. In the last resort, relations with France were still more important to the other five EC members than relations with the UK – their cohesion had been directly challenged in 1963 and 1967, leaving Britain as the embarrassed loser on both occasions. The link between state acquiescence to enlargement at the highest level, and the interests of existing EC members, had to be harnessed for the negotiation to succeed, and this time they were.

Membership and Leaving

This account makes clear that Britain's deep-seated political culture and ambitions were not primed for conflict-free Community membership[26]. When it finally joined in 1973, the British brought their own ideas of how its membership of the EC should play out. The economy was not in good shape either – and it is probably a truism worth remembering – that any successful EU enlargement has to be on the back of economic growth, for then there is more scope to cut the economic cake and share it out. Yet the early 1970s were dominated by the Yom Kippur War and the economic effects of the devastating oil supply crisis. At the same time, Ostpolitik and détente posed a double strategic dilemma for Britain. Diplomats realised that, on the European level of Ostpolitik and European détente, West Germany was rapidly becoming a comparatively more important player than France, while at the level of superpower détente, the status quo of all these three mid-ranking powers was challenged by direct US-Soviet negotiations. In their different ways, both Pompidou and Heath realised

26 Other chapters in this collection deal with some of these policy areas.

this strategic dilemma as one that challenged diplomatic relations between themselves and with the US.

This gives further significance to British efforts to develop one of a number of policy areas, that is, the non-supranational, intergovernmental cooperative aspect of the EC – established through European Political Cooperation (EPC) – to try to make a real impact as effective leaders within the Community. EPC was an intergovernmental development within the Community that was intended to support national diplomacy in partnership with the Community structures, but not as part of them. The EPC role in the Community was probably most successful in the delicate and quiet multilateral diplomacy within the wider Conference of Security and Cooperation in Europe (CSCE), which brought a diplomatic détente to Europe from the Helsinki Agreement of 1975 and beyond into the post-Cold War world[27].

Likewise, the contradictions in British policies inside the EC later came to be reflected in the championing of the Single European Act by Thatcher in the mid-1980s, in her instinctive reversion to pre-Community days as the Cold War ended, and in her rising fear of German domination, which finally brought her government down, along with the demanding negotiation over the Maastricht and later Amsterdam treaties. In one sense, one can understand Thatcher's world view, which was drawn from the 1940s and before, as politicians do draw from their personal experience of the past. In the 'Cold War' view, it seems clear that supranational integration could only work if it was firmly nested within a hard military alliance backed by the US and NATO in the face of an outside threat. For example, in the Cold War, Greece, Portugal, and then Spain were NATO members before being admitted to the EC. By 1990, with German unification, the security framework was shifting, with the emergence of Eastern European states as independent entities, thus creating the conditions for the slow burning implosion of the Soviet Union's

27 Brian White, *Britain, Détente and Changing East-West Relations* (London: Routledge, 1992). See further, Anne Deighton, 'The Basis of Ostpolitik and Détente: The Heath Government (1970–1974) and the Berlin Question', in Michael Borchard, Stefan Karner, Hanns Jürgen Küsters, and Peter Ruggenthaler, eds, *West German Ostpolitik, the Soviet Union, and East-West Détente in Europe*, Lexington (forthcoming); its German edition is entitled, *Entspannung im Kalten Krieg*, Leytamverlag (2020). For an authoritative multi-archival account from a British perspective, Kai Hebel, *Britain, Détente, and the CSCE: 'Fathers of the Final Act'* Routledge, 2025.

continental empire, and then the Russian Republic by 1991, which meant the old threat from communism in the east was now evaporating.

This brings us to today. Sadly, it is indeed the experience of Britain's 2016 referendum and subsequent departure from the EU which acts as a trigger to refresh our insights, and to inform the historian's work about our fifty-year relationship with the EU. The referendum campaign led to a bitter round of diplomacy and the eventual but incomplete Brexit settlement by 2020. Had Britain's EU membership been just an experiment, just a fifty-year adventure?

The Brexit experience – like defining 'European' as simply meaning being inside the EU – runs the risk of over-simplification for historians. Further, it would be wrong to assume that Britain's joining the EC in 1973, and its departure in 2020, was necessarily part of the same process. A holistic view of joining and then leaving the EC/EU creates an over-simplified historical interpretation. The later, Brexit period was also driven by new domestic and international political forces. Populism, social discontent, the experience of the 2008–9 crash, dire political calculations by Conservative Prime Ministers David Cameron and Boris Johnson, and perhaps also a popular misperception about 'sovereignty' in the twentieth century all contributed to negative perceptions in Britain about the EU by 2016. Yet the experience of the past, and of Britain's earlier reservations, also resonated through the gruelling Brexit process between 2016 and 2020, and there is no doubt that the run-up to membership in 1973, and the tensions that continued to exist, formed part of the wave of alienation from the EU, with 52 % of voters voting to leave in 2016[28].

We will probably never know whether it was indeed inevitable that Britain would leave the EU, and whether by leaving, the British reverted to a perception that what was 'normal' geopolitically did not include membership of a supranational institution. Historians will no doubt continue to debate this while the consequences of Brexit play out through the years.

Yet we do already know that Brexit has scarred both Britain and the EU itself. Britain still seems openly burdened by its past imperial inheritance.

28 Anand Menon and Geoffrey Evans, *Brexit and British Politics* (Cambridge: Polity Press, 2017). Scotland and Northern Ireland voted by a majority to remain in the EU, while voters in Wales voted to leave. For an extended assessment, Robert Saunders, 'Brexit and Empire: "Global Britain" and the Myth of Imperial Nostalgia', *The Journal of Imperial and Commonwealth History* 48/2 (2020), 1–35.

(The irony of all this is that Britain actively encouraged the post-Cold War states of Eastern Europe to make their own massive cultural and political shifts very quickly after communism, and to re-imagine themselves as members of a democratic EU, while then finding it impossible to do the same itself…). We see the Brexiters' obsession with the 'Anglosphere' and Commonwealth; the so-called Five-Eyes intelligence network; a desire for national sovereignty and our own legal and constitutional system; for a go-it-alone autonomy larded with non-specific hostility to some immigrants; and an attachment to sterling. These seem to be the cultural markers for British sentiment. However, those in favour of leaving the EU did not – and have not yet constructed – a realistic and coherent new strategy for the country. The Labour government has made considerable efforts to construct stronger bilateral, inter-state relations, especially with France, although the fear of anti-EU populism continues to haunt the government. Can it be the case that a new resetting of relations will once again depend upon Anglo-French relations?

As we have seen, the quest for British post-imperial leadership within the European Community was hard fought for but is now over. Conservative governments did not say what the sunlit uplands might look like beyond aspirations for global entrepreneurial leadership, free trade deals and greater bilateralism in foreign policy for a new 'global Britain', catch-phrases deployed like some post-imperial default button. It is also significant that Northern Ireland is now both trapped in a hideous crossover of Britain's post-imperial and European policy frames and is the victim of deeply intractable diplomatic issues relating to Brexit. Our French neighbours – partners in partial and tentative hard-power bilateralism – must be watching us closely, but breaches of trust, as well as some British bad diplomatic manners, will only be forgotten slowly.

Does this all matter, apart from the loss of British national prestige and the economic dangers that lie ahead? Yes it does. At crucial moments, historians can see the past through a new lens – and Brexit is just such a lens. States can be the positive builders of the international system: the UK was a positive builder of a new international system in the 1940s, until presented with the dilemma of supranational integration and a leadership challenge from France.

But states can also be destructive, for as you pull out one thread from the fabric (Brexit), you alter and begin to weaken the assumptions of the remaining international order. Although the British Conservative Government promised to continue the rules-based order after 2020, this is now in effect under challenge. This challenge is to both the EU and NATO, as Republicans under Donald Trump return to power, Russia seeks an expansionist role in Europe, the Middle East descends into fearful wars and repression, and China flexes its muscles on the international stage. Both the Commonwealth and the UN, in different ways, are now vulnerable to unravelling, as the wider balance of power starts to shift within the international system. Brexit contributed to the ongoing international institutional decline that has been developing since the 1990s, and the usually clear-headed leadership of European heads of state has clearly weakened badly since the end of the Cold War, as EU leaders struggle to redefine their role and place in the international system in a time of deep international crises.

Britons have found that Brexit has not in reality empowered its politicians to reconstruct the country but appears instead as a last gasp of national longing for a past world. Nostalgia provides only weak signposts for the future. Today we will not be able to recreate our past. Trust has diminished; transactional politics dominate; the wider international framework has changed; and the EU, also vulnerable as an institution now, seeks new policy priorities. Instead, at home the British face something of a shipwreck of post-Brexit domestic politics. British Europeanists are restricted to trying to make the most of our cultural common ground (including human rights, language, geography, wealth, perhaps shared imperial histories, and indeed the work of European Foundations and Archivists), and to tiptoe quietly ahead as they try to build a joint civil society, with security initiatives as willing Europeans, if not EUropeans.

Bibliography

Campbell, John, *Edward Heath: A Biography* (London: Jonathan Cape, 1993).

Cosgrove, Richard A., 'The Career of Sir Eyre Crowe: A Reassessment', *Albion* 4/4 (1972), 193–205.

Deighton, Anne, 'Brave New World – Brave Old World', *Contemporary European History* 28/1 (2019), 31–4.

———, Anne, 'Britain and the Three Interlocking Circles', in Antonio Varsori, ed., *Europe 1945–1990s: The End of an Era?* (London: Macmillan, 1995), 155–70.

———, Anne, 'Don and Diplomat: Isaiah Berlin and Britain's Early Cold War', *Cold War History* (2013), DOI:10.1080/14682745.2013.773213, and citations therein from the National UK Archives, FO/953/144, Berlin to FO, handwritten letter, 17 March 1948; FO/953/144, Rennie note, 19 March 1948.

———, Anne, 'The Basis of Ostpolitik and Détente: The Heath Government (1970–1974) and the Berlin Question', in Michael Borchard, Stefan Karner, Hanns Jürgen Küsters, and Peter Ruggenthaler, eds, *West German Ostpolitik, the Soviet Union, and East-West Détente in Europe*, Lexington (forthcoming); its German edition is entitled, *Entspannung im Kalten Krieg*, Leytamverlag (2020).

Dell, Edmund, *The Schuman Plan and the British Abdication of Leadership in Europe* (Oxford: Oxford University Press, 1995).

Documents on British Policy Overseas, Series 2/1, (London: Her Majesty's Stationery Office, 1986), PUSC (51)12.

Frank, Robert, 'Introduction', in *Être ou ne pas être européen: Les Britanniques et l'Europe du XVIIe siècle au Brexit* (Paris: Belin, 2018). For a perceptive overview, see also Richard Davis, *Britain, France and the Battle for the Leadership of Europe, 1945–2007* (London: Routledge, 2023).

Hannay, David, ed., *Britain's Entry into the European Community: Report on the Negotiations of 1970–1972 by Sir Con O'Neill* (London: Frank Cass, 2000).

Heuser, Beatrice, *NATO, Britain, France and the FRG: Nuclear Strategies and Forces for Europe, 1949–2000* (London: Macmillan, 1997).

Edward Heath Archive, Bodleian Libraries, University of Oxford.

———, Edward, *Old World, New Horizons: Britain, the Common Market and the Atlantic Alliance* (Oxford: Oxford University Press, 1970).

———, Edward, 'Realism in British Foreign Policy', *Foreign Affairs* 48/1 (1969), 39–50.

———, Edward, *The Course of My Life* (London: Hodder & Stoughton, 1998).

Hebel, Kai, *Britain, Détente, and the CSCE: 'Fathers of the Final Act'* (London: Routledge, 2025).

Hennessy, Peter, *The Prime Minister: The Office and its Holders since 1945* (London: Allen Lane, 2000).

Hill, Christopher, and Christopher Lord, 'The Foreign Policy of the Heath Government', in Stuart Ball and Anthony Seldon, eds, *The Heath Government 1970–1974: A Reappraisal* (New York: Longman, 1996).

Ludlow, N. Piers, *Negotiating the Gaullist Challenge: The European Community, 1963–1969* (London: Routledge, 2006).
Menon Anand, and Geoffrey Evans, *Brexit and British Politics* (Cambridge: Polity Press, 2017).
Parr, Helen, 'The Nuclear Myth: Edward Heath, Europe, and the International Politics of Anglo-French Nuclear Co-operation 1970–1973', *The International History Review* 35/3 (2013).
Pine, Melissa, 'British Personal Diplomacy and Public Policy: The Soames Affair', *Journal of European Integration History* 10/2 (2004), 59–76.
———, Melissa, *Harold Wilson and Europe: Pursuing Britain's Membership of the European Communities* (London: Bloomsbury, 2008).
Robert, Patrick, *The Heath-Pompidou Summit: Franco-British European Honeymoon or Marriage of Convenience?*, PhD diss. (University of Reading, 2019).
Saunders, Robert, 'Brexit and Empire: "Global Britain" and the Myth of Imperial Nostalgia', *The Journal of Imperial and Commonwealth History* 48/2 (2020), 1–35.
Ullman, Richard, 'The Covert French Connection', *Foreign Policy* 75 (1989), 3–33.
White, Brian, *Britain, Détente and Changing East-West Relations* (London: Routledge, 1992).

Turning the Tables: General de Gaulle's Vetoes of Britain's Applications to Join the EEC

Agnès Tachin

In 1963 and 1967, French President Charles de Gaulle twice vetoed the British application to join the Common Market. His decision triggered a crisis between France and its European partners, and poisoned relations between Paris and London for nearly a decade. The UK joined the EEC with Ireland and Denmark on 1 January 1973, after de Gaulle's successor, Georges Pompidou, lifted the veto. Over the past 40 years, the French vetoes have given rise to numerous publications and interpretations and have been more closely studied than the ensuing phase of enlargement[1]. They are part of an abundant historiography developed on both sides of the Channel on relations between France and the UK[2]. Many of these publications examine the respective relationship that both countries had with Europe[3]. The first works

---

1 Only one in-depth study has looked at the dialogue between Pompidou and Heath: Patrick Robert, *The Heath-Pompidou Paris 20–21 May 1971 Summit: Franco-British European Honeymoon or Marriage of Convenience? A Actor-centred Study of the Reasons for and Success of the Heath-Pompidou Meetings and of the Impact of 'Personal Diplomacy' in the Development of Franco-British and European Summitry under their Leadership*, PhD diss., University of Reading, 2020.

2 Antoine Capet, *Britain, France and the Entente Cordiale since 1904* (Basingstoke: Palgrave Macmillan, 2006); Philippe Chassaigne and M. L. Dockrill, *Anglo-French Relations, 1898–1998: From Fashoda to Jospin* (Basingstoke, Hampshire: Palgrave, 2002); Diana Cooper-Richet and Michel Rapoport, eds, *Cent ans de relations franco-britanniques (1904–2004)* (Paris: Créaphis, 2006); P. M. H. Bell, *France and Britain 1940–1994: The Long Separation* (London: Longman, 1997); Isabelle and Robert Tombs, *That Sweet Enemy: The French and the British from the Sun King to the Present* (London: William Heinenmann, 2006); Neville H. Waites, ed., *Troubled Neighbours: Franco-British Relations in the Twentieth Century* (London: Weidenfeld and Nicolson, 1971).

3 Oliver Daddow, *Britain and Europe since 1945: Historiographical Perspective on Integration* (Manchester: Manchester University Press, 2011); D. A. Gowland, Arthur Turner, and Alex Wright, *Britain and Europe Integration since 1945: On the Sidelines* (London: Routledge, 2010); Françoise de La Serre, Jacques Leruez, and Helen Wallace, eds, *Les politiques étrangères de la France et de la Grande-Bretagne depuis 1945 : l'inévitable ajustement* (Paris: Presses de la Fondation Nationale des Sciences Politiques, 1990);

on de Gaulle's vetoes in the 1970s were based on secondary sources, such as the memoirs and declarations of the central actors. By the late 1990s, access to primary sources from official British and French governmental archives, in addition to new approaches toward the subject, have enabled historians to better understand the genesis of his decision, as well as the reactions it provoked in France, England, and within the Community. Most of these works have analysed Gaullist opposition to British membership within the broader context of European integration and the Cold War.

In this paper, I will first look at the different approaches that have contributed to a better understanding of de Gaulle's thinking. I will then analyse the circumstances that led to the two vetoes, and the reactions they provoked among French politicians and public opinion.

The Genesis of the Vetoes: A Complex Issue with Multiple Approaches

Since the 1990s, the gradual opening up of governmental archives has made it possible to broaden the range of approaches, show the full complexity of the veto issue, and determine the responsibilities of leaders on both sides of the Channel. Anne Deighton has highlighted the UK government's errors which, through a policy of systematic obstruction of the Common Market, contributed to its own exclusion. From its withdrawal from the Messina Conference in 1955 to the creation of EFTA – a genuine war machine against the EEC – the British did everything in their power to prevent the Common Market from coming into force, and this policy had a counter-productive effect by strengthening the cohesion of the Six[4]. The governments of the Fourth Republic were not in favour of the free trade area proposed by the British and endeavoured to postpone negotiations. De Gaulle's return marked a stiffening in Franco-British relations, as he put an end to discussions on the free trade area, and then opposed Britain's

---

Alex May, *Britain and Europe since 1945* (London: Longman, 1999); Hugo Young, *This Blessed Plot: Britain and Europe from Churchill to Blair* (London: Macmillan, 1998); Alan Milward, *The Rise and Fall of a National Strategy: The UK and the European Community*, vol. 1 (London: Routledge, 2012).

4 Anne Deighton, 'La Grande-Bretagne et la Communauté économique européenne (1958–1963)', *Revue Histoire, Économie & Société* 13/1 (1994), 113–30.

application to join the Common Market. His motivations have given rise to several analyses. Maurice Vaïsse, and more recently Frédéric Gloriant, have explored the geopolitical reasons, and underscored the importance of security and defence[5]. Another trend has focused on economic issues: Piers Ludlow and Laurent Warlouzet have shown the importance of the Common Agricultural Policy that de Gaulle was determined to implement[6]. In addition to these factors, there were also historical and personal reasons. Historians such as Peter Mangold, or more recently Julian Jackson, have emphasised de Gaulle's complex relationship with 'Anglo-Saxons' since the Second World War[7]. All of these political, economic and historical reasons are closely intertwined. When he returned to power, de Gaulle wanted to restore France's greatness. His attitude was both pragmatic and guided by his grand design. He understood that his country needed the Common Market economically, and that through Europe it could once again play a leading role on the world stage, provided that Europe was independent of the United States, particularly in terms of defence and security.

Over the last two decades, historical studies focusing on the crises of the 1960s have also helped to sweep away a number of ideas conveyed by the classic narrative of European integration. They have tended to deconstruct the image of de Gaulle fighting alone against everyone, an image largely maintained by de Gaulle himself and the media and highlighted from the 1960s onwards by cartoonists such as Moisan and Leffel in France, and Cummings in England. Several studies have qualified the supposed unanimity of the Five against France. As Piers Ludlow has observed, the conditions set by the British government during the negotiations also worried the Italians and Germans. We should also distinguish between official positions and the reality of negotiations, where the French leaders were able to show themselves

---

5 Maurice Vaïsse, *La grandeur. Politique étrangère du général de Gaulle. 1958–1969* (Paris: Fayard, 1998); Frédéric Gloriant, *Le schisme franco-britannique : de Suez au veto de 1963* (Presses universitaires de Rennes: 2023).

6 N. Piers Ludlow, *The European Community and the Crisis of the 1960s: Negotiating the Gaullist Challenge* (London: Routledge, 2006); Laurent Warlouzet, *Le choix de la CEE par la France : l'Europe économique en débat de Mendès France à De Gaulle, 1955–1969*, Comité pour l'histoire économique et financière de la France, Paris, 2011.

7 Peter Mangold, *The Almost Impossible Ally: Harold Macmillan and Charles de Gaulle* (London: I. B. Tauris, 2006); Julian Jackson, *De Gaulle. Une certaine idée de la France* (Paris: Seuil, 2019).

to be more pragmatic and less intransigent[8]. The focus on French President de Gaulle and British Prime Ministers Macmillan and Wilson tends to reduce the history of European integration to a confrontation between great statesmen. Yet the role of close collaborators and public opinion also help to understand vetoes. The reactions to the French president's decision show that there was consensus surrounding the British candidacy, especially during the first veto. A cultural approach to the subject, and more specifically the study of representations and imaginations, sheds light on the French position in the face of British demands, which will be analysed in the discussion to follow[9].

The 1963 Veto

From 1958 onwards, de Gaulle's foreign policy aimed to restore France to a leading role on the international stage. This was done in two main ways: strengthening France's influence within the Atlantic Alliance and speeding up the entry into force of the Common Market. On the first point, de Gaulle's memorandum proposing a revision of the NATO command in September 1958 was rejected by US President Dwight D. Eisenhower and British Prime Minister Harold Macmillan. But he was more successful on the European question. As Anne Deighton has pointed out, there were in fact three vetoes: the first forgotten one was exercised on 14 November 1958, when France put an end to negotiations on the free trade area proposed by London[10]. This stop came two months after the proposed three-way *directoire* to review NATO's command structure. The refusal of Washington and London reinforced de Gaulle's conviction that France should expect nothing from the 'Anglo-Saxons'. He then refused the British request to postpone the date of entry into force of the Common Market to 1 January 1959. The Conservative government responded by setting up a rival association, the EFTA, which proved to be less successful economically than the EEC. In June 1959, de Gaulle received an official invitation from Queen Elizabeth II for a state visit, the timetable for which was only set by the Elysée Palace in the autumn to take place the following spring, on 5–8 April 1960.

---

8 Ludlow, *The European Community*.

9 Agnès Tachin, *Amie et rivale. La Grande-Bretagne dans l'imaginaire français à l'époque gaullienne* (Brussels, Peter Lang, 2009).

10 Deighton, 'La Grande-Bretagne', 115–19.

De Gaulle's lack of eagerness to visit London, despite the fact that Macmillan was the first leader to visit him in 1959 after his election to the presidency, is indicative of an increasingly asymmetrical relationship between the two men. Between 1958 and 1963, de Gaulle visited England just once, while Macmillan came to France three times. The British offered to extend his state visit with a weekend at Chequers, where they would have time to discuss the major issues of the day, East-West relations and above all Europe. In particular, Macmillan hoped to raise the issue of the latest directive from Brussels, the Hallstein resolution, which provided for the accelerated implementation of the Common External Tariff beginning on 9 July, and was deemed disastrous for British trade. But the Elysée refused, and talks were reduced to two hours during the visit. De Gaulle was also fussy about the programme, refusing to come by boat at the request of London, which feared that bad weather would delay his plane's landing, and finally travelling on board his Caravelle. His three-day visit, which was all about remembrance, was a real triumph for the former Resistance leader turned head of state. The British welcomed him as a sovereign, with a walk on the Mall alongside the Queen to a cheering crowd, a return to Carlton Gardens, his headquarters during the war, in the presence of around a hundred resistance fighters, and a sublime fireworks display at the end of the visit, illuminating a huge Lorraine cross, the last example of which, according to the press, dated back to 1914. Above all, de Gaulle had the exceptional honour of delivering his speech to both Houses of Parliament gathered in the Hall of Westminster. The energy expended during these three days to flatter de Gaulle was commensurate with the concerns of the British, but they were hardly rewarded for their efforts, as the president refused to give into any of the British demands.

This new balance of power was not lost on the media. The French press noted the British prime minister's feverishness as well as the self-assurance of de Gaulle, who showed no eagerness to discuss matters with him. A caricature published in *Le Canard enchaîné* a few days after the visit shows de Gaulle sitting in an armchair surrounded by courtesans, one of whom has Macmillan's face[11]. When Macmillan officially announced his country's application to join the Common Market in August 1961, de Gaulle did not react until September, and then only half-heartedly. In the second half of 1962, several events further distanced France from the UK. After the failure of the Fouchet

---

11 *Le Canard enchaîné*, 12 April 1960, p. 3.

plan, the strengthening of the Paris-Bonn axis made rapprochement with the British less essential. Transatlantic relations also weighed heavily on the British application. Kennedy's Multilateral Force (MLF) project and the Cuban crisis fuelled de Gaulle's mistrust of American intentions towards Europe, and in December the Skybolt affair made it clear that relations with the United States remained the priority for the British. The interplay between defence issues and the British candidacy was strikingly apparent at Rambouillet on 15–16 December, when Macmillan announced to de Gaulle that he would soon be meeting Kennedy to discuss replacing the Skybolt rockets with a new generation of missiles, the Polaris. For de Gaulle this choice in terms of defence confirmed that the British remained closer to the United States than Europe. While he noted the clear efforts on their part to move closer to Europe, he also frankly told the prime minister that Britain was not ready to join the Common Market. Macmillan was devastated and made no secret of his dismay. During this trying weekend, and no doubt to soften the blow, de Gaulle organised a hunt for his guest in Rambouillet. A British newspaper noted with irony that the prime minister did not return empty-handed: de Gaulle, a good prince, let him leave with seventy-seven pheasants[12].

Figure 3.1. Hunt in honour of Harold Macmillan, Rambouillet, 15 December 1962.
Source: National Archives, AG/SPH/31, AN

[12] *Daily Express*, 19 December 1962.

For de Gaulle, the crux of the problem remained Europe's independence, with respect to both the economy and defence. Both aspects were emphasised at the press conference on 14 January, when the president opposed the UK's entry into the Common Market and the MLF. The announcement of the veto shocked the British and triggered a crisis within the Community. It also surprised members of government. Edgar Pisani was informed of it while he was in Brussels negotiating and kept a bitter memory of the episode. Éric Roussel noted in his biography of Georges Pompidou that the prime minister remained in the background after the first veto, avoiding any 'untimely declarations' out of respect for the '*domaine réservé*'[13]. According to several witnesses and historians, Pompidou was concerned only with domestic affairs. But from the time of his appointment as head of government in April 1962, he followed the discussions underway in Brussels and took part in talks with the British. Although de Gaulle and Macmillan were able to meet face-to-face, Pompidou was quickly informed, as evidenced by his presence at important meetings in Champs-sur-Marne and Rambouillet.

Figure 3.2. Meeting in Champs-sur-Marne, 3 June 1962.

Source: National Archives, AG//SPH/28, reportage n°1489

[13] Éric Roussel, *Georges Pompidou* (Paris: Perrin, [1984] 2024).

Figure 3.3. Meeting in Rambouillet, 15–16 December 1962.
Source: National Archives, AG//SPH/31, reportage n°1550

In July 1962, at a restricted council meeting, Georges Pompidou said of the negotiations in Brussels: 'It would be in our interest to let the matter get bogged down in the sands'[14]. Like Maurice Couve de Murville, he thought that the negotiations would break down on their own, given the many disagreements on agricultural issues and relations with the Commonwealth. When questioned on the subject on other occasions, Pompidou never deviated from the line defined by de Gaulle. In absolute terms, France was not opposed in principle to British membership, but as things stood, the facts showed that it was not ready. This nuanced response, which was not a definitive 'no' but made membership conditional on British developments, reflects a general feeling, and explains the consensus around the first veto. Polls conducted shortly before the first veto showed that the French had little awareness of the British candidacy, with 9% of respondents ranking it as the third most important issue for the European Community, behind the

[14] 'Conseil restreint', 31 July 1962. 5AG 1/24, AN.

Common Agricultural Policy (22 %) and the Berlin problem (11 %)[15]. At the time of the opening of negotiations in September 1961, 49 % of French people were in favour of Britain's candidacy, but the number fell to 40 % after the press conference of 14 January, and unfavourable opinions rose from 9 % to 21 %[16]. The high and fairly stable abstention rate (42 and 39 % respectively) reflects either relative interest or indecision on a complex issue. Following the interruption of negotiations in Brussels, more French people agreed with de Gaulle: 44 % approved of his decision, with only 21 % still in favour of British membership, and 35 % undecided[17]. De Gaulle's popularity is not enough to explain this change. The hostile attitude of the British towards the Common Market, their intransigence on membership conditions during the negotiations, and the special relationship with the United States raised doubts regarding their sudden conversion to Europe. After the Nassau Conference, and just three weeks before the veto, the image of England as the Trojan Horse of the United States began to circulate in the press.

The study of representations may also explain the French turnaround. In his press conference, de Gaulle described England as a country apart, highly different from continental countries in every way; he insisted on the structural difference, but this was exactly how the French perceived England at the time. The British were seen as a conservative people, attached to their traditions. These were the dominant representations found in all sources. The media, school textbooks and tourist guides all conveyed the same image, of a country where nothing had seemingly changed since the reign of Queen Victoria and Hippolyte Taine's descriptions from his *Notes sur l'Angleterre* in 1872. These descriptions were subsequently taken up by other observers, such as Louis Cazamian, André Maurois and André Siegfried, whose works remained benchmarks in the early 1960s.

The Second Veto

At his conference on 14 January 1963 de Gaulle declared that England would have to change in order to join the EEC. Change did come in the following

---

15 IFOP, *Sondages. Revue française de l'opinion publique*, Paris, n°1, 1963, p. 42.

16 Ibid., p. 100.

17 Ibid., no. 2, 1963, p. 56.

years, but not where he expected it. In fact, from 1963 on, under the influence of its youth, England had changed its face. The cultural revolution with the arrival of the Beatles on the music scene, followed by Swinging London, made the country attractive to young French people, and had an effect on the French perception. The laws passed by the Wilson government legalising abortion, the status of homosexuality, and abolishing the death penalty reinforced the image of a country that was more progressive than France. For all that, Mary Quant's miniskirt was banned from schools by Education Minister Alain Peyrefitte in 1967. The feminisation of boys, following the fashion of wearing their hair long, was by far the most disturbing, provoking strong reactions in the press. The perception of England reflected intergenerational conflict in France, which found its most striking expression in May 68. Despite strong resistance, English fashions flooded into France. The magazine press, relayed by radio and television, showed a different image of the country, which was presented as a model by the new generations. London became the new trendy tourist destination, attracting 322,000 French visitors in 1966, and 500,000 in 1968[18]. Anglomania became a mass phenomenon and changed how the French saw the British. The Palme d'Or at the Cannes Film Festival was awarded in 1965 to Richard Lester for his film *The Knack … and how to get it*, and in 1967 to Michel-Angelo Antonioni for *Blow up*, two fictional films that faithfully recreated the atmosphere of the New England. The traditional mistrust of Perfidious Albion was derided. The publication of 'Asterix in Britain' illustrates this change in perception. In his book, René Goscinny described cultural differences with humour, the most comical effect coming from the literal translation of its English expressions. In April 1967, a poll revealed that 54 % of French people felt their country had more in common with England than with Germany (35 %)[19]. While baby boomers saw permissive society as a model to follow, the French government condescendingly interpreted these changes as a new symptom of British decline, the headlong rush of an England in the throes of an identity crisis. Its low growth rates compared to those in France reinforced this impression among the ruling class. The pessimistic judgement of the French was not only based on growth indices

18 *Digest of Tourist Statistics*, London British Authority, 1969, 28.

19 *Sondages*, n°2, 1967.

but also drew on the imaginary. The superiority felt by the French was exaggerated by their economic lead. It was only in 1965 that its per capita GDP exceeded that of the UK, but the gap was not very wide, which may also explain the fears aroused by Britain's accession. In a book published in 1985, entitled *De la supériorité de l'Angleterre sur la France. L'économique et l'imaginaire* (Regarding England's Superiority over France: Economics and Imaginary) the historian François Crouzet showed how England's supremacy had nurtured ambivalent feelings of fascination and jealousy in France for over two centuries. This inferiority complex disappeared when de Gaulle came to power. The success of the Common Market, France's rapid recovery on the international stage, and, as a counterpoint, England's growing difficulties and hesitations about Europe, gave rise to a new self-confidence in France that was brilliantly revealed by the first veto. Europe had helped reverse the Franco-British balance of power, placing Great Britain in the position of asking something of France. The veto looked like revenge for the past two hundred years.

After the first veto, dialogue between Paris and London did not resume until January 1965. De Gaulle met the new Labour Prime Minister, Harold Wilson, on the occasion of Churchill's funeral. The Empty Chair crisis and differences with Germany led French leaders to be more open to dialogue. In November, Pompidou told Edward Heath, who was visiting Paris at the time, that France was very much in favour of the Economic Community, and would 'like to see Great Britain join for geographical and human reasons, as a counterweight to German industry, and because a political Europe is unthinkable without it'[20]. At the Council of Ministers meeting in November, de Gaulle also said that things were evolving in a positive manner with Great Britain, but the following year, after the Luxembourg Compromise and France's withdrawal from NATO, his tone on British membership became firm once again. The Record of Decisions of the Restricted Council of 17 October 1966 states that 'France's position in this respect remains unchanged'[21]. With plans for a second application looming in the spring of 1967, the French tried to find a way to avoid repeating the bad impression created by the first

[20] Meeting between Charles de Gaulle, Georges Pompidou and Edward Heath, 22 November 1965, 'Entretiens et messages', Archives diplomatiques.

[21] Conseil restreint, 17 October 1966, 5AG 1/24, AN.

veto. Olivier Wormser, who had been the negotiator in Brussels for the first candidacy, suggested 'nipping the thing in the bud by opposing the very opening of negotiations', and also proposed 'preparing public opinion by informing it of the open hostility of the English towards the French'[22]. This second recommendation reflects a concern about the reaction of French public opinion, which might disapprove of a second veto. A fortnight after Harold Wilson's official announcement of the second candidacy, de Gaulle held a press conference on 16 May 1967, at which he reiterated the obstacles to British membership, albeit without expressing a firm refusal. But when Wilson came to see him on 18–20 June, he returned to political issues, notably British support for the Vietnam War, and concluded that British membership of the EEC would strengthen the Atlanticist camp. The devaluation of the pound in the autumn was used as a pretext for the second veto in November. While supporters of enlargement interpreted these efforts to put Britain's financial house in order as a positive sign, de Gaulle saw them as proof of British unpreparedness. At his press conference, he brandished the threat of dissolving the Common Market. The tone was harsh, the opposition more radical than in 1963. The president ironically recalled the Labour government's 'extraordinary insistence and haste' to join the EEC and pointed out the contradictory nature of the British government's position, which said it was ready to accept all the conditions, but at the same time wanted negotiations to be opened. He then discussed at length how the British opposed European integration, emphasising the 'fundamental hostility' of their leaders at the time to the Common Market, which Harold Macmillan compared to a 'continental blockade'. Although de Gaulle admitted that England had changed, he felt that these changes remained insufficient, and once again emphasised the structural nature of the problem, basing his view on the conclusions of the European Commission report drafted before the devaluation of the pound sterling:

> The Common Market remains incompatible with England's economy, whose chronic balance of payments deficit is proof of its permanent imbalance, and which, in terms of production, sources of supply, credit practices and working conditions, contains features that England could not change without altering its own nature'[23].

---

[22] Fond Maurice Couve de Murville, CM 8, Fondation Nationale des Sciences Politiques.

[23] Press Conference, 27 November 1967, *Discours et Messages*, tome 5, p. 241.

While De Gaulle cited Britain's financial situation to justify his opposition, for him the root of the problem was political. His more radical opposition ultimately highlighted the ambivalent view of Britain as a country in decline but feared its ability to transform the Common Market. While de Gaulle was more firmly opposed to the second British application, the French were less convinced than in 1963, with 41 % approving the second veto, compared with 44 % for the first one[24]. And when the question touched on feelings rather than objective reasons, favourable opinions were higher, with 50 % saying they were 'personally in favour' of British membership, 22 % opposed, and 28 % with no opinion[25]. The vetoes had no lasting effect on the number of favourable opinions, which continued to rise over the long term.

The second veto created a more serious crisis than the first and confirmed that no progress could be made on enlargement while de Gaulle was in power. France relied on the principle of unanimity of the Six contained in Article 237 of the Treaty of Rome to oppose the very opening of negotiations. De Gaulle skilfully exploited a legal loophole, as Article 237 did not specify whether unanimity of the Six was required to open negotiations, or only at the end of them[26]. The partner countries and the UK tried unsuccessfully to circumvent France's refusal through a series of initiatives in 1968 and 1969, notably by using the WEU as a forum for discussion. The second veto blocked the operation of the Community and posed a direct threat to French interests in terms of the Common Agricultural Policy, scheduled for completion in 1969. There was visible embarrassment among French leaders. Michel Debré, who succeeded Maurice Couve de Murville as foreign minister in July 1968, tried to break the deadlock by supporting the idea of resuming bilateral talks. At his request, de Gaulle agreed to meet the ambassador, Christopher Soames. But the meeting turned into a diplomatic scandal. The Soames affair, which broke out a few weeks after the meeting, was symptomatic of the impasse in Franco-British relations at the end of the decade. During the conversation, de Gaulle showed himself to be in favour of new cooperation in various fields (political, defence, technical). He suggested to the ambassador that this should

---

24 *Sondages*, n°4, 1967.

25 Ibid.

26 Guy Mollet reported on this skilful confusion between the decision on accession and the opening of negotiations at a press conference 30 November 1967, in *L'année politique*, 1967, p. 254–5.

be defined within the framework of bilateral talks, but these were to remain confidential pending a final agreement. Marked by the two vetoes, the Foreign Office thought de Gaulle's proposal was a trap, and advised Wilson, who was visiting Bonn, to inform Chancellor Kurt Kiesinger and the other European partners. Rumours immediately circulated on both sides of the Channel about these talks. According to *Le Figaro*, the British government had informed the Five of the talks in order to convince them to attend the WEU meeting in London. The British government reacted by publishing a full version of the talks, but the transcript was immediately contested by the Elysée. In particular, the transcript attributed to de Gaulle statements that he had not actually made, such as his desire to see European countries leave NATO[27]. De Gaulle's presidency came to an end with this episode, which reinforced France's isolation within the Community, and directly threatened its interests, as the Five had made the completion of the common policy conditional on the question of enlargement. Several facts and testimonies confirm that Georges Pompidou had decided to lift the veto even before becoming president. According to his close collaborator, Jean-René Bernard, he told Guy de Rothschild and Georges Rippon that, if elected president, he would lift the veto. His decision was taken before his election. The question of Britain's candidacy became one of the issues at stake in the presidential elections of June 1969. Pompidou campaigned on the theme of 'change and continuity' and announced his intention to resume negotiations with the United Kingdom, a promise that enabled him to win the votes of the centrists and beat their candidate, Alain Poher. The rallying of pro-Europeans behind his candidacy, followed by the appointment of Valéry Giscard d'Estaing to the Ministry of the Economy and Finance, and Maurice Schuman to Foreign Affairs – both of whom were in favour of British membership – were clear signals in this direction. Speaking to the British ambassador Christophe Soames on 10 October, Pompidou declared: 'I don't have an idea for a veto, I won't formulate one' and agreed that it was time to 'turn the page'. The economic and monetary problems at the end of the decade weighed heavily in his decision to lift the veto.

To conclude, it is important to highlight the changes that took place over the decade, and that prompted Pompidou to lift the veto. The situation

---

[27] Claire Sanderson, *Perfide Albion ? L'affaire Soames et les arcanes de la diplomatie britannique* (Paris: Publications de la Sorbonne, 2011).

was very different in 1969. Almost a decade had passed since the first application, and in the meantime the Community had grown stronger, demonstrating its ability to negotiate during the Kennedy Round. The French and British had also changed, with the transformation of lifestyles and the rapid evolution of mentalities under the influence of new generations helping to bring the two peoples closer together. The French view of their British neighbours had softened, with the most negative stereotypes tending to disappear. Likewise, Fachoda and Mers-El-Kébir no longer held much significance for the new generations, and Pompidou took note of these changes. While he may have doubted the sincerity of the British commitment to Europe at the beginning of the decade, he did not have the same experience and vision of England as de Gaulle, in other words he had no personal grievances against it. He thought that British membership would reinforce the Community and act as a counterweight to German power. Pompidou felt closer to Heath's ideas than Wilson's, and he may have seen, from his first meeting in 1965, the possibility of negotiating with him one day. A more in-depth study of his relationship with Prime Minister Edward Heath will shed light on all of these aspects and provide a clearer picture of his thinking.

Sources and Archives

Daily Express, 19 December 1962.
Digest of Tourist Statistics, London British Authority, 1969.
Fonds Maurice Couve de Murville, CM 8, Fondation Nationale des Sciences Politiques.
Gaulle, Charles de, *Discours et Messages*, tome 5 (Paris: Plon, 1970).
IFOP, *Sondages. Revue française de l'opinion publique* 1, Paris (1963).
L'année politique, 1967.
Le Canard enchaîné, 12 April 1960.

Bibliography

Bell, P. M. H., *France and Britain 1940–1994: The Long Separation* (London: Longman, 1997).
Capet, Antoine, *Britain, France and the Entente Cordiale since 1904* (Basingstoke: Palgrave Macmillan, 2006).

Chassaigne, Philippe, and M. L. Dockrill, *Anglo-French Relations, 1898–1998: From Fashoda to Jospin* (Basingstoke, Hampshire: Palgrave, 2002).
Cooper-Richet, Diana, and Michel Rapoport, eds, *Cent ans de relations franco-britanniques (1904–2004)* (Paris: Créaphis, 2006).
Daddow, Oliver, *Britain and Europe since 1945: Historiographical Perspective on Integration* (Manchester: Manchester University Press, 2011).
Deighton, Anne, 'La Grande-Bretagne et la Communauté économique européenne (1958–1963)', *Revue Histoire, Économie & Société* 13/1 (1994), 113–30.
De La Serre, Françoise, Jacques Leruez, and Helen Wallace, eds, *Les politiques étrangères de la France et de la Grande-Bretagne depuis 1945 : l'inévitable ajustement* (Paris: Presses de la Fondation Nationale des Sciences Politiques, 1990).
Dulphy, Anne, and Christine Manigand, *La France au risque de l'Europe* (Paris: Armand Colin, 2006).
Frank, Robert, Harmut Kaelbe, Marie-Françoise Levy et al., *Building a European Public Sphere: From the 1950s to the Present* (Brussels: Peter Lang, 2010).
Gowland, D. A., Arthur Turner, and Alex Wright, *Britain and Europe Integration since 1945: On the Sidelines* (London: Routledge, 2010).
Gloriant, Frédéric, *Le schisme franco-britannique : de Suez au veto de 1963* (Presses universitaires de Rennes: 2023).
Guieu, Jean-Michel, Christophe Le Dreau, Jenny Rafflik, and Laurent Warlouzet, *Penser et construire l'Europe, 1919–1992, historiographie, bibliographie, enjeux* (Paris: Belin, 2007).
Jackson, Julian, *De Gaulle. Une certaine idée de la France* (Paris: Seuil, 2019).
Loth, Wilfried, ed., *Crisis and Compromise: The European Project (1963–1969)* (Baden-Baden, Brussels: Nomos Verlag/Bruylant, 2001).
Ludlow, N. Piers, *The European Community and the Crisis of 1960s: Negotiating the Gaullist Challenge* (London: Routledge, 2006).
Mangold, Peter, *The Almost Impossible Ally: Harold Macmillan and Charles de Gaulle* (London: I. B. Tauris: 2006).
May, Alex, *Britain and Europe since 1945* (London: Longman, 1999).
Milward, Alan, *The Rise and Fall of a National Strategy: The UK and the European Community*, vol. 1 (London: Routledge, 2012).
Robert, Patrick, *The Heath-Pompidou Paris 20–21 May 1971 Summit: Franco-British European Honeymoon or Marriage of Convenience? A Actor-centred Study of the Reasons for and Success of the Heath-Pompidou Meetings and*

of the Impact of 'Personal Diplomacy' in the Development of Franco-British and European Summitry under their Leadership, PhD diss., University of Reading, 2020.
Roussel, Éric, *Georges Pompidou* (Paris: Perrin, [1984] 2024).
Sanderson, Claire, *Perfide Albion ? L'affaire Soames et les arcanes de la diplomatie britannique* (Paris: Publications de la Sorbonne, 2011).
Tachin, Agnès, *Amie et rivale. La Grande-Bretagne dans l'imaginaire français à l'époque gaullienne* (Brussels: Peter Lang, 2009).
Tombs, Isabelle and Robert, *That Sweet Enemy: The French and the British from the Sun King to the Present* (London: William Heinenmann, 2006).
Vaïsse, Maurice, *La grandeur. Politique étrangère du général de Gaulle. 1958–1969* (Paris: Fayard, 1998).
Waites, Neville H., ed., *Troubled Neighbours: Franco-British Relations in the Twentieth Century* (London: Weidenfeld and Nicolson, 1971).
Warlouzet, Laurent, *Le choix de la CEE par la France : l'Europe économique en débat de Mendès France à De Gaulle, 1955–1969* (Paris: Comité pour l'histoire économique et financière de la France, 2011).
Young, Hugo, *This Blessed Plot: Britain and Europe from Churchill to Blair* (London: Macmillan, 1998).

The Long Shadow of the Veto: Edward Heath, Georges Pompidou and the May 1971 Paris Summit

Daniel Furby

The May 1971 Paris summit meeting between French President Georges Pompidou and UK Prime Minister Edward Heath was punctuated by several poignant acts of symbolism. These include Heath laying a wreath on the Tomb of the Unknown Soldier in the Place Charles de Gaulle, and Pompidou's remarks during a banquet at the Élysée on 20 May: 'Through two men who are talking to each other, two peoples are trying to find each other again'[1]. In retrospect, a political cartoon published in the magazine *Punch* can also be said to afford one of the most evocative images of the summit talks. It depicts Heath and Pompidou facing each other across a negotiating table, while the shadows (or ghosts) of Winston Churchill and Charles de Gaulle loom above them, watching over proceedings[2]. While the reader is left to interpret the meaning behind the presence of these two momentous figures in British and French history (Churchill and de Gaulle), it seems reasonable to suggest that – at least in part – they represent the contrasting and at times conflicting approaches to European integration pursued by their respective countries after the Second World War[3]. Churchill was the progenitor of the idea that Britain stood at the centre of three interlinked circles: the Empire/Commonwealth; the English-speaking world (notably, the United States); and a united Europe[4]. During the 1950s, British govern-

1 Uwe Kitzinger, *Diplomacy and Persuasion: How Britain Joined the Common Market* (London: Thames & Hudson, 1973), 120–1.

2 Trog, 'Heath and Pompidou under the shadow Churchill and de Gaulle, discussing Europe', *Punch* (19 May 1971).

3 Clemens Wurm, 'Two Paths to Europe: Great Britain and France from a Comparative Perspective', in Clemens Wurm, ed., *Western Europe and Germany: The Beginnings of European Integration 1945–1960* (Oxford: Berg, 1995), 175–200.

4 Anne Deighton, 'Britain and the Three Interlocking Circles', in Antonio Varsori, ed., *Europe 1945–1990s: The End of An Era?* (London: Macmillan, 1995).

ments appeared to treat Europe as the least important of those circles. By contrast, French governments played a pivotal role in creating the three European Communities: the European Coal and Steel Community (ECSC), the European Economic Community (EEC) and the European Atomic Energy Community (Euratom) (hereafter the term 'European Community' or simply 'Community' will be used to refer collectively to the ECSC, EEC and Euratom).

When de Gaulle returned to power in 1958, he too accepted the EEC, despite its supranational characteristics, for the benefits it would afford to France's economy and his foreign policy goals[5]. Then, as British policy changed in the 1960s, two applications for membership – that of the Conservative government of Harold Macmillan in 1961, followed by the Labour government of Harold Wilson in 1967 – were each met by a veto from de Gaulle[6]. The consequential breakdown of trust in French-British relations was vividly exposed by the 1969 'Soames affair', which centred on a conversation between de Gaulle and Britain's recently appointed ambassador to Paris, Cristopher Soames (a former Conservative Cabinet minister, and Churchill's son-in-law). De Gaulle proposed initiating confidential, bilateral talks on the possibility of a wider Europe (such as a free trade area) with an 'inner political association' of Britain, France, Germany and Italy. Fearing that de Gaulle's offer might be less than wholly sincere, and that to even discuss such a proposal could rebound to the detriment of Britain's efforts to join the EEC, the Foreign Office persuaded Wilson to disclose the French proposal to German Chancellor Kurt Georg Kiesinger during his visit to Bonn on 12 February. Given de Gaulle's emphasis on confidentiality, Wilson's actions produced a furious

5 Maurice Vaïse, *La grandeur: Politique étrangère du général de Gaulle, 1958–1969* (Paris: Arthème Fayard, 1998); Jeffrey Vanke, 'Charles de Gaulle's Uncertain Idea of Europe', in Desmond Dinan, ed., *Origins and Evolution of the European Union* (Oxford: Oxford University Press, 2006), pp.141–65; Laurent Warlouzet, 'De Gaulle as a Father of Europe: The Unpredictability of the FTA's Failure and the EEC's Success (1956–1958)', *Contemporary European History* 20/4 (2011), 419–34.

6 James Ellison, 'Separated by the Atlantic: The British and de Gaulle, 1958–67', *Diplomacy and Statecraft* 17/4 (2006), 853–70; N. Piers Ludlow, *Dealing with Britain: The Six and the First UK Application to the EEC* (Cambridge: Cambridge University Press, 1997); Helen Parr, *Britain's Policy towards the European Community: Harold Wilson and Britain's World Role, 1964–1967* (Abingdon: Routledge, 2006).

response from the French government. Relations would not recover prior to de Gaulle's resignation in April 1969[7].

Held a little more than two years later, at a crucial moment in the UK's renewed negotiations to join the European Community, the Paris summit undoubtedly took place under a weight of history. Yet as evocative as the imagery of Churchill and de Gaulle may be, it has limitations as a means of explaining the character and substance of the Heath-Pompidou talks. This chapter advances a more specific and analytically more useful metaphor – the long shadow of the French veto. I will argue that memories of de Gaulle's 1961 and 1967 vetoes, and British anxiety that there should be no third veto, strongly influenced the origins of the summit and its dynamics. De Gaulle's vetoes also help understand the content of the summit talks; for while the topics discussed by Heath and Pompidou may not have been those that primarily motivated de Gaulle's decisions, some of them – notably the international reserve role of sterling and the preservation of French as the main working language of the Community – have been seen as contributing factors in French opposition to British membership in the EEC during the 1960s[8]. Finally, I will argue that the legacy of the veto in French politics is central to understanding Pompidou's presentation of the summit's purpose. More specifically, Pompidou strove to demonstrate consistency with de Gaulle's thinking on British membership of the Community, while in practice deciding that the veto should be withdrawn.

This chapter is based on a wide range of primary and secondary source material, including UK government papers (held at The National Archives

---

[7] On the Soames Affair see Daniel Furby, 'The Revival and Success of Britain's Second Application for Membership of the European Community, 1968–71', unpublished PhD thesis (Queen Mary, University of London, 2010), 51–78; Daniel Furby and N. Piers Ludlow, 'Christopher Soames', in Rogelia Pastor-Castro and John W. Young, eds, *The Paris Embassy: British Ambassadors and Anglo-French Relations*, 1944–79 (London: Palgrave Macmillan, 2013); Melissa Pine, 'British Personal Diplomacy and Public Policy: The Soames Affair', *Journal of European Integration History* 10/2 (2004), 59–76; Claire Sanderson, *Perfide Albion? L'affaire Soames et les arcanes de la diplomatie britannique* (Paris: Publications de la Sorbonne, 2012).

[8] Helen Parr, 'Saving the Community: The French Response to Britain's Second EEC Application in 1967', *Cold War History* 6/4 (2006), 425–54; David Hannay, ed., *Britain's Entry to the European Community: Report on the Negotiations of 1970–72 by Sir Con O'Neill* (London: Frank Cass, 2000), 337.

in Kew), the Archive of Edward Heath (held at the Bodleian Library in Oxford), Georges Pompidou's presidential papers (held at the Archives Nationales in Paris), newspapers, memoirs, and an extensive secondary literature on the UK's entry into the European Community.

Heath, Pompidou and the Politics of European Community Enlargement

Edward Heath is rightly remembered as the most pro-European of all British prime ministers. However, a degree of legend also surrounds the origins and development of his attitudes towards European unity – due in part to Heath's own cultivation of his reputation in that area[9]. Having travelled to Nazi Germany and civil war Spain in the late 1930s, Heath participated in the liberation of Europe during the final year of the Second World War[10]. As a newly elected MP in 1950, his maiden speech called for British participation in the Schuman Plan. From that point on, it is often claimed, Heath held a consistent view on the need for Britain to participate in efforts towards European unity – a view that distinguished him from mainstream opinion in British politics[11]. While there is no reason to doubt that Heath was profoundly affected by his experiences in the 1930s and 1940s, historians have often uncritically accepted the version of Heath's biography presented above[12]. To take one example, discussion of Heath's maiden speech often omits the fact that he was speaking in support of a motion, moved by the Conservative front bench (notably shadow foreign secretary Anthony Eden), that was critical of the Attlee government's decision not to participate in negotiations on the Schuman Plan[13]. As would become clear when the Conservatives returned to office the following year, Churchill (as prime minister) and Eden (as foreign secretary)

---

9 Edward Heath, *The Course of My Life* (London: Hodder and Stoughton, 1998), 141–9.

10 Philip Ziegler, *Edward Heath: The Authorized Biography* (London: HarperCollins, 2010), 28–48.

11 Ziegler, *Edward Heath*, 68–70 (for example).

12 An exception to this is John Campbell, *Edward Heath: A Biography* (London: Jonathan Cape, 1993), 112–14.

13 Ziegler, *Edward Heath*, 68–70 (for example).

proved sceptical towards British involvement in European integration[14]. As Heath served in the whips' office for much of the 1950s, little is known about his attitudes towards European policy during that time. As Chief Whip from 1955, he would have been responsible for maintaining party discipline during the Free Trade Area negotiations (1957–58) – the British government's attempt to minimise the negative economic consequences of Britain being outside the EEC. Prime Minister Harold Macmillan's subsequent decision to appoint Heath to the Foreign Office, responsible for Britain's relations with the Community, was very likely informed by the knowledge that Heath would be supportive of an attempt to move Britain closer to the Community. It may also have reflected Heath's loyalty and perceived capabilities as a minister[15].

Heath would earn plaudits for his role as Britain's chief negotiator during the 1961–63 accession negotiations. In May 1963, he was awarded the Charlemagne prize for his contribution to the cause of European unity[16]. Then, in July 1965, Heath became the leader of the Conservative party, eliminating any possibility that the party would seek domestic political advantage by criticising Labour's 1967 decision to apply for Community membership. Where Heath did seek to distance himself from Labour's approach was at the level of diplomatic strategy. After the 1967 veto, the British government was (rightly) perceived as seeking to pressure France by supporting (and even sponsoring) European initiatives outside of the Community[17]. Heath, however, maintained that the UK could not hope to join the Community in the face of French opposition[18]. Mirroring a debate taking place within Whitehall in the lead up to the Soames affair, the logic of Heath's position appeared to be that improved bilateral relations with Paris provided a surer

---

14 Alan Milward, *The United Kingdom and the European Community, Volume 1: The Rise and Fall of a National Strategy, 1945–1963* (London: Franck Cass, 2002), 78–115.

15 Campbell, *Edward Heath*, 113–14.

16 The Times Special Correspondent, 'Mr Heath "Among Great Pace Setters of Europe"', *The Times* (24 May 1963).

17 Furby, 'The Revival and Success of Britain's Second Application for Membership of the European Community', 31–51.

18 Edward Heath, *Old World, New Horizons: Britain, the Common Market and the Atlantic Alliance* (London: Oxford University Press, 1970), 2–3.

means of facilitating British accession (perhaps after de Gaulle had left the political scene) than a policy of confrontation[19].

By comparison with Heath, Pompidou's thinking on foreign policy was relatively unknown prior to him becoming president in June 1969. As president, he proved more pragmatic than de Gaulle, while seeking to avoid any appearance of rupture with the policies of his predecessor – an approach the historian Georges-Henri Soutou has described as 'rationalised Gaullism'[20]. One of the earliest foreign policy challenges he would face was the future of the European Community. Following France's 1967 veto, little progress had been made on the internal development of the EEC. This presented a clear risk to one of France's priorities within the Community – the need to agree on a permanent system for financing the Common Agricultural Policy (CAP). In December 1969, at Pompidou's initiative, the heads of state and government of Community member states met for an historic summit meeting in The Hague. The summit saw Pompidou withdraw French opposition to enlargement negotiations, in return for an agreement to conclude (in the first half of 1970) a permanent mechanism for financing the CAP. In parallel, the summit communiqué emphasised the need for further development of the Community, notably in the areas of (i) economic and monetary integration and (ii) 'political' (i.e. foreign policy) cooperation[21].

Several analyses, including those of Jean-René Bernard, Pompidou's principal foreign affairs adviser, Sir Con O'Neill, Britain's chief negotiator at official level during the 1970–72 accession negotiations, and (most recently) Piers Ludlow, the leading historian of the European Community in the 1960s, have concluded that The Hague summit marked the moment when Pompidou effectively took the decision to admit Britain to the Community[22]. While

---

[19] Furby, 'The Revival and Success of Britain's Second Application for Membership of the European Community', 31–51; Lord Gladwyn, 'The Problems of Breathing Life into the European Idea', *The Times* (15 November 1968).

[20] Georges-Henri Soutou, 'Georges Pompidou and US-European Relations', in Marc Tractenberg, ed., *Between Empire and Alliance: America and Europe During the Cold War* (Maryland: Rowman & Littlefield, 2003), 159–60; Frédéric Bozo, *French Foreign Policy since 1945: An Introduction* (New York: Berghahn Books, 2016), 81–96.

[21] N. Piers Ludlow, *The European Community and the Crises of the 1960s: Negotiating the Gaullist Challenge* (Abingdon: Routledge, 2006), 174–98.

[22] Jean-René Bernard, 'Britain into Europe', in Douglas Johnson, Richard Mayne and Robert Tombs, eds, *Cross Channel Currents: 100 Years of Entente Cordiale* (London:

this chapter also endorses that conclusion, it is important to stress that this was by no means clear to most contemporary observers. Concerns over the potential for an additional veto persisted until the outcome of the May 1971 Paris summit became clear.

The Path to Paris: The Accession Negotiations and a Premeditated Impasse

Heath and Pompidou met on two occasions in 1970: the first meeting took place in May (while Heath was still leader of the opposition); the second in November when Heath, by then prime minister (following the June 1970 General Election), visited Paris for de Gaulle's funeral. Both encounters are notable for Pompidou's invocation of the Anglo-American 'special relationship' – one of the factors often thought to have influenced de Gaulle's opposition to British membership of the Community. In May, Pompidou complained of a British 'tendency to remain too closely wedded to the United States'. It was not enough, Pompidou insisted, 'just to have European sentiments', the Community 'would have to be prepared to defend to the hilt European interests in the face of likely economic and political onslaughts from outside'[23]. In November, Pompidou opened a copy of *Le Monde* in front of Heath, displaying an advertisement by the state-owned British airline BOAC, which read: 'America begins in London on board a VC 10 of BOAC'[24]. The Foreign Office reminded Heath of Pompidou's apparent concern regarding British attachment to the United States when briefing him for the Paris summit, furnishing him with counter-arguments should Pompidou revert to the same line of criticism[25]. Relations with the US were ultimately not a major subject of discussion during the summit, however.

Routledge, 2004), 164–75. See also, Jean-René Bernard, 'L'élargissement de la Communauté, vu de Paris', in *Georges Pompidou et L'Europe: Colloque* (Brussels: Editions Complexe, 1995), 237–52; Hannay, ed., *Britain's Entry.to the European Community*, 14–15; Ludlow, *The European Community and the Crises of the 1960s*, 197.

23 Oxford, Bodleian Libraries, EH/4/2/14/E, Soames to Greenhill, 8 May 1970.

24 The National Archives (hereafter TNA), London, PREM15/370, Paris to FCO, tel.1142, 12 November 1970.

25 TNA, CAB133/422, PMVP71(1), 14 May 1971.

In late 1970, the British government tabled its opening bids on the three British priorities in the accession negotiations. The first was the need to ensure a gradual increase in British contributions to the Community budget over a (long) transitional period. Under the normal operation of Community rules, the UK expected to face contributions significantly in excess of its share of Community GDP, with potential risks to the UK's balance of payments. The second and third priorities focused on market access arrangements for New Zealand dairy products and Caribbean sugar. Satisfactory solutions were deemed vital to securing parliamentary approval for UK entry to the Community at the conclusion of negotiations.

During the first three months of 1971, it became clear that an impasse was emerging in the accession talks. The unmistakable reason for that was the hardline stances adopted by French negotiators on the UK's priority topics – as a result of which, the Community could not agree on responses to Britain's opening bids. Then, during the ministerial meeting in March, France pushed an additional issue to the forefront of the negotiations: sterling, the relative weakness of which had been a major theme in de Gaulle's November 1967 press conference presaging the second veto.

The contention of this chapter is that the impasse in the spring of 1971 was a French tactic to create circumstances in which a summit meeting between Heath and Pompidou was seen to be necessary[26]. Pompidou's desire for France to adopt an uncompromising negotiating stance was conveyed at a meeting between the president and senior ministers, including Foreign Minister Maurice Schumann, on 16 February 1971. After considering the British application in general terms, as well as French priorities in the negotiations, Pompidou concluded the discussion by stating: 'In relation to Great Britain, it is necessary, for the moment, for the Minister of Foreign Affairs to be very firm and even malicious'[27].

In parallel with the formal negotiations, however, a confidential bilateral channel of communication was opening between Christopher Soames and the secretary general of the Élysée, Michel Jobert. The possibility of a

---

[26] This argument is set out in more detail in Furby, 'The Revival and Success of Britain's Second Application for Membership of the European Community', 198–220.

[27] *Archives Nationales* (hereafter AN), Paris, 86/AJ/127, Compte-rendu du Conseil restreint sur la négociation entre la CEE et la Grande Bretagne, 16 février 1971.

meeting between Heath and Pompidou was first broached during a conversation between the two in mid-February[28]. On 1 March, Heath authorised Soames to tell Jobert that the prime minister believed an understanding with Pompidou would be 'an important element in the negotiations', and that 'the timing of any meeting between them was important in view of the need to avoid the Brussels negotiations turning sour'[29]. When Soames met Jobert again on 6 March, he relayed Heath's message. On the question of timing, Jobert remarked that a summit:

> would clearly have to be either before the Ministerial negotiating meeting in May or before the Ministerial meeting in June. A point for consideration was how much of a crisis atmosphere was desirable for the holding of the Prime Minister/President meeting. Jobert tended to think that the best situation would be one that was short of a crisis, but where there was a sufficient degree of impasse for people to appreciate the need for a meeting.[30]

Following the Easter recess, intensive bilateral preparations for the summit proceeded, including the preparation of the summit agenda. The May ministerial meeting then resulted in the first significant advances of the accession negotiations, with progress made on two of Britain's priority topics: arrangements for Caribbean sugar and the formula for determining British contributions to the Community budget during a transitional period. While neither issue was resolved on that occasion, the shift in French positions generated a sense of momentum in Brussels ahead of the Heath-Pompidou meeting[31].

Deciphering the Summit: Presentation and Substance

One important aspect of the Paris summit that calls for explanation is Pompidou's public presentation of the meeting's purpose. In his media

---

[28] Furby, 'The Revival and Success of Britain's Second Application for Membership of the European Community', 203.

[29] TNA, PREM15/368, Note of a meeting between Heath and Soames, 1 March 1971.

[30] TNA, PREM15/369, Soames to Greenhill, 10 March 1971.

[31] On the preparation of the summit and the May ministerial meeting, see Furby, 'The Revival and Success of Britain's Second Application for Membership of the European Community', 198–230.

appearances, Pompidou placed particular emphasis on the need to ascertain whether the British government's outlook was truly 'European'[32]. In an interview with French television on 24 June, Pompidou claimed that the most important question he had put to Heath was 'Whether Britain, which is an island, had decided to moor itself to the continent, and if she was therefore ready to come in from the wide seas which had always drawn her'[33]. As will be seen, this is far from being an accurate guide to the substance of the summit talks. To understand why Pompidou chose to present the purpose of the talks this way, it is crucial to recall the arguments and narratives that de Gaulle used to justify his vetoes of British membership of the Community. For experienced observers of French foreign policy, it should have been evident that Pompidou was employing language almost identical to that used by de Gaulle in his famous January 1963 press conference[34]. Moreover, de Gaulle had been careful to leave open the possibility of Britain joining the Community in the future – once its international relationships and trading patterns had evolved in a way that aligned with the aims and policies of the Community: 'it is possible that one day England might manage to transform herself ... to become part of the European community, without restriction, [and] without reserve'. In such circumstances, de Gaulle insisted, 'the Six would open the door' to Britain, 'and France would raise no obstacle'[35]. In this light, Pompidou's public presentation of the summit's purpose clearly reveals itself as an attempt to show consistency with the principles

32 CVCE, Interview by Georges Pompidou given to the BBC, 19 May 1971, <https://www.cvce.eu/en/obj/interview_given_by_georges_pompidou_to_the_bbc_17_may_1971-en-c9915b40-223e-4ee3-b1e4-5abae8003f97.html> (accessed on 5 January 2025); CVCE, excerpt from television interview with Georges Pompidou, 24 June 1971.

33 CVCE, Excerpt from television interview with Georges Pompidou, 24 June 1971.

34 In his January 1963 press conference, De Gaulle concluded his remarks on Britain's application by stating that 'it is very possible that Britain's own evolution ... might bring the English little by little towards the Continent, whatever delays the achievement might demand, and for my part, that is what I readily believe, and ... it will in any case have been a great honour for the British Prime Minister, for my friend Harold Macmillan, and for his Government, to have discerned in good time ... and to have led their country in the first steps down the path which one day, perhaps, will lead it to moor alongside the Continent'. WEU Assembly, 'Press conference by President de Gaulle', 14 January 1963, University of Pittsburgh Archive of European Integration, <https://aei.pitt.edu/5777/>, accessed on 5 January 2025.

35 Ibid.

that de Gaulle had set out regarding when, and under what circumstances, Britain might join the Community. The Soames affair was also helpful to Pompidou, as it suggested that towards the end of his presidency, de Gaulle too might have been reconsidering his stance on Britain's place in Europe[36].

Pompidou's substantive objectives at the summit were far more specific, and more oriented towards concrete French interests, than an abstract assessment of Britain's European outlook, as implied by his media statements. At the core of Pompidou's approach stood four main concerns related to the potential consequences of the UK's accession to the EEC: (i) the impact of sterling's status as an international reserve currency, especially in light of the goal of greater economic and monetary coordination within the Community; (ii) the need to reinforce the French government's view on the role of unanimity in the Council of Ministers; (iii) a desire to preserve French as the principal working language of Community institutions; and (iv) protection of the benefits that former French African colonies derived from EEC association arrangements under the Yaoundé Convention. With the exception of sterling, these issues fell outside the scope of the Brussels negotiations. In the case of sterling and the use of French within Community institutions, they have also been seen as contributing factors in French opposition to British membership in the Community during the 1960s[37]. The summit thus provided a last opportunity for Pompidou to explore, with Heath, ways of addressing these French concerns in advance of the UK's accession.

For Heath, the objective was straightforward: to arrive at an understanding with Pompidou on Britain's priorities in the accession negotiations. Given the progress made on Caribbean sugar at the May ministerial meeting, the key items for discussion between Heath and Pompidou would be British contributions to the Community budget during a transitional period, and

---

36 In his 24 June television interview, Pompidou also referred to this episode: 'as you know ... in the last months of his presidency, he [de Gaulle] made a step toward Britain which failed because of the British Government at the time'. CVCE, Excerpt from television interview with Georges Pompidou, 24 June 1971 <https://www.cvce.eu/en/collections/unit-content/-/unit/df06517b-babc-451d-baf6-a2d4b19c1c88/f0d3b03b-cbe2-484a-8d17-466e7a6bf34a/Resources#341aa357-871d-4440-bc3f-a7290fc1c7a1_en&overlay>, accessed on 5 January 2025.

37 Hannay, ed., *Britain's Entry to the European Community*, 337; Parr, 'Saving the Community', 425–54.

arrangements for New Zealand dairy products. For Heath, timing was also critical; in order to initiate the parliamentary processes necessary for Britain to join the Community, including a vote on the principle of membership in the autumn of 1971, the major issues would need to be resolved by the end of June.

The Four French Concerns

Of Pompidou's four concerns, the simplest for Heath to address was unanimity within the Council of Ministers. In 1965, French representatives boycotted EEC institutions during the so-called Empty Chair crisis. One of the issues was the planned introduction of majority voting within the Council. The crisis was eventually resolved through the Luxembourg Compromise. The French interpretation of the compromise held that if a member state considered a vital national interest to be at stake, unanimity should apply, i.e. that state should not be outvoted[38]. In January 1971, Pompidou publicly confirmed that the French interpretation of the Luxembourg Compromise remained of paramount importance for him[39]. During the preparatory talks for the summit, the French interpretation of the Luxembourg Compromise was included on the annotated agenda. At the summit itself, Pompidou explained that this was 'in the hope of obtaining the Prime Minister's complete agreement to it'[40]. As Pompidou would likely have been aware, the implications of Community decision-making for national sovereignty was an area of sensitivity in British politics as well. Pompidou thus referred to the French interpretation of the Luxembourg Compromise as 'conforming to the British genius'[41]. Heath too had previously stated in the House of Commons that the Community should not take a decision against the expressed vital interests of one of

---

38 On the Empty Chair crisis and the Luxembourg Compromise, see Ludlow, *The European Community and the Crises of the 1960s*, 71–124.

39 Charles Hargrove, 'M. Pompidou's Attitude to European Unity', *The Times* (23 January 1971).

40 TNA, PREM15/2241, Record of Conversation (RoC) between Heath and Pompidou, 20 May 1971, 10am. Quotations in this chapter are based on the British record of the talks, but references are also provided for the corresponding French record: AN, 5AG2/108, Premier tête-à-tête entre M. Pompidou et M. Heath, 20 Mai 1971, 10h.

41 TNA, PREM15/2241, RoC Heath and Pompidou, 20 May 1971.

its member states[42]. It was thus with little difficulty that the record of the summit made clear Heath's agreement to the French interpretation of the Luxembourg Compromise, thereby navigating the first of Pompidou's concerns[43].

The desire to preserve French as the Community's primary working language was related not just to the possible entry of the UK, but the broader enlargement context too. Denmark, Ireland, and Norway were all in negotiations to join the Community, and in each case English was a preferred working language for the officials and representatives of those governments. At the summit, Pompidou emphasised the importance France attached to the issue 'for intellectual, national and even European reasons'. At the same time, he conceded that it was 'not a fundamental issue', and that there was a limited amount that he and Heath could do to solve it. Nonetheless, if Heath 'had something to say', Pompidou would be 'happy to listen'[44]. Heath then made a proposal, prepared by the Foreign Office in advance and included in the agreed record of summit conclusions, that the UK government would always send to Brussels 'officials qualified to conduct business in French'[45]. Turning next to association arrangements under the Yaoundé Convention, Pompidou's concern centred on the risk that if such arrangements were opened to all Commonwealth countries in Africa, then the benefits derived by former French colonies might be diluted. Of particular concern, given its relative size in population terms, was the case of Nigeria. Heath again proposed a potential solution: in view of its expected oil revenues, Nigeria could be treated separately for aid purposes (for example through the provision of technical support and training)[46].

The most complex of the four French concerns, and the one that consumed greatest attention during the summit talks, was the international reserve role

---

42 Hansard, House of Commons Debates, 25 February 1970, c.1223.

43 TNA, PREM15/2241, Agreed English text of record of conclusions, Heath-Pompidou meetings, 20–21 May 1971.

44 TNA, PREM15/2241, RoC Heath and Pompidou, 15.30, 20 May; AN, 5AG2/108, Deuxième tête-à-tête entre M. Pompidou et M. Heath, 20 Mai 1971, 15h 30.

45 TNA, CAB133/422, PMVP(71)4, 14 May 1971; TNA, PREM15/2241, RoC Heath and Pompidou, 15.30, 20 May 1971; TNA, PREM15/2241, Agreed English text of Record of Conclusions, meetings between Heath and Pompidou, 20–21 May 1971.

46 TNA, PREM15/2241, RoC Heath and Pompidou, 15.30, 20 May 1971.

of sterling. One aspect of the problem, from a French perspective, was the possibility that the UK might, as a member of the Community, and in the event of a balance of payments crisis, request financial assistance from EEC member states under Articles 108 and 109 of the Treaty of Rome[47]. Another aspect was the sterling balances (an arrangement dating back to the Second World War under which certain Sterling Area countries held part of their foreign currency reserves in London). In the context of British accession and the movement towards greater economic and monetary coordination within the Community, Pompidou wanted to see the sterling balances run down. Pompidou told Heath that 'he was profoundly convinced that the pound as a reserve currency was a relic of the British Empire of an earlier era and was incompatible with the British decision to become a member of the European Community'[48]. Heath in turn made clear that the British government was fully prepared to take action to that end, but argued that the speed and timing of any reductions must be based on Britain's financial position in any year. From the beginning of its transitional period, the UK would also be required to make contributions to the Community budget, which would also place a burden on the balance of payments. It was therefore impossible to specify in advance how quickly the sterling balances could be run down. The agreed record of the summit conclusions thus included a compromise formula, which indicated the British intention to stabilise the sterling balances in advance of accession, and to progressively reduce them thereafter[49]. In the absence of further specificity, however, it was a commitment in principle only, subject to the unpredictability of events in the years following British entry.

---

47 AN, 86AJ/129, J-R Bernard, Note pour information pour le Président de la République, 23 Avril 1971. On French concerns in relation to sterling, also see: Patrick Robert, 'The Heath-Pompidou Paris 20–21 May 1971 Summit: Franco-British European Honeymoon or Marriage of Convenience?', unpublished PhD thesis (University of Reading, 2019); and Katrin Rücker-Guitelmacher, 'Le triangle Paris-Bonn-Londres et le processus d'adhésion britannique au marché commun 1969–1973. Quel rôle pour le trilatéral au sein du multilatéral?', unpublished PhD thesis (Sciences Po, 2009).

48 TNA, PREM15/2241, RoC Heath and Pompidou, 15:30, 20 May 1971; AN, 5AG2/108, Troisième tête-à-tête entre Pompidou et Heath, 21 May 1971, 10h.

49 TNA, PREM15/2241, Agreed English text of Record of Conclusions, meetings between Heath and Pompidou, 20–21 May 1971.

UK Priorities and the Summit Outcome

Turning to the issues at the heart of the accession negotiations, Pompidou was evidently reluctant to take the summit discussions too far. He emphasised that he had no authority to negotiate on behalf of the Community and, if he and Heath were to agree on figures, 'this would make the Brussels talks seem meaningless'[50]. During the preparatory talks for the summit, however, Soames impressed upon Jobert that Heath would want to ensure that a satisfactory resolution of the British priorities was within sight[51]. Pompidou therefore did engage with Heath on potential starting figures for British contributions to the Community budget. On New Zealand, he offered Heath an assurance of goodwill: France would 'try to be helpful … taking account of the moral, sentimental and political aspects of the problem as much as the economic ones'[52]. Pompidou's meaning was clear: provided he received satisfactory assurances on the four French concerns (which proved to be the case), France would show flexibility on New Zealand within the accession negotiations. Emphasising this point, Pompidou insisted that 'he did not intend to allow Europe to fail over the issue of New Zealand'[53].

As the summit approached its conclusion, the talks overran by approximately one hour. Among the gathered media and diplomats, the sense of anticipation grew. At approximately 7:00 p.m., Heath and Pompidou entered the Salle des Fêtes of the Élysée – the same room from which de Gaulle had pronounced his veto in January 1963[54]. Pompidou addressed the audience first, and in words that met the drama of the moment, made clear that France no longer posed an obstacle to British membership in the Community: 'There were many people', Pompidou explained, 'who believed that Great Britain was not European and did not wish to become European'. Similarly, many people 'thought France was prepared to use all kinds of means and pretexts to propose a new veto to the entry of Great Britain into the Community'. 'Well, ladies and gentlemen', Pompidou

50 TNA, PREM/2241, RoC Heath and Pompidou, 21 May 1971, 4pm.

51 Furby, 'Revival and Success', 219–20.

52 TNA, PREM15/2241, RoC Heath and Pompidou, 15:30, 20 May 1971; AN, 5AG2/108, Deuxième tête-à-tête entre M. Pompidou et M. Heath, 20 Mai 1971, 15h 30–17h 30.

53 Ibid.

54 Furby, 'The Revival and Success of Britain's Second Application for Membership of the European Community', 194 and 273.

concluded, 'you see tonight before you two men who are convinced to the contrary'[55].

As has been argued above, Pompidou's public presentation of the summit consistently sought to emphasise continuity with de Gaulle – above all the need to be sure that the British outlook was now truly European. In practice, the core of the summit deal was a bilateral understanding or *quid pro quo*: Heath provided satisfactory assurances on the four French concerns, and Pompidou made clear that French stances in the accession negotiations would allow for agreements to be reached by the end of June. And so it proved: during the two ministerial meetings that took place the following month, agreements were progressively concluded on Caribbean sugar, New Zealand dairy products and UK contributions to the Community budget[56]. On 7 July, the UK government published a White Paper outlining the terms negotiated and recommending, on that basis, that the UK should proceed to join the Community[57].

For both Heath and Pompidou, the summit also represented a vivid foreign policy success. Pompidou had withdrawn France's veto on enlargement, yet had done so in a way that limited the scope for criticism from 'orthodox Gaullists'[58]. In return, Pompidou had secured a permanent mechanism for financing the CAP from his Community partners, and a series of bilateral assurances from Heath that helped to address remaining French concerns about the consequences of enlargement. For Heath, the consequences of the summit were of even greater significance. A decade on from the first application, the road to British membership in the Community (at a diplomatic level) was finally clear. Still today, British entry to the EEC is a defining feature of Heath's political career and legacy.

---

55 Charles Hargrove, 'Mr Heath and M Pompidou Agree the Way is Now Open for Britain', *The Times* (22 May 1971).

56 Furby, 'The Revival and Success of Britain's Second Application for Membership of the European Community', 275–82.

57 Hansard, *House of Commons Papers*, Cmnd 4751, July 1971.

58 On 'orthodox Gaullists' see Frank L. Wilson, 'Gaullism without de Gaulle', *The Western Political Quarterly* 26/3 (1973), 485–506.

Conclusion

In the days following the Paris summit, Soames wrote to Heath to congratulate him on the successful outcome. In his letter, Soames recalled the events of January 1963 when – in the wake of de Gaulle's veto – Heath delivered his concluding statement to the ministerial conference of the 1961–63 accession negotiations:

> My mind went back to that ghastly meeting round the green baize table at Brussels when the veto finally fell and to the speech you then made reminding them all that we would be back. How right you have been proved – and in a very personal way.[59]

Soames's letter affords just one further illustration of the varied ways in which memories of de Gaulle's vetoes shaped the Paris summit. As this chapter has argued, the 'long shadow of the veto' influenced the character, content and presentation of the summit talks. Regarding the summit's character, the overriding British concern was to ensure that there would be no third veto, and that agreements on the major issues in the accession negotiations could be reached by the end of June. Heath therefore approached the summit fully prepared to explore with Pompidou ways of addressing the four French concerns about the consequences of enlargement. At least two of those concerns (sterling and the status of French as the Community's primary working language) had likely influenced French attitudes towards British membership in the EEC during the 1960s – and it is in this sense that the shadow of the veto can be seen in the substance of the summit talks. Finally, Pompidou's presentation of the summit, as a means of ascertaining the truth of Britain's European outlook, reflected the legacy of de Gaulle's vetoes in French domestic politics. Pompidou sought to demonstrate consistency with his predecessor's approach while in practice implementing a reversal of the policy that had done so much to shape Community politics, and French-British relations, over the previous decade.

---

[59] Oxford, Bodleian Libraries, EH4/2/14/E, Soames to Heath, 26 May 1971.

Bibliography

Bernard, Jean-René, 'Britain into Europe', in Douglas Johnson, Richard Mayne and Robert Tombs, eds, *Cross Channel Currents: 100 Years of Entente Cordiale* (London: Routledge, 2004), 164–75.

———, 'L'élargissement de la Communauté, vu de Paris', in *Georges Pompidou et L'Europe: Colloque* (Brussels: Editions Complexe, 1995), 237–52.

Bozo, Frédéric, *French Foreign Policy since 1945: An Introduction* (New York: Berghahn Books, 2016).

Campbell, John, *Edward Heath: A Biography* (London: Jonathan Cape, 1993).

Deighton, Anne, 'Britain and the Three Interlocking Circles', in Antonio Varsori, ed., *Europe 1945–1990s: The End of An Era?* (London: Macmillan, 1995).

Ellison, James, 'Separated by the Atlantic: The British and de Gaulle, 1958–67', *Diplomacy and Statecraft* 17/4 (2006), 853–70.

———, The United States, Britain and the Transatlantic Crisis: Rising to the Gaullist Challenge, 1963–68 (Basingstoke: Palgrave Macmillan, 2007).

Furby, Daniel, 'The Revival and Success of Britain's Second Application for Membership of the European Community, 1968–71', unpublished PhD thesis (Queen Mary, University of London, 2010).

———, and Ludlow, N. Piers, 'Christopher Soames', in Rogelia Pastor-Castro and John W. Young, eds, The Paris Embassy: British Ambassadors and Anglo-French Relations, 1944–79 (London: Palgrave Macmillan, 2013).

Gladwyn (Lord), 'The Problems of Breathing Life into the European Idea', *The Times* (15 November 1968).

Hannay, David ed., *Britain's Entry to the European Community: Report on the Negotiations of 1970–72 by Sir Con O'Neill* (London: Frank Cass, 2000).

Hargrove, Charles, 'M. Pompidou's Attitude to European Unity', *The Times* (23 January 1971).

Heath, Edward, *Old World, New Horizons: Britain, the Common Market and the Atlantic Alliance* (London: Oxford University Press, 1970).

——— *The Course of My Life* (London: Hodder and Stoughton, 1998).

Kitzinger, Uwe, *Diplomacy and Persuasion: How Britain Joined the Common Market* (London: Thames & Hudson, 1973).

Ludlow, N. Piers, *Dealing with Britain: The Six and the First UK Application to the EEC* (Cambridge: Cambridge University Press, 1997).

———, *The European Community and the Crises of the 1960s: Negotiating the Gaullist Challenge* (Abingdon: Routledge, 2006).

Milward, Alan, *The United Kingdom and the European Community, Volume 1: The Rise and Fall of a National Strategy, 1945–1963* (London: Franck Cass, 2002).
Parr, Helen, *Britain's Policy towards the European Community: Harold Wilson and Britain's World Role, 1964–1967* (Abingdon: Routledge, 2006).
———, 'Saving the Community: The French Response to Britain's Second EEC Application in 1967', *Cold War History* 6/4 (2006), 425–54.
Pine, Melissa, 'British Personal Diplomacy and Public Policy: The Soames Affair', *Journal of European Integration History* 10/2 (2004), 59–76.
Robert, Patrick 'The Heath-Pompidou Paris 20–21 May 1971 Summit: Franco-British European Honeymoon or Marriage of Convenience?', unpublished PhD thesis (University of Reading, 2019)
Rücker-Guitelmacher, Katrin, 'Le triangle Paris-Bonn-Londres et le processus d'adhésion britannique au marché commun 1969–1973. Quel rôle pour le trilatéral au sein du multilatéral?', unpublished PhD thesis (Sciences Po, 2009).
Sanderson, Claire, *Perfide Albion? L'affaire Soames et les arcanes de la diplomatie britannique* (Paris: Publications de la Sorbonne, 2012).
Soutou, Georges-Henri, 'Georges Pompidou and US-European Relations', in Marc Tractenberg, ed., *Between Empire and Alliance: America and Europe During the Cold War* (Maryland: Rowman & Littlefield, 2003).
The Times Special Correspondent, 'Mr Heath "Among Great Pace Setters of Europe"', *The Times* (24 May 1963).
Trog, 'Heath and Pompidou under the shadow Churchill and de Gaulle, discussing Europe', *Punch* (19 May 1971).
Vaïsse, Maurice, *La grandeur: Politique étrangère du général de Gaulle, 1958–1969* (Paris: Arthème Fayard, 1998).
Vanke, Jeffrey 'Charles de Gaulle's Uncertain Idea of Europe', in Desmond Dinan, ed., *Origins and Evolution of the European Union* (Oxford: Oxford University Press, 2006), pp.141–65.
Warlouzet, Laurent, 'De Gaulle as a Father of Europe: The Unpredictability of the FTA's Failure and the EEC's Success (1956–1958)', *Contemporary European History* 20/4 (2011), 419–34.
Wurm, Clemens, 'Two Paths to Europe: Great Britain and France from a Comparative Perspective', in Clemens Wurm, ed., *Western Europe and Germany: The Beginnings of European Integration 1945–1960* (Oxford: Berg, 1995), 175–200.
Ziegler, Philip, *Edward Heath: The Authorized Biography* (London: HarperCollins, 2010).

Fighting the 'Economic War': Georges Pompidou, Edward Heath and Industrial Policy at the End of the 'Glorious Thirty' (1969–1974)

Cesare Vagge

Introduction

The British historian Martin Conway recently used the phrase 'state-led democracy' to describe the democratic polities that took shape in Western Europe between 1945 and 1968[1]. According to Conway, the 'state-led' nature of these new democracies was largely due to the significant expansion in the powers of the administrative state, which became 'the agent of economic prosperity' and 'the comprehensive problem solver for modern society'[2]. This gave state planners the claim to having become the autonomous 'technical agents of effective government'[3].

One of the chief protagonists of 'the Glorious Thirty' (1945–75) was therefore the 'developmental state', more specifically, 'a particular type of state bureaucracy [...] animated by a certain kind of ambition [...] not only one of economic growth, but also one of protection and promotion of national interests, as perceived or determined by the administrative elite'[4]. The industrial policies pursued by Georges Pompidou and Edward Heath between 1969 and 1974 reflect the resilience of this post-war consensus over the merits of state-sponsored economic planning. These two conservative leaders firmly believed that the challenges of the 1970s – above all the state of 'economic war' generated by the collapse of the Bretton Woods system in 1971 – could still be met by relying on the developmental state's modernising thrust. Their ambitions therefore

1 Martin Conway, *Western Europe's Democratic Age 1945–1968* (Princeton NJ: Princeton University Press, 2020), 216.
2 Ibid., 206–7.
3 Ibid., 208.
4 Michel Loriaux, "The French Developmental State as Myth and Moral Ambition', in Meredith Woo-Cummings, ed., *The Developmental State* (Ithaca NY: Cornell University Press, 1999), 235; Jean Fourastié, *Les Trente Glorieuses* (Paris: Fayard,1979), 27, 276.

suggested a common techno-nationalist equation between industrial and national grandeur, which the state guaranteed through the mobilisation of its experts and social partners.

Georges Pompidou's Industrial Ambition and the Concerted Economy

Georges Pompidou's industrial policy cannot be discussed without addressing his relationship with the General Planning Commissariat (CGP) and its network of sectorial Modernisation Commissions (CMs), which constituted the core of the post-war French developmental state. Created in 1946 by the quasi-legendary Jean Monnet, the CGP was the chief coordinator of France's post-war industrial rebirth within the framework of a 'concerted economy', which involved the civil service, business and labour in the elaboration of long-term economic plans[5]. Within this techno-corporatist framework, engineers constituted the key mediators between the state, trade organisations, nationalised enterprises, and private firms. The prototypical industrial strategy developed by the CGP and its twenty-four original CMs was the First Modernisation and Equipment Plan for 1947–52 – the 'Monnet Plan' – which implemented the reconstruction and modernisation of the six 'basic sectors' necessary for the rehabilitation of the French economy: coal, electricity, steel, means of transportation, agricultural machine tools, and construction materials[6].

Some scholarly interpretations emphasise the increasingly indicative and liberal character that French planning acquired under Pompidou, as well as the loss of independence by the CGP in the context of his industrial policy. According to Frédéric Tristam, the Sixth Economic and Social Development Plan (PDES) for 1971–75 particularly 'lacked ambition and reflected an adaptation to the liberal economy'[7]. Michel Margairaz has also emphasised the weakening of French planning in the late 1960s and early 1970s, due

---

5 Commissariat Général au Plan [henceforth CGP], *Rapport Général sur le Premier Plan de Modernisation et d'équipement* (Paris: Imprimerie Nationale, 1947), 101.

6 Frances M. B. Lynch, *The French Economy* (London: Agenda Publishing, 2021), 26.

7 Frédéric Tristam, 'Quelle temporalité pour l'action publique au tornant des années 1970?', in Gilles le Béguec and Frédéric Tristam, eds, *Penser l'avenir au temps de Georges Pompidou* (Paris: Peter Lang, 2018), 85.

to multiple factors: the French economy's exposure to international competition; the increasingly anti-*dirigiste* stances of French business leaders; and Pompidou's own preference for 'political' appointees such as Francois Xavier Ortoli (1925–2007) – General Planning Commissioner in 1966–67 and Minister of Industrial and Scientific Development in 1969–72 – who failed to defend the CGP's independence[8]. The result was the CGP's loss of influence over the policy-making process and the definitive rupture between the planners and the labour movement, exemplified by the withdrawal of the French Democratic Confederation of Labour (CFDT) from the preparation of the PDES in 1970[9]. By contrast, Pascal Griset has acknowledged the role played by the Sixth Plan in the formulation of Pompidou's industrial policy, which was centred upon 'the strategic equipment goods for the economic war': machine tools, chemicals, telecommunications, and computers[10].

It would therefore be misleading to portray Pompidou as a precursor of the late twentieth-century neo-liberal challengers of the developmental state. The account of the *Polytechnicien* and *Mines* engineer Bernard Ésambert (1934-) – the chief industrial adviser to the prime minister and later the president from 1967 to 1974 – suggests that during Pompidou's presidency concerted planning survived as a means to orient France's industrial core. According to Ésambert, Pompidou was 'statist when it was necessary' and 'liberal when it was necessary'[11]: he accepted liberalism in trade policy, but also believed that liberalism had to be 'tempered' to guarantee national industrial autonomy[12]. He therefore rejected the protectionist component of twentieth-century *Colbertisme*, but embraced its other essential trait: the 'internal mobilisation and stimulus' of national industrial production[13]. This was the policy stance that Pompidou and his advisers took in the face

---

8 Michel Margairaz, 'De l'apogée au double infléchissement de la planification à la française sous Georges Pompidou', in *Penser l'avenir*, 198–99, 201.

9 Ibid., 203.

10 Pascal Griset, 'Entre pragmatisme et ambition: la politique industrielle de Georges Pompidou face au contexte des années 1970', in Éric Boussière, ed., *Georges Pompidou face à la mutation économique de l'Occident, 1969–1974* (Paris: Presses Universitaires de France, 2001), 288.

11 Bernard Ésambert, 'Temoinage sur les années Pompidou', in *Penser l'avenir*, 302.

12 Archives Orales Georges Pompidou [henceforth AOGP] 'Bernard Ésambert-Entretien du 12.02.1999'

13 Ésambert, 'Témoinage', 299.

of the 'economic war' unleashed by the renewal of the General Agreement on Tariffs and Trade in 1967 and the August 1971 'Nixon shock' or dollar devaluation, which led to the breakdown of the Bretton Woods System in December 1971[14]. The 1971–75 Plan was therefore meant to create the 'consensus behind growth among the living forces of the nation' (an expression already utilised by Monnet in 1946–47) in order to promote a doubling of French industrial production over 10 years through the constitution of 'national champions of international size' capable of overtaking the United States within this new trade war[15].

According to Ésambert, the chief interpreters and agents of Pompidou's 'industrial ambition' were the engineers from the French *Grands Corps*, nicknamed 'musketeers of industrialisation'[16]. The *Polytechnicien* and *Mines* engineer René Montjoie (1926–82) – industrial adviser to the prime minister from 1962 to 1967, and General Planning Commissioner from 1967 to 1974 – 'played an eminent role in defining Pompidou's economic policy'[17]. In the late 1960s Montjoie led the CGP's Committee on Industrial Development, which identified recasting industrial policy and the 'necessity of growth focused on a competitive industry' as the 'number one priority of planning'[18].

In conformity with these industrial priorities, Montjoie had brokered a series of binding special 'conventions', aimed at expanding and restructuring key industrial branches such as steel, computers – the so-called '*plan calcul*' – and naval constructions in exchange for subsidies provided by the Treasury's Economic and Social Development Fund (FDES)[19]. These binding agreements strongly resembled the 'imperative' contracts that the private producers negotiated with the CGP and the Directorates of the Ministry of Industry during the Monnet Plan[20].

---

14 Bernard Ésambert, *Pompidou Capitaine d'industries* (Paris: Odile Jacob, 1994), 42, 78.

15 AOGP, 'Ésambert, 12.02.1999'; B. Ésambert, 'Un industrie pour la France', *Annales des Mines* (June-July 1971), 8, 22.

16 Ésamebrt, *Pompidou*, 17.

17 Ibid., 17.

18 Archives Nationales [henceforth AN], CGP, 19890575/215–216, 'L'éxperience française de planification industrielle', 6.

19 Ibid., 5.

20 CGP, *Rapport Général*, 108.

Montjoie was therefore neither a partisan of economic liberalism nor an unambitious political appointee, but rather a convinced developmental technocrat, determined to reaffirm the CGP as the chief enforcer of national industrial modernisation. Far from reflecting a shift from *dirigisme* to liberalism, Montjoie's appointment reflected the affirmation of a particularly targeted form of sectorial planning aimed at developing the industrial core of the economy in the face of growing international pressures.

In December 1969, the CGP Commissioner explicitly praised the example of the Monnet Plan as the 'selective instrument of the accelerated reconstruction of a war-torn nation', and identified 'industrial development as the essential vector of our growth and national independence'[21]. To this end, in September 1969 Montjoie appointed a new Industrial Commission at the CGP. Led by the fellow *Polytechnicien* and *Mines* engineer Roger Martin (1915–2008), the Chairman and General Manager of the *Pont à Mousson* Company, the Industrial Commission relied on a network of twenty-two sub-committees, tasked with developing sectorial programmes for the industries targeted by the plan[22].

Margairaz has interpreted the choice of Roger Martin as the sign of 'the overtly active role of business representatives, who were called to join planning organs during Pompidou's presidency'[23]. Yet, it would be reductive to identify Martin's appointment as a sign of Montjoie's subservience to business interests. Martin was no ordinary businessman, but a former civil servant, who served as deputy head of the Ministry of Industry's Iron and Steel Directorate from 1942 to 1947, and deputy rapporteur of the Modernisation Commission for Steel (CMSID) during the preparations for the Monnet Plan[24]. It was therefore no accident that Montjoie chose this veteran of post-war techno-corporatist planning and industrial expansion to help the CGP encourage French business to invest further in the hypercompetitive atmosphere of the 1970s.

Martin had also taught Montjoie at the École des Mines in Paris, and specifically attributed his decision to accept the leadership of the Commission

---

21 AN, CGP, 19890575/151–152, 'Project d'article sur les innovations du VI Plan', 1, 8.

22 AN, CGP, 19890575/93–94, 'Commission de l'industrie', 1; AN, CGP, 19890575/93–94, 'VI Plan: Liste des Comités Sectoriels', 1.

23 Margairaz, 'De l'apogée', 200.

24 CGP, *Rapport Général*, 190.

to his 'vague nostalgia for [his] civil servant status', which 'pushed [him] not to refuse a task that constituted a good civic action'[25]. The resilient esprit des corps of Mines engineers – and self-perception as the privileged technical mediators of the relationship between the developmental state and private industry – prompted Martin to undertake the task demanded by Montjoie.

Reprising the traditional tripartite structure of the original CMs, the Industrial Commission's permanent members consisted of eleven civil servants, twelve business leaders, and five labour representatives[26]. Martin's chief advisers were the *Inspecteur des Finances* Claude Sarrazin (1929–2009), programmes director at the Ministry of Industrial and Scientific Development, and the naval engineer Guy Zarrouati (1931–2019), the head of the CGP's Industrial Office[27]. The Commission also included the *Inspecteur des Finances* François Bloch-Lainé (1912–2002), President of the Credit Lyonnais since 1967, and the manager Pierre Dreyfus (1907–94), the Chairman of Renault since 1955[28]. Both men had been key actors of the Monnet Plan. As Treasury Director from 1947 to 1953, Bloch-Lainé had instituted the Modernisation and Equipment Fund (FME) – the predecessor of the FDES – to back the Plan's industrial restructuring programmes, while Dreyfus had served as Cabinet Director of the Ministry of Industry and its chief liaison with the CGP in 1947–49[29]. The choice of these men confirmed Montjoie's intention to rely on experts, who had contributed to the immediate post-war renewal of France's industrial structures, and pair them with a new generation of technocrats.

The Commission's final report, published in early 1971 confirms the central role played by the CGP in defining the priorities of Pompidou's industrial policy: machine tools, chemicals, electronics and telecommunications[30]. The report also recommended a series of 'specific sectorial actions', which included

---

25 Roger Martin, *Patron de droit divin* (Paris: Gallimard, 1984), 313.

26 AN, CGP, 19890575/217–218 'Rapport des commissions du 6e plan 1971–1975: Industrie', 131–3.

27 Ibid., 131.

28 Ibid., 131–2.

29 François Bloch-Lainé and Jean Bouvier, *La France Restaurée: Dialogue sur les choix d'une modernisation, 1944–1954* (Paris: Fayard, 1986), 186; Pierre Dreyfus, 'Débats-le Ministère de l'industrie et le Plan', in Henry Rousso, ed., *De Monnet à Massé: Enjeux politiques et objectifs économiques dans le cadre des quatre premiers Plans (1946–1965)* (Paris: Editions du CNRS, 1986), 71.

30 AN, CGP, 19890575/217–218, 'Rapports: Industrie', 105–11.

an ambitious aeronautics programme, featuring the 'project of the 10 tons civil engine': the future CFM-56 jet engine jointly developed by SNECMA and General Electric[31]. The report also featured encouragement to continue the 'necessary pursuit of the rationalisation effort', which the steel industry had commenced in the late 1960s[32].

The report also illustrates the resilience of traditional statist instruments, which had played a significant role in orienting industrial investments since the original Monnet Plan. Despite calling for progressive 'disengagement of the Treasury in relation to the banking system' as the chief financer of industrial investments, the Commission acknowledged that the key sectors targeted by the plan might 'refuse to risk the dilapidation of their financial structures and thus not undertake the supplementary investments necessary to grow at the desired pace'[33]. As a result, 'Priority public support should be accorded to these sectors to stimulate their growth'[34]. One of the instruments advocated by the planners was the Treasury's FDES, where the CGP retained considerable influence through the chairmanship of the key sub-committees charged with financing the investments of both public and private firms[35].

The report also highlighted the creation of the new Institute of Industrial Development (IDI), a special financial institution designed to promote mergers and 'put small and medium enterprises in the position to find the resources needed to fund their growth'[36]. Furthermore, citing the special conventions of the late 1960s, the planners stressed the necessity of an 'analogous policy of conditional support', in which the private sector agreed to use public resources only to fulfil the plan's objectives[37]. Rather than calling for the state's retreat from industrial life, the planners and their business partners stressed that French industry still required vigorous state intervention and orientation to sustain the challenge of the economic war.

The plan's call for public funding of private industrial initiatives, however, received considerable criticism from the General Confederation of

---

31 AN, CGP, 19890575/217-218, 'Rapports: Industrie', 111–13.
32 Ibid., 114–15.
33 Ibid., 87.
34 Ibid., 88.
35 Ibid., 88; AN, CGP, 19890575/215–216 'l'éxperience française', 16.
36 AN, CGP, 19890575/217–218, 'Rapports: Industrie', 62.
37 Ibid., 62–3.

Labour (CGT). Communist trade unionists reiterated their 'firm opposition to the accumulation of state transfers to private industry', and declared that only the nationalisation and democratic management of key industries and credit institutions constituted the 'precondition to any industrial policy in keeping with the national interest'[38]. This indicates that the rupture between the CGP and the labour movement under Pompidou was not due to the increasingly market-oriented nature of planning, but to the planners' aversion to the structural reforms advocated by the Communists.

One of the key private sectors that benefited from the kind of public funding advocated by the planners and deprecated by the CGT was the steel industry. The CGP charged a special Steel Sub-Committee to develop a programme for this still crucial basic sector, with a view to continuing the rationalisation effort of the late 1960s. The Sub-Committee consisted of seven civil servants, fourteen business representatives and four trade unionists[39]. Its chairman was the *Mines* engineer Jean Latourte (1910–76), then one of the chief board members of the Wendel-SIDELOR group, the leader of the Lorraine steel industry[40]. Like Roger Martin, Latourte was a former civil servant and veteran of France's state-led industrial modernisation, who had been the chief rapporteur of the CMSID during the Monnet Plan[41]. Other former CMSID members in the new sub-committee were the fellow *Mines* engineers Maurice Borgeaud (1909–2006), Chairman and General Manager of the Union Sidérurgique du Nord de la France (USINOR), and Henri Malcor (1906–91), Chairman and General Manager of Creusot-Loire. Also worth noting was the membership of Jacques Ferry (1913–96), the President of the *Chambre Syndicale de la Sidérurgie Française* (CSSF) and chief negotiator of the agreement that had led to the rationalisation efforts of the late 1960s. The business representatives chosen by the CGP were therefore veterans of the concerted economy and partisans of industrial expansion within the sector, schooled into coming to terms with the plans and demands of the French developmental state.

---

38 AN, CGP, 19890575/217–218, 'Rapports: Industrie', 126, 128.

39 AN, CGP, 19890575/215–216, 'Rapports des comités du 6e Plan 1971–1975 : Sidérurgie et Mines des Fer', 67–9.

40 Ibid., 67.

41 CGP, *Rapport Général,* 190.

Drawing from the Japanese model, the investment programme developed by the Sub-Committee sought to expand French basic oxygen integrated coastal steelworks supplied with foreign minerals in order to substitute the Thomas and Martin-Siemens steelworks reliant on iron ore from Lorraine[42]. The latter was deemed significantly more expensive than foreign ores, and it was estimated that its reserves would be depleted by the end of the century[43]. The Sub-Committee thus recommended the construction of a new basic oxygen steel plant in the new southern industrial centre of Fos sur Mer, and the expansion of the productive capacity of the existing USINOR plant of the same type in Dunkirk, resulting in a productive capacity of 14 million annual tons of raw steel[44]. Both USINOR and Wendel-SIDELOR would manage the new Fos plant through the constitution of a joint venture: SOLMER[45]. Investments in the new basic oxygen steelworks were estimated at 1.3 billion francs, and the Treasury's FDES would provide SOLMER with a loan of 1.85 billion francs for the construction of the new Fos plant and its milling facilities[46]. This constituted over 10% of the 16.5 billion-investment programme forecasted for 1971–75[47]. Nearly 25 years since the launch of the Monnet Plan's steel programme, the French developmental state was therefore once again actively involved in the restructuring of the French steel industry in the face of the economic war of the 1970s.

A key figure in the creation of SOLMER was Georges Dominjon (1929–2018) – then head of the Directorate for Metallurgical Industries and Cabinet Director of the Ministry of Industrial and Scientific Development – who also served as Deputy Chairman of the Steel Sub-Committee[48]. A graduate of the National School of Administration (ENA), Dominjon presented himself as a liberal financial expert after retiring, opposed to the industrial *dirigisme* practiced by the *Mines* engineers[49]. Nevertheless, the heavy involvement of the FDES in the construction of the Fos steelworks suggests that his allegedly

42 Ésambert, *Pompidou*, 244.
43 Ibid., 244.
44 AN, CGP, 19890575/215–216, 'Rapports : Sidérurgie', 21.
45 Ibid., 21.
46 Ibid., 20, 32.
47 Ibid., 20.
48 Ibid., 67.
49 AOGP, 'Georges Dominjon-Entretien du 10.09.2001'.

liberal views did not result in the state's withdrawal from the orientation of the steel sector.

The new Fos plant began operating on 6 April 1974, four days after Pompidou's death. The business historian Harold James described the Fos project as the victory of 'government gigantomania' over the traditional risk aversion of French family capitalism[50]. Philippe Mioche and Ésambert emphasised how the SOLMER solution resulted from the nationalist and corporatist pressures of both the CSSF and the then Finance Minister Valery Giscard-D'Estaing, who firmly opposed the prospect of a merger between Wendel-SIDELOR and the German Thyssen group, an option initially favoured by Pompidou himself[51].

Above all, the Fos experience indicates how Georges Pompidou's industrial policy still took place within the framework of a state-led democracy, where the civil service engaged in dialogue with the productive forces within the framework of a techno-corporatist 'concerted economy'. This framework allowed the CGP and its managerial allies to co-opt the private sector into executing a new sectorial plan, in line with the president's industrial ambition. Yet, the very same framework ensured that the project would still benefit national and corporatist interests. Rather than the triumph of economic liberalism over state planning, the project thus exposed the compromise between technocracy and corporatism, which still characterised French state-led democracy at the twilight of the Glorious Thirty.

Edward Heath and Industrial Policy

Edward Heath's changing relationship with industrial policy from 1970 to 1974 was quite indicative of the resilience of the 'state-led' post-war trajectory of British democracy. Although initially elected on the liberal-conservative promise to dismantle the industrial planning bodies created in the 1960s, Heath eventually emerged as an upholder of the developmental state akin to Georges Pompidou.

---

50 Harold James, *Family Capitalism: Wendels, Falcks, Haniels and the Continental European Model* (Princeton NJ: Princeton University Press, 2006), 314.

51 Philippe Mioche, 'Georges Pompidou et la modernisation manquée de la sidérurgie française', in *Georges Pompidou face*, 306; Ésambert, *Pompidou*, 243.

The papers of the Conservative Party's Research Department (CRD) are illustrative of Heath's shifting attitude towards industrial policy. In 1969–70 the CRD attacked the Labour Party's acceptance of the 'fallacy that government and industry [were] in a partnership' and denounced that Harold Wilson's government had 'wrecked the mechanism of spontaneous change', which was supposed to guide industrial development[52]. The CRD's liberal experts particularly criticised of the then Minister of Technology, Tony Benn (1925–2014), accusing him of nurturing the fallacy that 'government economic planning and company planning [were] basically the same'[53]. This allegedly misguided belief, had led to the formation of a 'bloated bureaucracy', which had undermined British industry's creative initiative[54]. One of the planning bodies targeted by Heath's advisers was the Industrial Reorganisation Corporation (IRC), which had engineered key mergers such as British Leyland and the Upper Clyde Shipyards (UCS) to further modernise and rationalise their plants. The CRD mocked the IRC's 'evangelical patriotism', accused the agency of having 'involved itself in industries in disarray' and concluded that under an improved fiscal regime 'much of the work that the IRC [set] itself, would be done spontaneously by the market'[55].

Conservatives therefore accused Wilson's industrial policy of having created unnecessary governmental bodies, which further bureaucratised British industry, undermined entrepreneurial creativity, and contributed to preserving inefficient enterprises in the name of irrational nationalistic considerations. The key to revitalising British industrial growth, innovation and productivity was therefore eliminating these planning bodies in favour of market forces and indirect fiscal incentives.

In keeping with these prescriptions, in 1970–71 Heath's Secretary for Trade and Industry John Davies (1916–79) former Director General of the Confederation of British Industry (CBI) abolished both the IRC and the Ministry of Technology[56]. Additionally, the Heath cabinet diminished

---

52 Bodleian Archives & Manuscripts [henceforth BA&M], Conservative Party Research Department [CRD], 3/45/1, 'Summary', 1.

53 Ibid., 3.

54 Ibid., 2.

55 Ibid., 11–12.

56 David Edgerton, *The Rise and Fall of the British Nation: A Twentieth-century History* (London: Allen Lane, 2018), 326.

the influence of the National Economic Development Council (NEDC), the national planning agency created by Harold MacMillan's government in 1962 on the model of the French General Planning Commissariat (CGP). As the political commentator Anthony Sampson remarked in 1971, Heath and his Chancellor of the Exchequer, the liberal-minded Anthony Barber (1920–2005) regarded the NEDC 'more as a sounding-board than an instrument of national policy making'[57]. They hence entrusted it to Frank Figgures (1910–90), a Treasury official 'without great planning ambitions'[58].

Paired with the passing of the 1971 Competition Credit Control (CCC) financial liberalisation experiment, the abolition of the Ministry of Technology and the IRC seemingly marked a challenge to the British developmental state. The disbanding of the IRC stood in sharp contrast to Pompidou's creation of the Industrial Development Institute (IDI), whose functions and structure mirrored those of its British counterpart.

The far-sighted Sampson nevertheless warned that Heath's intention to join the European Economic Community (EEC), paired with the emergence of menacing foreign multinational corporations, would likely result in the abandonment of *laisser-faire*. Sampson remarked that in the face of European governments that saw themselves as 'the mediators between the defensive interests of small societies and the aggressive interests of big businesses [...] Ted Heath's talk about industry '"standing on its own feet" will not make much long-term difference to this trend'[59]. Furthermore, echoing Ésambert's rhetoric of the 'economic war', Sampson argued that government was 'now interlocked with every industry', while enterprises had become 'the chosen instruments of the nation's aggrandisement'[60]. Confronted with new 'economic war' of the early 1970s Heath's industrial *laisser-faire* would thus prove anachronistic, misguided and harmful.

It did not therefore take long before the Conservative government rediscovered the British developmental state. The first significant signs of what has been described as a 'U-turn of enormous proportions' on industrial policy came in the spring of 1971, when the government decided to bail out and

---

57 Anthony Sampson, *The New Anatomy of Britain* (London: Book Club Associates, 1971), 284.

58 Ibid., 284.

59 Ibid., 664–5.

60 Ibid., 665.

nationalise the struggling Rolls Royce Company[61]. Ironically, the company's need for government aid was strictly connected with its development of the RB 211 jet engine, one of the projects that had been strongly supported by Benn's Ministry of Technology[62]. Another sign of the imminent U-turn was the government's rescue and restructuring of the UCS shipyards – a creation of the IRC – in February 1972[63].

The formalisation of the government's new course in industrial policy eventually came in April 1972 with the passing of the Industry Act. This legislation granted the new Department of Trade and Industry (DTI) with pervasive planning powers, which exceeded those of the Labour government's 1968 Industrial Expansion Act[64]. Under the new Act, the DTI and the Treasury would be able to extend grants worth 250 million pounds per year 'to promote the development or modernisation of an industry [...] to promote the efficiency of an industry' and 'to promote the reconstruction, reorganisation or conversion of an industry or of undertakings in an industry'[65]. The targeted sectors were the exact same the Wilson government prioritised: computers, shipbuilding and machine tools[66].

The agency charged with coordinating these new tasks was the DTI's new Industrial Development Executive (IDE), aided by network of Regional Offices and tripartite corporatist Regional Development Councils[67]. One of the chief differences between the IDE and the IRC was the new agency's direct attachment to the DTI, which made its activities directly accountable to parliament[68]. IDE's chairman was not a technocrat, but the Conservative MP and former broadcaster Christopher Chataway (1931–2014), Davies' junior Minister for Industrial Development. Davies justified the Act by arguing that 'government [could] not stand aside when situations [arose]

---

61 Dominic Sandbrook, *State of Emergency – The Way we were: Britain, 1970–1974* (London: Allen Lane, 2010), 300.

62 Edgerton, *The Rise*, 326.

63 Ibid., 326.

64 Ibid., 334.

65 BA&M, CRD, 4/25/1–4, 'Industry Act 1972', 8.

66 Trevor Smith, 'The United Kingdom', in Raymond Vernon, ed., *Big Business and the State: Changing Relations in Western Europe*, (London: Macmillan, 1974), 98.

67 BA&M, CRD, 4/25/1–4, 'The Industry Act 1972 and the new framework', 161.

68 Ibid., 161.

which industry and financial institutions [could] not meet alone'[69]. Davies particularly emphasised the need 'to help industry to modernise, adapt and rationalise (...) in preparation for entry in Europe'[70].

Less than two years from its appointment, the Heath cabinet therefore reversed its attitude towards industrial policy. Like his Labour predecessors and his future French partners, Heath was therefore determined to mobilise the planning powers of the developmental state to modernise British industrial structures. Preparing British industry for imminent competition within the EEC was one of the chief concerns of British policymakers. This state corporatist industrial planning framework heavily relied on personnel recruited from the civil service and had a particularly 'political' management, personified by Chataway and Davies. This last characteristic distinguished the British DTI from the significantly more 'expert-led' French CGP.

State technocrats were nevertheless heavily involved in developing the Industry Act and its executive framework. Its chief inspirer was undoubtedly Sir William Armstrong (1915–80), the head of the home civil service since 1968 and one of Heath's closest advisers. Although not an experienced industrial expert of the likes of Ésambert and Montjoie, Armstrong was 'an unusually political civil servant' and 'a convinced interventionist in economic management'[71]. As Sampson noted, Armstrong saw civil servants 'as the instruments through which our fellow countrymen [sought] to exercise their collective will'[72]. This kind of activist thinking rendered Armstrong akin to Pompidou's 'musketeers of industrialisation'. The other two intellectual fathers of the Industry Act were Sir William Nield (1913–94), former head of the defunct Department of Economic Affairs (DEA) under Wilson, and Leo Pliatzky (1919–99) Deputy Secretary of the Treasury and a firm opponent of the IRC's abolition[73]. The British civil service was therefore determined to safeguard the developmental state built by Macmillan and Wilson from Heath's initial liberal tendencies.

The main executive champion of the Industry Act was Peter Walker (1932–2008), who replaced Davies as Secretary for Industry and Trade in

---

69 BA&M, CRD, 4/25/1–4, 'The Industry Act", 159.

70 Ibid., 159.

71 John Campbell, *Edward Heath: A Biography* (London: Jonathan Cape, 1993), 446.

72 Sampson, *The New Anatomy*, 251.

73 Campbell, *Edward Heath*, 446–7.

November 1972. According to Robert Taylor, Walker was an enthusiast of a 'new capitalism where a dynamic state was to be the catalyst for industrial change' modelled on the 'mainland European dirigiste experience'[74]. In his memoirs Walker explicitly praised the French model of state-industry relations, and praised their expedients to counter overseas competition without explicitly resorting to protectionism[75]. Walker also made no secret of his resentment of British entrepreneurs, who had 'inherited with no idea to run the business' and preferred to live as 'gentlemen', contributing to British industrial decline[76]. Walker thus comprehended that the intensification of world competition would lead to an economic war, which could not be fought by an inadequate and leisurely British entrepreneurial class. What was needed was 'to look at the practices of all [our] competitors'[77]. As in France, the British developmental state had to step in to help national industry expand and modernise.

One particular sector that was central to Walker's aggressive industrial strategy was the steel industry. Since its creation in 1967 the state-owned British Steel Corporation (BSC) had controlled over 90% of British crude steel output, thus making it 'the largest steel business in the free world outside the USA'[78]. Shortly after its creation BSC had devised a long-term modernisation strategy, aimed at 'rationalising production facilities, and for concentrating production whenever possible on those plants having the lowest through costs' and 'matching those already developed by several overseas steel industries'[79]. The plan was intended to be achieved by 1975 and would have relied on financial assistance from the IRC.

As a response to the BSC's strategy, in January 1970 the British Independent Steel Producers Association (BISPA) provided the CRD with a reform proposal, which would turn the BSC into a 'commercial entity committed to

---

74 Robert Taylor, 'The Heath government, industrial policy and the "new capitalism"', in Stuart Ball and Anthony Seldon *The Heath Government, 1970–74* (London: Routledge, 1996), 154.

75 Peter Walker, *Staying Power: An autobiography*, (London: Bloomsbury, 1991), 103.

76 Ibid., 100.

77 Ibid., 103.

78 British Steel Corporation [henceforth BSC] *Annual Reports and Accounts 1967–68*, (London: Her Majesty's Stationery Office, 1969), 1.

79 Ibid., 5, 16.

paying its way' and permit 'the private sector to be suitably expanded', especially in the field of secondary processing of raw steel[80]. At the same time private producers agreed with the merits of the rationalisation strategy and recommended 'the bulk of steelmaking plants to be preserved in a public owned corporation' and that 'a framework of comparable discipline, fair trading, and adequate capacity planning, be established and overseen by a new Iron and Steel authority responsible to a Minister'[81].

BISPA's reform proposal therefore amounted to neither the de-nationalisation of the sector, nor the abolition of industrial planning in favour of the restoration of unfettered competition. Private producers instead advocated a 'state corporatist' solution, which would allow a governmental office to coordinate the long-term investment programmes of the BSC and its private producers. Far from being a neo-liberal solution, this proposal did not distance itself from the model of the European developmental state. Instead of resorting to total public ownership, industrial modernisation would be achieved within the framework of a strategy coordinated by a ministerial office in agreement with both public and private producers.

The corporatist option, however, was eventually scrapped. In December 1972 Walker and Lord Julian Melchett (1925–73) – BSC's Chairman since 1967 – introduced a new Steel Act that confirmed the Corporation's structure and re-launched its sectorial modernisation plan. The plan's cornerstones were the expansion of the Port Talbot integrated plant, and the construction a new integrated basic oxygen steelworks in South Teesside capable of producing 12.5 million tons of steel per year. The cost of the overall strategy amounted to 3 billion pounds[82]. The plan's aim was to create 'an efficient and profitable business, capable of withstanding international competition'[83]. Britain's entry into the EEC was regarded as a major incentive for the strategy's implementation. The Teesside plant was indeed presented as 'the most modern steel complex in the European Community'[84]. The particular case study of the steel industry therefore indicates that a combination of Walker's distaste for the

80 BA&M, CRD, 3/7/25/1, 'A Policy for the Steel Industry', 3, 4.
81 Ibid., 5.
82 BSC, *Annual Reports and Accounts, 1972–73*, (London: Her Majesty's Stationery Office, 1973), 26.
83 Ibid., 26.
84 Edgerton, *The Rise*, 326.

risk aversion of British private entrepreneurs, and the threat of competition with heavily subsidised European partners, prompted the Heath government to regard nationalised enterprises as industrial modernisation instruments rather than inefficient 'lame ducks'.

The cabinet's incapacity to find a settlement with the Trades Unions Congress (TUC) over the incomes policy that would have facilitated the success of Walker's industrial strategy in the context of the hyperinflationary 'oil shock of 1973–74', however resulted in a governmental crisis, which led to Heath's defeat in the February 1974 elections. The 1974–79 Labour governments nevertheless carried on with the implementation of the BSC investment strategy, albeit without closing down the inefficient plants identified by Walker and the deceased Melchett[85]. Conservative free marketers never forgave Heath for pursuing a policy, which had given the DTI 'far more extensive powers than any Labour government hitherto had dreamed of talking'[86].

Yet it would be unfair to label Heath's industrial policy as socialist. As Brian Harrison has pointed out, the 'corporatist planning' pursued in 1972–74 was 'all the more attractive to Heath because [it was] compatible with EEC structures and attitudes'[87]. For Heath tasking the developmental state and its social partners with re-launching British industry was therefore a means to adjust the management of national industrial affairs to the practices of Britain's future European partners. As Sampson had predicted in 1971, if it intended to truly become European, British democracy had to remain a state-led democracy.

Conclusion

State-led democracy did not survive the wave of inflation and unemployment that hit Western European industrial economies after the 1973–74 oil shock, thus unleashing a new era of neo-liberal government disengagement from economic, and particularly industrial affairs. As the economic historian Barry Eichengreen put it, it 'in this brave new world, it became

---

85 Walker, *Staying Power*, 112.

86 Campbell, *Edward Heath*, 453.

87 Brian Harrison, *Finding a role? The United Kingdom 1970–1990*, (Oxford: Oxford University Press, 2011), 290.

more difficult for government holding companies, planning commissions, and bureaucrats to identify high-return for funds'[88]. The Western European developmental state therefore did not endure the stagflation of the 1970s.

Nevertheless, Georges Pompidou and Edward Heath belonged to the last generation of conservative European politicians, who firmly believed that even the challenges of the 1970s – above all the revitalisation of global competition that Ésambert defined the 'economic war' – could still be fought by mobilising the developmental state and its social partners. In their pursuit of a common 'techno-nationalist' vision, which saw the renewal of national industrial structures as the necessary condition for economic prosperity in the face of globalisation and European integration, the two political leaders extended the lifespan of industrial planning bodies, which would either be abandoned or disempowered in the 1980s and 1990s. Pompidou and Heath's handling of industrial policy at the twilight of the Glorious Thirty therefore qualifies them as two of the very last French and British conservative upholders of post-war European state-led democracy.

Bibliography

Bloch-Lainé, François, and Jean Bouvier, *La France Restaurée: Dialogue sur les choix d'une modernisation, 1944–1954* (Paris: Fayard, 1986).

British Steel Corporation, *Annual Reports and Accounts 1967–1968* (London: Her Majesty's Stationery Office, 1969).

Campbell, John, *Edward Heath: A Biography* (London: Jonathan Cape, 1993).

Commissariat Général au Plan, *Rapport Général sur le Premier Plan de Modernisation et d'équipement* (Paris: Imprimerie Nationale, 1947).

Conway, Martin. *Western Europe's Democratic Age 1945–1968* (Princeton, NJ: Princeton University Press, 2020).

Dreyfus, Pierre, 'Débats-le Ministère de l'industrie et le Plan', in Henry Rousso, ed., *De Monnet à Massé: Enjeux politiques et objectifs économiques dans le cadre des quatre premiers Plans (1946–1965)* (Paris: Editions du CNRS, 1986).

[88] Barry Eichengreen, *The European Economy since 1945: Coordinated Capitalism and beyond* (Princeton: Princeton University Press, 2007), 48.

Edgerton, David, *The Rise and Fall of the British Nation: A Twentieth-century History* (London: Allen Lane, 2018).

Eichengreen, Barry, *The European Economy since 1945: Coordinated Capitalism and beyond* (Princeton: Princeton University Press, 2007).

Ésambert, Bernard, *Pompidou, Capitaine d'industries* (Paris: Odile Jacob, 1994).

——— Bernard, 'Temoinage sur les années Pompidou', in Gilles le Béguec and Frédéric Tristam, eds, *Penser l'avenir au temps de Georges Pompidou* (Paris: Peter Lang, 2018).

——— Bernard, 'Une industrie pour la France', *Annales des Mines* (1971).

Fourastié, Jean, *Les Trente Glorieuses* (Paris: Fayard, 1979).

Griset, Pascal, 'Entre pragmatisme et ambition: la politique industrielle de Georges Pompidou face au contexte des années 1970', in Éric Boussière, ed., *Georges Pompidou face à la mutation économique de l'Occident, 1969–1974* (Paris: Presses Universitaires de France, 2001).

Harrison, Brian, *Finding a Role? The United Kingdom 1970–1990* (Oxford: Oxford University Press, 2011).

James, Harold, *Family Capitalism: Wendels, Falcks, Haniels and the Continental European Model* (Princeton, NJ: Princeton University Press, 2006).

Loriaux, Michel, 'The French Developmental State as Myth and Moral Ambition', in Meredith Woo-Cummings, ed., *The Developmental State* (Ithaca, NY: Cornell University Press, 1999).

Lynch, Frances M. B., *The French Economy* (London: Agenda Publishing, 2021).

Margairaz, Michel, 'De l'apogée au double infléchissement de la planification à la française sous Georges Pompidou', in Gilles le Béguec and Frédéric Tristram, eds, *Penser l'avenir au temps de Georges Pompidou* (Paris: Peter Lang, 2018).

Martin, Roger, *Patron de droit divin* (Paris: Gallimard, 1984).

Mioche, Philippe, 'Georges Pompidou et la modernisation manquée de la sidérurgie française', in Éric Boussière, ed., *Georges Pompidou face à la mutation économique de l'Occident, 1969–1974* (Paris: Presses Universitaires de France, 2001).

Sampson, Anthony, *The New Anatomy of Britain* (London: Book Club Associates, 1971).

Sandbrook, Dominic, *State of Emergency – The Way we were: Britain, 1970–1974* (London: Allen Lane, 2010).

Smith, Trevor, 'The United Kingdom', in Raymond Vernon, ed., *Big Business and the State: Changing Relations in Western Europe* (London: Macmillan, 1974).

Taylor, Robert, 'The Heath Government, Industrial Policy and the "New Capitalism"', in Stuart Ball and Anthony Seldon, *The Heath Government, 1970–1974* (London: Routledge, 1996).

Tristam, Frédéric, 'Quelle temporalité pour l'action publique au tornant des années 1970?', in Gilles le Béguec and Frédéric Tristam, eds, *Penser l'avenir au temps de Georges Pompidou* (Paris: Peter Lang, 2018).

Walker, Peter, *Staying Power: An Autobiography* (London: Bloomsbury, 1991).

Competition and Credit Control (CCC)

Marie-Claude Esposito

During the 1970s, the United Kingdom (UK) was considered 'the sick man of Europe', with inflation reaching its highest levels ever recorded, and the performance of its real economy being worse than it had been since the late nineteenth century. As the Conservative Party returned to power in June 1970, the British economy experienced stagflation, which is to say both high inflation (6 % in June compared to 5 % in 1969) and growing unemployment (2.5 % in June compared to less than 2 % since the end of the Second World War except for 1963). While inflation in the late 1960s and 1970s was a worldwide phenomenon, it was more pronounced in the UK than in most Western counties. At the time, there was still the belief that inflation was sensitive to the level of unemployment (cf. Philips Curve), and that it was a non-monetary phenomenon resulting from rising costs, wage costs in particular. The Bank of England (BoE)/the Bank was just beginning to accept that the money supply might be more important than it had previously thought.

The recurring sterling crises of the previous decade, which resulted in the November 1967 devaluation, had shown that it was impossible to simultaneously pursue full employment and economic growth with growing government expenditure and a pegged exchange rate. This resulted in strong pressures on the balance of payments and inflation. In other words, there was a conflict between the domestic and external objectives of economic policy. Britain's position was all the more difficult, as sterling was still a reserve currency with the unsolved problem of sterling balances.

During the 1960s, the BoE had become increasingly wary of ceilings on bank advances (loans) and other forms of quantitative controls that were damaging the Bank's relationship with the City, increasingly difficult to enforce, and less and less efficient. They also poisoned relations with the clearing banks and the Treasury. These ceilings had been lifted in April 1967 but were put back in place just a few months later at the time of devaluation. The severe tightening of credit resulted in opposition from clearers, who complained that it was impossible to meet the imposed limits. In early 1969, bank advances exceeded £140 m[1]. The BoE insisted on compliance, and used persuasion and threats with little success, while the Treasury tried to avoid confrontation with the clearers[2]. Fines were imposed in May 1969, as every big bank was 5% over the target[3]. The governor's exhortations had done nothing, and in September bank lending was once again above the target, pushing the crisis to a climax. Beside the growing dissatisfaction with controls on bank lending, there was a recognition that a more competitive banking sector was desirable. There was also concern about operations in the money and gilt-edged markets.

During the 1960s, there were several attempts to address some of the issues, but they were hampered by short-term crises. Pressure for change also came from outside – from the International Monetary Fund (IMF) in particular – during the negotiation of stand-by agreements to help sterling navigate recurrent exchange rate crises. Following the 1967 devaluation, the IMF asked the UK to follow a target for Domestic Credit Expansion (DCE), and from mid-1968 onward there were intensive discussions at the Bank and Treasury regarding DCE and the money supply. That year, the BoE set up an internal Money Supply Group in advance of a monetary seminar with IMF experts.

In opposition, Heath and the Conservative Party prepared an economic strategy entitled 'a quiet revolution'. It sought radical changes in British economic life by relying on individual responsibility, freedom of business, greater competition, reduced state intervention, and membership in the European Economic Community (EEC) in order to spur growth. One could say that CCC was linked to the 'quiet revolution', even if the consultative document published in May 1971 was entirely the BoE's work, and not part of the government legislative process. This is hardly surprising, since it dealt with the Bank's fields of expertise: lending control, and knowledge of the foreign exchange and gilt-edged markets, which played a very important role in public debt management.

1 Forrest Capie, *The Bank of England, 1950s to 1979* (Cambridge: Cambridge University Press, 2010), 431.

2 Capie, *The Bank*, 432.

3 BoE: 3A8/4 CHIEF CASHIER'S POLICY FILES: MONETARY POLICY – ADVANCES AND CONTROL OF INFLATION, 1 Jun 1969–31 Aug 1969. Hancock, 'Note of a meeting… 27 August 1969'; Hollom to O'Brien, 'The banking figures', 29 August 1969.

What is surprising is that the Treasury was notified of the proposed changes at a late stage. Treasury officials were informed in January, and meetings were held in February 1971[4]. It was only on 12 March that Governor O'Brien sent a letter to Chancellor of the Exchequer Anthony Barber outlining the proposals[5]. However, according to Reid, CCC had been presented to the chancellor previously at a private dinner[6].

CCC was a four-page consultative document published by the BoE on 15 May 1971. The aims of the reform were threefold: to increase competition within the banking sector; to improve the bank regulatory system, which was chaotic before 1971; and to increase the money-stock control of monetary authorities (Bank of England and Treasury).

Academics were given the opportunity to discuss the CCC proposals at the BoE from May to September 1971. The Bank also consulted the main banking associations, together with a few individual banks. These discussions were all the more important as the Bank wanted to secure a uniform system of credit control. An agreement was soon concluded with the discount houses, but it was more difficult with the clearing banks, which felt that the new approach 'discriminated' against them[7]. They wanted the BoE to widen the definition of the reserve asset ratio, but the Bank was unwilling to do so, because it would leave bank liquidity too high[8]. The problem of funding was a very difficult one. To get the Treasury and the Chancellor's approval for the new arrangement, the Bank had to show that the clearing bank's capacity to increase credit was limited. But clearers complained to Governor O'Brien that with the funding proposals, the Bank would for the first time be intervening directly in their policy concerning gilts. The Bank

---

4 BoE: 3A8/10 CHIEF CASHIER'S POLICY FILES: MONETARY POLICY – ADVANCES AND CONTROL OF INFLATION, 1 Jan 1971–31 Jan 1971. Fforde to O'Brien, 13 January 1971; BoE: 3A8/12, CHIEF CASHIER'S POLICY FILES: MONETARY POLICY – ADVANCES AND CONTROL OF INFLATION, 1 Mar 1971–31 Mar 1971. D. A. Harding 'Minutes of a meeting… 9 February 1971…', 1 March 1971.

5 BoE: 3A8/12, Ibid., O'Brien to Barber, 12 March 1971.

6 Margaret Reid, *The Secondary Banking Crisis, 1973–1975: Its Causes and Course* (London and Basingstoke: Macmillan, 1982), 31.

7 Capie, *The Bank*, 502–3.

8 BoE: 3A8/18 CHIEF CASHIER'S POLICY FILES: MONETARY POLICY – ADVANCES AND CONTROL OF INFLATION, 17 Jul 1971– 31 Jul 1971. Page to O'Brien, 'London Clearing Banks: funding', 27 July 1971.

disagreed[9]. Data presented by the Committee of London Clearing Bankers (CLCB) showed that reserve assets amounted to 16.6% (£1,752 m) in July, compared to the proposed 12.5%. In the end, the Bank and clearers agreed that £750 m of the total amount of gilts and outstanding special deposits would be funded[10]. Problems were encountered with other banks, especially Scottish clearers and Northern Irish banks. The main complaints were about the universal characteristics of the reserve asset ratio. After lengthy discussions, an agreement was struck with Scottish clearers by abolishing a stamp duty on the note issue worth £600,000 per year[11]. With Northern Irish banks, the BoE recognised that the political and economic situation of Northern Ireland was a special case and secured an agreement for a reserve ratio that would be defined after further consideration[12].

Negotiations with finance houses took a very long time. The Finance Houses Association (FHA) disagreed with the universal asset reserve ratio; their main point of contention was that if they were to be treated as banks for credit control, they had to be considered banks for the purposes of the Protection of Depository Act. Some concessions were offered: FHA banks whose total assets were greater than £5 m were offered the status of banks, and in the end a 10% reserve asset ratio was offered by the Bank to sixteen finance houses[13].

After four months of discussion with the Treasury and consultation with the City, CCC became operational in September 1971. At the end of the summer session, the prime minister explained the new policy to the party's 1922 Committee, and the reform was introduced on 16 September 1971.

---

9 BoE: 3A8/19 CHIEF CASHIER'S POLICY FILES: MONETARY POLICY – ADVANCES AND CONTROL OF INFLATION, 1 Aug 1971–18 Aug 1971. Hollom, Note for record: 'The Governor's conversation with Archibald Forbes', 3 August 1971.

10 Ibid. Page to Fforde, O'Brien/Hollom, 'Competition and Credit Control. Clearing Banks: Funding', 13 August 1971.

11 Capie, *The Bank*, 505.

12 BoE: 3A8/20 CHIEF CASHIER'S POLICY FILES: MONETARY POLICY – ADVANCES AND CONTROL OF INFLATION, 19 Aug 1971–31 Aug 1971. Fforde to O'Brien/Hollom, 'New Approach: Northern Ireland', 24 August 1971.

13 Ibid. Ryrie, Note for the record, 24 August 1971; BoE: 3A8/21 CHIEF CASHIER'S POLICY FILES: MONETARY POLICY – ADVANCES AND CONTROL OF INFLATION, 1 Sep 1971–30 Sep 1971. G. A. Cooke to Fforde, 2 September 1971. (Cooke was FHA's chairman).

The Arrangements of the Reform

Because CCC was meant to respond to different problems at the same time, each institution had a different conception of how it would work[14]. Another difficulty was linked to the fact that Bank and Treasury civil servants had been brought up on Radcliffian thinking[15], which granted a very minor role to monetary policy. For the Bank, CCC's success rested on the use of interest rates, and for the Treasury on the more frequent use of special deposits. Since the Bank had played up the reform's competitive side to win the Conservative government's approval, it is quite reasonable to think that Prime Minister Edward Heath never understood that CCC was essentially about controlling the money supply by varying interest rates.

- Cartels were dissolved.
- Quantitative ceilings were removed. The 28 % liquidity ratio was replaced by a reserve asset ratio at 12.5 % that applied to all private sector banks, near banks and finance houses. It included a narrower range of assets to make it more effective. Special deposits would be used in a more flexible manner.
- According to John S. Fforde[16], M3[17] became the 'one simple aim' of monetary policy[18]. Bank and Treasury framed monetary policy using the Bank's demand for money functions to forecast M3 growth, and to control it with interest rates and special deposits.
- Support for the gilt-edged market was withdrawn.

The document was welcomed by *The Times*, the *Economist* – whose headline was 'Yes, at last revolution for the City' – and *The Banker*[19]. The Economist

---

14 Duncan Needham, *UK Monetary Policy from Devaluation to Thatcher, 1967–1982* (London: Palgrave Macmillan, 2014), 45.

15 In May 1957, Chancellor of the Exchequer Thorneycroft established, under the chairmanship of Lord Radcliffe, a committee 'to enquire into the working of the monetary and credit system, and to make recommendations'. It produced a unanimous report in August 1959 that did not trust monetary policy to achieve the main objectives of economic policy, namely full employment, low inflation and external balance.

16 At that time, he served as the Bank's executive director for home finance.

17 M3 is a broad measure of the money supply. It includes the currency in circulation, Demand deposits, time deposits and Long-term savings and deposits.

18 BoE: 6A50/8 MONETARY POLICY Jan 1973–Apr 1973. Fforde, 'Unhappy Monetary Policy', 27 March 1973.

19 David Kynaston, *Till Time's Last Sand: A History of the BoE, 1694–2013* (London: Bloomsbury Publishing, 2017), 494.

observed: 'It really is worth remarking that this radical change of Britain's whole internal financial system ... has not been the subject of a single clause of legislation. Parliament has barely discussed it. It has all been fixed up as a gentlemen's agreement in private conclaves in the City'[20].

CCC in Operation: Results from October 1971 to December 1973

CCC resulted in heightened competition within the banking sector. Clearing banks entered 'wholesale money' markets as both borrowers and lenders in their own right, rather than through subsidiaries. Differences between clearing banks and non-clearing banks became blurred. The size of networks began diminishing in over-banked regions.

Greater attention was given to the money stock, and a wider definition of the money stock was adopted: M3 was published every month. The new approach ascribed a greater role to more flexible use of interest rates, including Bank Rate; but it had not been decided how this flexibility would operate when CCC was introduced.

Monetary growth was very strong in the first half of 1972: M3 increased by 4.5 % in the first quarter, and 7.5 % in the second[21]. From 1971 to the end of 1973, bank loans in sterling to UK residents rose by no less than 148 %[22]. Most of that lending was not directed to industry, but to property and finance. It was linked to the Heath government's objective of economic growth at all costs. For the BoE, it meant a loss of control over the money supply, which would prove to be a central problem[23]. Governor O'Brien was being criticised for not defending his position on interest rate policy, although he was powerless in the context of a weak chancellor and a very determined prime minister. In early 1972, he was told that the chancellor and prime minister had diverging views[24].

---

20 Quoted by Capie, *The Bank*, 507.
21 Capie, *The Bank*, 509.
22 Reid, *The Secondary Banking Crisis*, 59–60.
23 Capie, *The Bank*, 509.
24 Kynaston, *Till Time's Last Sand*, 495.

Bank Rate was increased from 5 to 6 % in June 1972. It had been announced in the March Budget that sterling would float. The prime minister finally accepted to raise Bank Rate on 22 June, with the sterling crisis resulting in the British pound's ejection on 23 June from the European currency 'snake' it had joined in May[25,26]. Markets were highly sceptical about Barber's 'dash for growth'. Due to market pressure, sterling began floating: it was a 'dirty' float, since the Bank continued to intervene in foreign exchange markets in an attempt to stop the outflow of capital. The Bank recommended another rise of Bank Rate to 7 %. Heath, however, was adamantly opposed to such a move, fearing that an increase just three months after the launch of the 'dash for growth' budget would be seen as a return to the 'stop and go' policies of the previous decade. He was in favour of reintroducing quantitative controls[27], while the governor was in total disagreement.

With the outflow of capital during the June sterling crisis, bank reserves were below the new 12.5 % reserve asset ratio. Because of the severity of the crisis – overnight borrowing rates reached 200 % – the BoE had to bail out the clearing banks and replenish their reserves thanks to a £358 m gilt sale and repurchase agreement[28]. Despite the outflow of capital, M3 growth

---

25 In August 1971, President Nixon put an end to the dollar's convertibility into gold. The following December, leading developed countries met in Washington to try to rescue the Bretton Woods System of fixed exchange rates. The Smithsonian Agreement of December 1971 allowed currencies to fluctuate within a broader band of ±2.25 % around the new fixed parities, whereas under Bretton Woods, the band was narrower: ±1 % around the parity. The 'snake' was created on 24 April 1972 to promote a zone of relative stability within a chaotic International Monetary System. It asked the six EEC member states to limit fluctuations of the exchange rate to 2.25 % around the fixed parity. This meant that the margin that had been agreed to at the Smithsonian Institute was reduced by half.

26 This was even more of a concern considering that a summit was held in Paris, on 20–21 May 1971, between French President George Pompidou and British Prime Minister Edward Heath to discuss the United Kingdom's accession to the European Economic Community. The international status of sterling as a reserve currency was high on the agenda, and Britain was asked to reduce sterling balances and to stabilise sterling before joining the EEC. Marie-Claude Esposito, 'Britain Joining The European Economic Community: the Pompidou-Heath Summit, 20–21 May 1971', in Stéphane Porion, ed., *Fresh Perspectives on the UK in crisis1970–1979* (Paris: Atlande, 2017), 227–39.

27 Needham, *UK Monetary Policy*, 56.

28 Ibid., 57.

reached a record 3.5 % growth in June. Barber was warned by Treasury officials that this growth rate was 'without precedent' and would contribute to 'inflationary psychosis'[29].

Incomes policy was in tatters after the miners' 30 % rise in pay, and with inflation running at an annual rate of 7.2 %. On 8 August, the governor decided to issue the first lending guidance under CCC, asking banks to 'make credit less available to property companies and for financial transactions associated with the maintenance of expansion of industry'[30]. Newspapers did not miss the opportunity to show the obvious contradiction between that request and the precepts of CCC, which undermined its credibility. A week later, O'Brien circulated a memo to a few of his colleagues stating:

> I do not think it too alarmist to say that the Bank's whole authority in the City is in some jeopardy [...]. We pride ourselves on the lack of banking law and specific regulations, and on the superior merits of the Governor's eyebrows. This is only justified if the latter are used with firmness to give unmistakeable messages which are accepted as just and fair by all concerned [...]. The real trouble there is that the Bank, despite its apparent conversion to modern 'scientific' credit management, still loves its traditional ways too. It clings to the ancient rituals of 'nod, nod, wink, wink' but whereas in the good old days a nod was a nod and a wink a wink, now a nod may turn out to be a wink, a wink a nod, a nod 'good morning', and a wink no more than 'hello darling'. What is more, you can't learn this sign language: it is liable to change every week [...]. The dilemma for the Bank is between going completely modern, which it has not yet the will to do, and going back, which it can't do. It should face up to it soon.[31]

In early September, the Treasury Bill Rate was above Bank Rate. Bank Rate was the penalty rate at which the Bank pumped money into the market via the discount houses. If Bank Rate was below market rates, the market could borrow from the Bank and invest in other assets. Ministers continued to reject the recommendations of the Bank and Treasury for a higher Bank Rate. The Bank feared it would be stuck with a Bank Rate that was frozen by politicians. To defuse the political significance of Bank Rate, monetary

---

29 Ibid.

30 O'Brien, 'Bank lending: the Governor's letter to the banking system', 7 August 1972, *BEQB* 12 (3), September 1972, 327.

31 BoE: G3/276 GOVERNOR'S DUPLICATE MEMORANDA, Jul 1972–Dec 1972. O'Brien's memoranda, November 1972.

authorities (Treasury and Bank) decided to replace it with a Minimum Lending Rate (MLR). The new formula linked the Bank's discount rate to the market rates for Treasury bills, as monetary authorities hoped that changes in MLR would have a smaller 'announcement effect' than changes in Bank Rate. The new mechanism was introduced in October 1972, putting an end to Bank Rate, which had been in place for 270 years[32]. It would be announced on each Friday afternoon at the same time as the Treasury bill tender, a decision that brought an end to the tradition of simultaneously announcing Bank Rate in the hall of the Bank and on the floor of the London Stock Exchange every Thursday[33]. As the chief cashier explained: 'We adopted the Minimum Lending Rate technique basically because it was better than having Bank Rate completely frozen by ministers, not because we thought it was technically a superior arrangement'[34].

Operation of the MLR had an immediate impact: the first MLR on 13 October was 7.25 %, whereas Bank Rate was 6 %. It reached 9 % at the end of the year, and the chief cashier was convinced that these rates could not have been reached without a change in the system[35]. At that time, the prime minister was particularly irritated by commentaries in the Bank's bulletin. Tensions developed between the government and the BoE, and the governor had to make it clear that he was not prepared to publish a bulletin subject to Treasury approval[36].

Concerning special deposits, O'Brien recommended that a call of 1 % should be made in November[37]. The first call of special deposits was made on 15 November 1972, with 0.5 % to be paid on 30 November, and 0.5 % a month later. It was followed by a call for 2 % in January 1973[38]. In April and May, the Bank was in favour of a 0.5 % reduction to show the flexible use of special deposits, hoping that the freed-up cash could be used to buy more

---

32 BoE: C42/10 CHIEF CASHIER'S PERSONAL FILES: INTEREST RATES, 17 Feb 1969–4 May 1977. Page to O'Brien/Hollom, 'Special deposits and Bank Rate', 18 September 1972.

33 Capie, *The Bank*, 510.

34 BoE: 6A50/8 op. cit., J. B. Page, 'Monetary policy', 2 April 1973.

35 BoE: C42/10 op. cit. Page to Fforde/Richardson/Hollom, 'Bank rate versus minimum lending rate', 31 December 1976.

36 Kynaston, *Till Time's Last Sand*, 495.

37 BoE: 5A148/2 CHIEF CASHIER'S POLICY FILES: ADVANCES & CONTROL OF INFLATION – SPECIAL DEPOSITS, 7 Jan 1972–21 Dec 1973. O'Brien to Barber, 7 November 1972.

38 Ibid.

gilts. The Treasury advised the chancellor of the Exchequer to agree, but special deposits remained at 3 %[39].

Following the June sterling crisis and the changes in how the Bank intervened in the gilt-edged market, prices started to fall from the end of 1971. By the summer of 1972, Heath wanted to know if something could be done to support the market, and if interventions in the market could be made by operators other than the Government Broker, in order to hide the operation[40]. The Treasury explained that under CCC fluctuations, interest rates would be larger than in the past, and that they were satisfied with the arrangements concerning market interventions: 'Discreet operations could be disguised, and large operations would, in any event, be identified'[41].

The autumn of 1972 forecasts relied again on a set of interest rate assumptions, and not on a money supply target. The Bank forecast that M3 would have to increase by 13 % in 1973–74 in order to accommodate 5 % real GDP growth, which was much less than the 20 % estimated in March[42].

A New Approach

Tensions between O'Brien and Heath intensified, as did those between O'Brien and Barber. In the aftermath of President Nixon's decision to suspend the convertibility of the dollar into gold in August 1971, and the resulting disturbance in the International Monetary System, O'Brien announced on 8 February 1973 that he would retire at the end of June. He had probably hoped to stay a little bit longer, but Heath was adamant: the governor had to go[43]. O'Brien's successor was Gordon Richardson, who like his predecessor took over at a difficult time.

In March, the prime minister asked for a reappraisal of CCC. The main question was to determine whether 'competition' and 'credit control' were compatible, and whether credit controls might not be a better option[44]. The reappraisal was completed in May, and a simplified version

39 Capie, *The Bank of England*, 512.
40 Ibid., 512.
41 Ibid., 513.
42 Needham, *UK Monetary Policy*, 61.
43 Kynaston, *Till Time's Last Sand*, 499–500.
44 BoE: 6A50/8 op. cit., Willets to Fforde, 'Review of the New Approach', 10 April 1973.

was produced for the prime minister and chancellor[45]. One of the major criticisms was that there had been no control on bank lending and the money supply since CCC. This resulted in rampant inflation since 1972. The review considered that the reform made it impossible for the BoE to control the quantity of money or credit. This was due to 'reintermediation', which resulted in monetary growth: funds that had left clearing banks, to the benefit of fringe banks because of quantitative controls imposed exclusively on clearing banks before CCC, returned to clearing banks, and were now counted in the statistics. However, it was very difficult to estimate the amount of M3 due to reintermediation. Moreover, the enormous growth of lending was to individuals and the property sector, not industry. It resulted in a property boom that mostly benefited fringe banks.

The London Discount Market Association (LDMA) was critical of the MLR formula. The fact that short-term interest rates were lower in London than other countries was also a source of concern, because London was less attractive for short-term capital flows, which resulted in pressures on sterling. The Bank was very critical of the Heath government's refusal to give the interest rate the required flexibility, with the review concluding that CCC should not be jettisoned because of the limited experiment (it had been operating for 18 months)[46].

The chief cashier agreed that the MLR formula should be amended; in June he proposed to the Treasury changes that would suppress distortions without undermining the arrangement put in place in October 1972[47].

In July 1973, Richardson warned the chairman of the CLCB that if the increase in lending and the money supply continued, restrictive measures would follow, potentially including direct controls[48]. A governor's guidance letter was issued in the second week of September asking banks to limit the interest on any deposit of less than £10,000 to no more than 9.5 %. Richardson also asked that finance for industrial investment and exports should be given priority, and that loans to persons and real estate be limited. The wording of

---

45 BoE: 6A50/10 MONETARY POLICY, May 1973–Jul 1973. O'Brien to Barber, 4 May 1973, enc 'Competition and Credit Control: a Review and Reappraisal', 4 May 1973.

46 Capie, *The Bank of England*, 515.

47 Ibid., 516.

48 BoE: 5A148/2 op. cit. Note on a meeting at the Bank of England between the clearing bank chairman and the Governors on 6 August 1973.

the governor's guidelines was very similar to the letters on ceilings from the 1960s. For the first time, building societies were subject to the same guidance. The governor's letter also addressed the issue of interest rate arbitrage activities, especially 'round tripping'. Under this form of arbitrage, borrowers could draw on their unused overdraft facilities and use the proceeds to make deposits at higher rates in parallel markets, for example in the inter-bank market or the market for certificates of deposit (CD market), which resulted in an increase both in M3 and interest rates[49]. Richardson asked clearing banks to limit this type of arbitrage.

October 1973 saw the first round of OPEC oil price increases. The United Kingdom also experienced severe industrial unrest, with the prime minister declaring a state of emergency on 13 November. On the same day, the BoE made a call for special deposits of 2 %, and the MLR was raised from 11.25 to 13 %[50]. The market was taken by surprise; trading in gilts was temporarily suspended, and the gilt-edged market experienced the biggest fall since the Second World War[51].

On 15 November, the chancellor of the Exchequer wrote to the governor about the impact of CCC and the effect of high interest rates[52]. The prime minister complained that despite its merits, CCC '[…] had had unforeseen and undesirable consequences from the point of view of the government's overall economic strategy and its political and social priorities'. Heath wanted an alternative with less adverse consequences both short-term and long-term, while Barber pressed the BoE to find a method that '[…] did not raise interest rates to levels which were intolerable politically'.

The BoE came up with a new technique – the 'supplementary scheme' – that was added to CCC arrangements. Banks were asked to deposit with the BoE, interest-free, a percentage of their interest-bearing deposits. It became

---

49 BoE: 3A8/26 CHIEF CASHIER'S POLICY FILES: MONETARY POLICY – ADVANCES AND CONTROL OF INFLATION, 1 May 1973–31 Aug 1973. Fforde to Hollom, 'Managing upward pressures on the parallel rates', 29 August 1973.

50 BoE: 5A148/2, op. cit. Richardson to Barber, 13 November 1973.

51 Capie, *The Bank of England*, 520.

52 BoE: G1/255 GOVERNOR'S FILE: FINANCIAL AND MONETARY POLICY – EXCHANGES OF VIEWS PRINCIPALLY AT GOVERNOR, CHANCELLOR, CLEARING BANK CHAIRMAN LEVEL (AND OTHERS), WITH BACKGROUND PAPERS ON THE BANK AND TREASURY (HMT), 8 Jan 1969–11 Dec 1974. Barber to Richardson, 15 November 1973.

quickly known as the 'supplementary special deposits' (SSD) and later 'the corset', although it had no link with special deposits.

Further tightening measures (tax increases and cuts in public spending) were announced by Barber on 17 December 1973[53]. Hire purchase controls were re-introduced for the first time since July 1971.The 'supplementary special deposit scheme' was imposed not only on clearing banks, but also on all finance houses[54]. These measures marked a return to reliance on quantitative controls in the banking sector, a total U-turn for proponents of CCC, because monetary growth had continued unabated during 1973.

Conclusion

In May 1971, CCC was announced as being a tremendous shift in postwar monetary policy. Two years later, it was considered a 'disaster', because of the dramatic growth of M3, caused by several factors: the Heath Government's 'dash for growth' policy, about which the BoE could do little; the failure of the Bank to anticipate reintermediation; and the failure, due to political reasons, to use interest rates to limit the growth of the money supply.

In late 1973 a secondary bank collapsed, precipitating the Secondary banking crisis, whereas the British banking system had been stable since the third quarter of the nineteenth century. The year 1974 began with a 3-day workweek, and on 7 February, after negotiations with miners stalled, Heath announced there would be a general election in 3 weeks' time.

Bank of England Archives

BoE: 3A8/4 CHIEF CASHIER'S POLICY FILES: MONETARY POLICY – ADVANCES AND CONTROL OF INFLATION, 1 Jun 1969– 31 Aug 1969. Hancock, 'Note of a meeting… 27 August 1969'; Hollom to O'Brien, 'The banking figures', 29 August 1969.

BoE: 3A8/10 CHIEF CASHIER'S POLICY FILES: MONETARY POLICY – ADVANCES AND CONTROL OF INFLATION, 1 Jan 1971– 31 Jan 1971. Fforde to O'Brien, 13 January 1971.

53 House of Commons Debate, 17 December 1973, *Hansard*, Vol. 866, cc. 952–66.

54 *Bank of England Quarterly Bulletin*, Vol. 14, Issue 1, March 1974, p. 37–8.

BoE: 3A8/12, CHIEF CASHIER'S POLICY FILES: MONETARY POLICY – ADVANCES AND CONTROL OF INFLATION, 1 Mar 1971–31 Mar 1971. D. A. Harding 'Minutes of a meeting… 9 February 1971…', 1 March 1971; O'Brien to Barber, 12 March 1971.

BoE: 3A8/18 CHIEF CASHIER'S POLICY FILES: MONETARY POLICY – ADVANCES AND CONTROL OF INFLATION, 17 Jul 1971– 31 Jul 1971. Page to O'Brien, 'London Clearing Banks: funding', 27 July 1971.

BoE: 3A8/19 CHIEF CASHIER'S POLICY FILES: MONETARY POLICY – ADVANCES AND CONTROL OF INFLATION, 1 Aug 1971–18 Aug 1971. Hollom, Note for record: 'The Governor's conversation with Archibald Forbes', 3 August 1971; Page to Fforde, O'Brien/Hollom, 'Competition and Credit Control. Clearing Banks: Funding', 13 August 1971.

BoE: 3A8/20 CHIEF CASHIER'S POLICY FILES: MONETARY POLICY – ADVANCES AND CONTROL OF INFLATION, 19 Aug 1971– 31 Aug 1971. Fforde to O'Brien/Hollom, 'New Approach: Northern Ireland', 24 August 1971; Ryrie, Note for the record, 24 August 1971.

BoE: 3A8/21 CHIEF CASHIER'S POLICY FILES: MONETARY POLICY – ADVANCES AND CONTROL OF INFLATION, 1 Sep 1971–30 Sep 1971. G. A. Cooke to Fforde, 2 September 1971.

BoE: 6A50/8 MONETARY POLICY Jan 1973–Apr 1973. Fforde, 'Unhappy Monetary Policy', 27 March 1973; J. B. Page, 'Monetary policy', 2 April 1973.

BoE: C42/10 CHIEF CASHIER'S PERSONAL FILES: INTEREST RATES, 17 Feb 1969–4 May 1977. Page to O'Brien/Hollom, 'Special deposits and Bank Rate', 18 September 1972; Page to Fforde/Richardson/Hollom, 'Bank rate versus minimum lending rate', 31 December 1976.

BoE: G1/255 GOVERNOR'SFILE: FINANCIAL AND MONETARY POLICY – EXCHANGES OF VIEWS PRINCIPALLY AT GOVERNOR, CHANCELLOR, CLEARING BANK CHAIRMAN LEVEL (AND OTHERS), WITH BACKGROUND PAPERS ON THE BANK AND TREASURY (HMT), 8 Jan 1969–11 Dec 1974. Barber to Richardson, 15 November 1973.

BoE: G3/276 GOVERNOR'S DUPLICATE MEMORANDA, Jul 1972–Dec 1972. O'Brien's memoranda, November 1972.

BoE: 3A8/26 CHIEF CASHIER'S POLICY FILES: MONETARY POLICY – ADVANCES AND CONTROL OF INFLATION, 1 May 1973–31 Aug 1973. Fforde to Hollom, 'Managing upward pressures on the parallel rates', 29 August 1973.

BoE: 5A148/2 CHIEF CASHIER'S POLICY FILES: ADVANCES & CONTROL OF INFLATION – SPECIAL DEPOSITS, 7 Jan 1972–21 Dec 1973. O'Brien to Barber, 7 November 1972; Note on a meeting at the Bank of England between the clearing bank chairman and the Governors on 6 August 1973; Richardson to Barber, 13 November 1973.

BoE: 6A50/8 op. cit., Willets to Fforde, 'Review of the New Approach', 10 April 1973.

BoE: 6A50/10 MONETARY POLICY, May 1973–Jul 1973. O'Brien to Barber, 4 May 1973, enc 'Competition and Credit Control: a Review and Reappraisal', 4 May 1973.

Bibliography

Capie, Forrest, *The Bank of England, 1950s to 1979* (Cambridge: Cambridge University Press, 2010).

Esposito, Marie-Claude, 'Britain Joining The European Economic Community: The Pompidou-Heath Summit, 20–21 May 1971', in Stéphane Porion, ed., *Fresh Perspectives on the UK in Crisis 1970–1979* (Paris: Atlande, 2017), 227–39.

Kynaston, David, *Till Time's Last Sand: A History of the BoE, 1694–2013* (London: Bloomsbury Publishing, 2017).

Needham, Duncan, *UK Monetary Policy from Devaluation to Thatcher, 1967–1982* (Palgrave Macmillan, 2014).

Reid, Margaret, *The Secondary Banking Crisis, 1973–1975* (London and Basingstoke: Macmillan, 1982).

Enoch Powell's Stance on Europe in the Heath Years: The Development of 'Euroscepticism' Within the Conservative Party *Avant la Lettre*

Stéphane Porion

Introduction

At the end of the summit held on 20–21 May 1971, French President Pompidou declared that his European stance was 'similar and even analogous' to that of British Prime Minister Edward Heath, putting an end to a feeling of distrust between France and the UK. Pompidou anticipated a positive outcome to British entry in the EEC:

> We are both aware that the questions we are debating come at an important moment in the history of our nations and the history of Europe. Many believed that Great Britain is not European, and that it wanted to get into the Common Market only to destroy it. Many others also believed that France was prepared to use all means of veto to prevent Great Britain from getting into the Common Market. Well, ladies and gentlemen, tonight you see before you two men who are convinced that this is not the case.[1]

Enoch Powell, on the other hand, ruled out the idea of a European future that Pompidou wanted to impose on the United Kingdom with Heath's collusion:

> We know the crucial question which M. Pompidou administered to Mr Heath in Paris [in May 1971]. [...] "Are you determined to tie yourself to the Continent, and consequently to loosen your ties with the open sea to which you have always looked?" [...] In return for accepting the irreversible agricultural policy of Western Europe – that may be a shrewd bargain for others. For us it would be manifest folly.[2]

---

1 Pompidou as quoted in 'The World: Europe: The British are Coming', *Time* (31 May 1971), <https://time.com/archive/6877510/the-world-europe-the-british-are-coming/>, accessed 30 December 2024.

2 Enoch Powell, *Still to Decide* (Kingswood: Elliot Right Way Books, 1972), 233–4.

Just before the Act of Entry was ratified on 22 January 1972, Powell expressed a foreboding sense of harmful changes to come: 'In order for Britain to join the Community, the House of Commons has to be told, and to accept, that it will progressively lose its executive power to control legislation and government. [...] Parliament has to drink deadly poison, and not in a single draught but drop by fatal drop'[3].

At the turn of the 1970s, Powell had laid out all the hardships Britain would face if it joined the Common Market, namely economic, strategic and political issues, including a loss of sovereignty. He had thus become the most vocal opponent to British membership in the EEC within the Conservative Party. According to David Shiels, 'his views have undoubtedly shaped the modern Tory critique of European integration. In some respects, he can be regarded as the founding father of modern Tory Euroscepticism'[4]. However, as some have pointed out, Powell 'fluctuated in his opinions' on British integration in the EEC[5], supporting it to some extent in the 1960s, before 'emerging as the leading advocate of the anti-Market cause' in 1969[6], when he delivered his first Eurosceptic speech[7]. In Powell's view, Heath betrayed the sacrosanct principle of the supremacy of British institutions, which Disraeli reasserted in his 1872 speech, in favour of the European super-parliament[8]. This accounted for Powell's ultimate sacrifice of standing down as a Tory MP and casting a

3 Enoch Powell, 'Speech to the Liechtenstein Press Club' (15 January 1972), 3, POLL 4/1/8 File 4, Powell Papers.

4 David Shiels, 'How Enoch Powell Helped to Shape Modern Tory Euroscepticism', LSE blogs (3 June 2016), https://blogs.lse.ac.uk/brexit/2016/06/03/how-enoch-powell-helped-to-shape-modern-tory-euroscepticism/, accessed 10 December 2024.

5 See for example Paul Corthorn, *Enoch Powell: Politics and Ideas in Modern Britain* (Oxford: OUP, 2019), 105; Roy Lewis, *Enoch Powell: Principle in Politics* (London: Cassell, 1979), 145; Nick Pearce, Michael Kenny and Lindsay Aqui, 'The Empire of England: Enoch Powell, Sovereignty and the Constitution of the Nation', *Twentieth Century British History* 32/2 (2021), 21, <https://purehost.bath.ac.uk/ws/portalfiles/portal/210524969/The_Empire_of_England_final_version_with_copyediting_changes.pdf>, accessed 28 November 2024.

6 Enoch Powell, *Common Market: Renegotiate or Come Out* (Tadworth: Elliot Right Way Books, 1973), 9.

7 Douglas E. Schoen, *Enoch Powell and the Powellites* (London: Macmillan, 1977), 74.

8 Stéphane Porion, 'Disraeli's Significant Influence on Enoch Powell's Tory Conception of Nationhood', *Cahiers victoriens et édouardiens*, 101, (Spring 2025), <https://journals.openedition.org/cve/15721>.

vote for the Labour Party in the February 1974 general election[9], earning him calls of 'Judas'[10]. Heath depicted this as an act of betrayal: Powell as 'a champion of the right showed that he would sacrifice all his principles for a remote chance that Labour might take Britain out of Europe'[11].

The aim of this chapter is to reconsider Powell's intellectual journey with respect to British membership in the EEC in the Heath years by redefining the concept of Euroscepticism before the 1980s, which gained prominence in the aftermath of Thatcher's 1988 Bruges speech. It will complement biographical works and recent analyses, notably by Paul Corthorn and Nick Pearce, Michael Kenny, and Lindsay Aqui in the UK[12], and Laetitia Langlois and Richard Davis in France[13]. It will exclude Powell's campaign against the EEC during the 1975 referendum, as Robert Saunders already wrote a substantial analysis on this topic in 2018[14]. To this end, I will use E. H. H. Green's methodological approach to writing an intellectual history of the Conservative Party[15], in which Powell should be seen as an intellectual Eurosceptic Conservative. The chapter will focus on Powell's fluctuating stance on European integration, with his eventual defence of British national sovereignty in the early 1970s as a protection of the British nation, clashing with Heath and Pompidou's

---

9 Simon Heffer, *Like the Roman: The Life and Times of Enoch Powell* (London: Weidenfield, 1998), 705–7.

10 'Enoch Powell – Judas?', YouTube (27 January 2017), <https://www.youtube.com/watch?v=GYy8ORPz1nE>, accessed 3 January 2025.

11 Edward Heath, *Course of My Life: The Autobiography of Edward Heath* (London: Hodder and Stoughton, 1998), 516.

12 Corthorn, *Enoch Powell*; Paul Corthorn, 'Enoch Powell, the Original Anti-immigrant, Anti-Europe, Pro-unionist Tory', *The Irish Times* (27 August 2019), <https://www.irishtimes.com/culture/books/enoch-powell-theoriginal-anti-immigrant-anti-europe-pro-unionist-tory-1.3997786>, accessed 10 December 2024. Nick Pearce, Michael Kenny and Lindsay Aqui, 'The Empire of England: Enoch Powell, Sovereignty and the Constitution of the Nation', *art. cit.*

13 Richard Davis, 'Euroscepticism and Opposition to British Entry into the EEC, 1955–1975', *Revue française de civilisation britannique* 22/2 (2017), <https://journals.openedition.org/rfcb/1364>, accessed 2 April 2024; Laetitia Langlois, 'Le Parti conservateur et l'adhésion à la Communauté européenne : coulisses d'un vote historique', *Outre-Terre* 49 (2016).

14 Robert Saunders, *Yes to Europe: The 1975 Referendum and Seventies Britain* (Cambridge: Cambridge University Press, 2018).

15 E. H. H. Green, *Ideologies of Conservatism: Conservative Political Ideas in the Twentieth Century* (Oxford: OUP, 2002).

pro-European move. It will be based on archival material (mainly the Powell and Heath Papers), as well as Powell's published writings.

Powell's 'Eurosceptic Instinct' in the Aftermath of the War

Powell started his political career in the Conservative Research Department (CRD)[16], and was trained in a Disraelian vein when he became one of Rab Butler's 'backroom boys'[17]. Under Butler's influence, the Conservatives working within the CRD had to draw intellectually on the tutelary figures of the past in order to recast Conservative ideas, for instance Disraeli[18]. Powell had become a staunch champion of imperialism, remembering Disraeli's eloquent words in his 1872 Crystal Palace speech in defence of the British Empire – the cornerstone of Britain's prestige. Powell therefore submitted a report to Churchill in 1946 listing all the reasons why the Conservative Party should oppose Labour's policy on India's independence[19]. Churchill dismissed Powell's plan as 'crazy and unrealistic', as he believed there was no alternative[20].

In September 1946, Churchill called for setting up a 'United Europe', which in practice could mean the necessary pooling of national sovereignty. Churchill became honorary president of the European Movement, created on 25 October 1948 to bring together all of the organisations supporting European unity, and to implement a system of close cooperation in order to avoid federalism and supra-national wishful thinking. While there was an overall acceptance of European unity among the Conservatives, Powell's top priorities were the Empire and the preservation of British sovereignty.

---

16 Powell's job was to prepare memos and briefs for ministers or members of the Conservative Party.

17 In Butler's views, these young ambitious people were ready to work hard in the CRD before emerging and pursuing a good political career in the House of Commons. Rab Butler, *The Art of the Possible: The Memoirs of Lord Butler* (London: Purnell Book, 1971), 140.

18 Butler, *The Art*, 154.

19 Enoch Powell, 'Indian Memorandum' (16 May 1946 & 3 December 1946), POLL 3/1/4, Powell Papers.

20 Heffer, *Like the Roman*, 109.

In November 1949, he declared: 'Within the Empire we were working to diminish and destroy the remaining vestiges of that sovereignty which had given unity to a quarter of the inhabited world. At the same time, we were apparently ready to contemplate a European Union which, if it meant anything at all, meant the surrender of effective sovereignty over these realms to some external body'[21]. He reasserted the same concern a year later: 'The continental countries are each separate units whereas the United Kingdom is only one part of a greater whole, namely the British Empire. Britain cannot, therefore, agree to any pooling of sovereignty with the European countries which would automatically result in severing her from the non-European countries of the Empire'[22]. As a matter of fact, as Paul Corthorn has observed, 'in 1950, as the Labour government rejected the French ultimatum to decide promptly whether to join the European Coal and Steel Community (ECSC), Powell was one of six Conservative MPs who abstained when the Conservative Party opposed the government's decision'.[23] When the Conservatives returned to power in 1951, there was a shift in their pro-European stance, as they no longer intended to join the ECSC. At the time, Powell was concerned by defence commitments that lay overseas in the British Empire.

While Eurosceptic ideas can be traced back to the aftermath of the war in the UK, the term itself is recent: 'it was not used during the first decades of European integration, when opponents of integration were referred to as nationalists, "anti-marketeers". [...] Euroscepticism is a term that originated in a specific context, that of British public debate on the EC in the mid-1980s'[24]. Agnès Alexandre-Collier has pointed out that in her dictionary of new words, Sara Tulloch alludes to an article in *The Times* of 30 June 1986, which used the term to describe Margaret Thatcher's specific attitude to Europe[25]. The term was popularised in 1988 following Thatcher's Bruges speech at the College

---

21 Enoch Powell, 'Speech at Annual Meeting of Divisional Young Conservatives' (29 November 1949), D3123/223, Staffordshire Record Office.

22 Enoch Powell, 'Speech at the Annual General Meeting of the Penn Ward Branch at the Rose and Crowns' (between 26th October and 5th November 1950), D3123/223, Staffordshire Record Office.

23 Corthorn, *Enoch Powell*, 105.

24 Cécile Leconte, *Understanding Euroscepticism* (Basingstoke: Palgrave Macmillan, 2010), 3.

25 Sara Tulloch, *The Oxford Dictionary of New Words: A Popular Guide to Words in the News* (Oxford: OPU, 1996), 105–7, in Agnès Alexandre-Collier, 'Le Phénomène eurosceptique au sein du Parti conservateur britannique', *Politique Européenne* 6 (2002), 54.

of Europe. In the words of Richard Davis, 'defining the historical expressions of British Euroscepticism, and seeking to understand its origins and ideological bases, is not, therefore, easy'[26]. According to Menno Spiering, 'one could argue that using the term Eurosceptic in such a wide, temporal context [post-war Britain] is anachronistic'[27]. Using the studies of Anthony Forster and Martin Holmes[28], Spiering adds that 'every British doubt, past and present, about the European institutions is a sign of Euroscepticism'. The term can be used 'in a non-specific way, as a portmanteau for every British reservation ever expressed about post-war European cooperation and integration'[29]. One key element of Powell's British Euroscepticism was a distinctive conception of sovereignty through a nationalist view, including the British Empire, which clashed with the intergovernmentalism of the European integration process[30].

To establish an overall picture of Britain's post-war situation, one should also consider Britain's sense of exceptionalism. Agnès Alexandre-Collier has shown that the debate on European construction in post-war Britain was perceived as a pacification issue specific to continental nations and, in this sense, far removed from British concerns. This attitude was based on a deep and enduring sense of belonging to an exceptional, thriving, powerful, and imperial island nation, much closer to the United States than to continental Europe[31]. In Powell's case, there were a deep and long-standing distrust of the US that had crystallised during the Second World War[32], and critical distance from Churchill's three-circles theory. Powell's priority was the British

---

26 Davis, 'Euroscepticism', 2.

27 Menno Spiering, 'British Euroscepticism', in Robert Harmsen and Menno Spiering, eds, *Euroscepticism: Party Politics, National Identity and European Integration* (Amsterdam: Rodopi, 2004), 127.

28 Anthony Foster, *Euroscepticism in Contemporary British Politics: Opposition to Europe in the British Conservative and Labour Parties* (London: Routledge 2002); Martin Holmes, *The Eurosceptic Reader* (Houndmills and New York: Palgrave, 1996).

29 Spiering, 'British Euroscepticsm', 128.

30 Robert Harmsen, 'Is British Euroscepticism still Unique', in Justine Lacroix and Ramona Coman, *Les Résistances à l'Europe : Cultures nationales, idéologies et stratégies d'acteurs* (Brussels : Éditions de l'Université de Bruxelles, 2007), 70–1.

31 Agnès Alexandre-Collier, *La Grande-Bretagne eurosceptique ? L'Europe dans le débat politique britannique* (Paris : Éditions du Temps, 2002), 11.

32 Stéphane Porion, 'Enoch Powell et le powellisme : entre tradition disraélienne et anticipation néo-libérale, 1946–1968' (unpublished Phd thesis, Université Sorbonne-Nouvelle Paris 3, 2011), 49.

Empire, not European integration. It is subsequently more accurate to talk of Powell's 'Eurosceptic instinct' than 'Hard Euroscepticism' at this stage[33], as Britain had opted out both of the European Coal and Steel Community (ECSC) and the Treaty of Rome. Powell's Eurosceptic instinct nevertheless meant a 'rejectionist attitude' towards European integration, which he saw as 'a negative construction'[34]. Hugo Young has argued that Hugh Gaiskell was 'the first Eurosceptic' in post-war Britain[35]. As for Powell, he had been an MP since 1950 but could be seen as the most Eurosceptic among the Conservatives. His attitude can also be accounted for by focusing on Britain's specific historical and constitutional context: 'Powell pointed to the fact that four of the six initial member states of the EEC were recent creations in European history and that all of them had recently created constitutions and assemblies which, he argued, made them more amenable to the creation of another new, European, political structure'[36].

Powell's Move to Europragmatism in the 1960s

In July 1960, Prime Minister Harold Macmillan appointed Edward Heath as Lord Privy Seal to negotiate Britain's entry in the Common Market. Macmillan had thus turned the Conservative Party into a pro-European party. As for Heath, he had pro-European convictions since his Maiden speech in 1950[37], and viewed Britain in 1960 'at the end of a glorious era, that of the British Empire, and at the beginning of a whole new chapter of British history'[38]. Being part of the EEC was thus seen as the panacea to Britain's sluggish economy. Powell acknowledged that at the time he had

---

33 Paul Taggart and Aleks Szczerbiak, eds, *Opposing Europe?: The Comparative Party Politics of Euroscepticism* (Oxford: OUP, 2008).

34 Benjamin Leruth, Nicholas Startin and Simon Usherwood, eds, *The Routledge Handbook of Euroscepticism* (London and New York: Routledge, 2018), 4 and 41.

35 Hugo Young, *This Blessed Plot: Britain and Europe from Churchill to Blair* (London: Macmillan, 1998), 161.

36 Davis, 'Euroscepticism', 3.

37 Edward Heath, 'Maiden Speech in the House of Commons' (Political Speech Archive, 1950), <https://www.ukpol.co.uk/edward-heath-1950-maiden-speech-in-the-house-of-commons/>, accessed 6 November 2024.

38 Heath, *Course of My Life*, 203.

supported Britain's membership application[39], as he embraced economic arguments in joining the EEC, and deliberately overlooked concerns regarding diminished British sovereignty. He had also made up his mind: British membership would not undermine trade with the Commonwealth. There were potential benefits of British membership for trade, industry, and agriculture. Powell thought that British people were starting to perceive advantages in the larger European market[40]. He was aware of bureaucratic disadvantages but contended that they were 'outweighed by the advantage of not being left outside the tariff wall. It was a *pis aller*; but it seemed on balance worth going for'[41]. Powell had thus converted to Europragmatism. As Paul Corthorn has indicated, 'developing his case for a "free economy", Powell argued that Labour's main priority – in contrast – was to keep Britain's economy sufficiently insulated from the outside world to be in the control of the national planners, which was the root of their antagonism to the Common Market'[42]. But in 1963, De Gaulle's veto dashed British hopes; Britain was a potential danger to European construction, being seen as 'the American Trojan horse'.

In 1964, Powell once again joined the One Nation Group (ONG) when its members decided to tackle the European question in the aftermath of De Gaulle's veto. ONG members believed that the Conservative Party should not only occupy the pro-European political space, with the Labour Party showing entrenched opposition to European integration[43], but also take advantage of a change in attitude within Conservative local branches, which were becoming less and less opposed to European integration[44]. Powell gave the impression of being a staunch pro-European, since he contributed to the

39 For example, see Enoch Powell, 'Speech to Conservative Women's Rally' (Clacton, 21 March 1969), 3, POLL 4/1/5, Powell Papers; Enoch Powell, *The Common Market: The Case Against* (Kingswood: Elliott Rightway, 1971), 9.

40 South European Service, 5 April 1965, POLL 4/1/27, Powell Papers.

41 Enoch Powell, 'Speech to Conservative Women's Rally', 8.

42 Corthorn, *Enoch Powell*, 106.

43 Reginald Maudling, 'The Conservative Party in Europe' (LCC (65) 24, 25 March 1965), POLL 3/2/1/7, Powell Papers.

44 '"One Nation" Tories Regroup for Europeanism', 1965, LONGDEN 4/1, Longden Papers.

drafting of *One Europe*[45], but without including his name[46]. Robert Shepherd contends that he wrote a quarter of the document[47].

In *One Europe*, the authors argue that Britain 'can no longer develop her economy, her defence, her influence from outside the Common Market'[48]. They explain that before 1962, 'no association in one form or another' was possible due to British exceptionalism[49], 'a feeling of distrust of the French'[50], and Churchill's three-circles theory, which did not prioritise European integration[51]. A change occurred in 1962 when 'British people were awakened to the dangers of being excluded'[52]. In the early 1960s, Britain was already hit by stagnation and was seeking to boost her industry and economy. While the European Free Trade Association (EFTA) seemed to be less successful than the Common Market, British trade with the Commonwealth did not turn out to be the panacea either. ONG members thought that being out of the Common Market was a hindrance to British trade: 'As free trade is established within the Six, so it becomes harder for Britain outside the Common External Tariff to sell her goods competitively with the Common Market'[53].

In addition to being more competitive, they listed all of the benefits that Britain would enjoy from being part of the Common Market: the free movement of labour; a larger labour market in Europe; rising wages; reduced trade restrictions by either management or labour; and the implementation of the very reforms that British industry and agriculture needed. They thus argued that 'by joining Europe we would gain more say in the policies which control our economic destinies'[54]. It would also develop technological cooperation in four fields (nuclear, aircraft, research, and the military)[55]. In their view, 'those who regarded European integration as an infringement of our

45 Nicholas Ridley, ed., *One Europe* (London: CPC, 1965), 1–27, POLL 6/2/2, Powell Papers.
46 Andrew Roth, *Enoch Powell: Tory Tribune* (London, Macdonald & Co, 1970), 329.
47 Robert Shepherd, *Enoch Powell: A Biography* (London: Pimlico, 1997), 285.
48 Ridley, ed., *One Europe*, 5.
49 Ridley, ed., *One Europe*.
50 Ridley, ed., *One Europe*, 6.
51 Ridley, ed., *One Europe*.
52 Ridley, ed., *One Europe*, 7.
53 Ridley, ed., *One Europe*, 9.
54 Ridley, ed., *One Europe*, 11.
55 Ridley, ed., *One Europe*, 8.

sovereignty were to protect our society from [positive and vital] change'[56]. All in all, ONG members adopted a Europragmatic or Eurorealist stance on British integration in the EEC: 'we have already lost our ability to pursue an independent economic policy, the economic crisis at the end of the 1964 has emphasised our dependence upon Europe. No country can be an economic island today. We depend upon Europe to guarantee the strength of sterling as a world currency'[57].

In *One Europe*, the authors also tackled the 'political argument': 'Economic union in Europe, or a combined military force, presupposes that the political will to unite is present (…) it involves a cession of national sovereignty on the part of the participating countries'[58]. In their view, political integration was 'inevitable' as it came hand in hand with 'economic and military combination'[59], even though they acknowledged that there had been 'resistance' to the 'idea of participating in a European political union' in Britain. Once again, their stance stemmed from a Eurorealist view, because Britian had decided to be part of international organisations in which the decision-making process involved pooling the decisions of members: 'we have lost much sovereignty in monetary, defence and foreign political matters by joining IMF, GATT, NATO and UN'[60]. ONG members, including Powell, were well aware that European integration would result in Britain's potential loss of sovereignty, but at this stage they preferred calling for 'a looser association', and had no 'prior commitment' on the debate between 'confederalism' and 'federalism' – whether Europe should become an association of sovereign states (*'L'Europe des Patries'*) or 'a closer knit political whole' like the United States[61]. Within this political union, ONG members expected Britain to regain strength and prestige, 'wield Britain's influence', 'influence the European Community to [Britain's] point of view', and avoid being 'excluded and isolated'. That way Britain could 'rise again in strength'[62]. The Conservative Party should thus

56 Ridley, ed., *One Europe*, 10.
57 Ridley, ed., *One Europe*, 11.
58 Ridley, ed., *One Europe*, 15.
59 Ridley, ed., *One Europe*.
60 Ridley, ed., *One Europe* 16.
61 Ridley, ed., *One Europe*.
62 Ridley, ed., *One Europe*, 17.

show 'enthusiasm for this European ideal' and pledge to create 'a Minister for European Affairs'[63].

As for the members of the Conservative Shadow Cabinet, they approved the content of *One Europe*, because the Conservative Party still had to strategically reassert its pro-European position following General de Gaulle's 1963 veto against Britain's entry, before formalising specific measures supporting European integration[64]. As the question of national sovereignty was concerned, Duncan Sandys thought that 'we would not be expected to say how far or how fast political integration should go or what form it should take. In particular, we would not be expected to express our readiness to renounce any part of our sovereignty in the political field, to which the French government are in any case firmly opposed'[65].

Powell's lack of lucidity in participating in the drafting of *One Europe* with respect to the political consequences of British membership within the EEC can be criticised, for as early as the late 1940s, he had fully grasped what it would mean for Britain: 'Economic co-operation and, even more, co-operation in defence is not possible without a degree of political unity. We must be ready to sacrifice in this cause some portion of our independence of action'[66].

As the Shadow Cabinet Defence minister, Powell was convinced in 1966 that Britain could still be a world power if 'it remains a maritime and oceanic power'. Britain should maintain 'substantial strength and efficiency outside Europe' and 'secure British interests'. Powell showed again he had adopted a Eurorealist stance, as Britain should be part of the EEC despite a potential loss of sovereignty:

> History and Geography have decreed that the British Isles are part of Europe. [...] Britain needs to be an integral part of the arrangements for defending the mainland of Western Europe. [...] Economically Britain seems destined to be absorbed into the life of the adjacent mainland, and the ever-increasing advantages of this may be expected to break down political obstacles on both sides, especially as the masses in

63 Ridley, ed., *One Europe*, 22.

64 Charles Longbottom, 'Correspondence with One Nation members' (8 February 1965), LONGDEN 4/1, Longden Papers.

65 Duncan Sandys, 'Britain and Europe' (LCC (65) 25, 25 March 1965), 3, POLL 3/2/1/7, Powell Papers.

66 Enoch Powell, 'Speech at Graiseley School in Fellows Street' (14 December 1949), D3123/223, Staffordshire Record Office.

> Britain come to realise that the continent is outstripping them. There will always be enough that is unique in the situation and characteristics of Britain to ensure that the national identity we prize is not submerged. Economic integration does not, in itself, imply political integration; but I would expect that continuous collaboration in both the military and the economic spheres is bound to be reflected in permanent political institutions.[67]

Powell's view contrasted with Heath's deep pro-European stance. Despite De Gaulle's veto, Heath thought that 'we are a part of Europe, by geography, history, culture, tradition and civilization. [...] There have been times in the history of Europe when it has been only too plain how European we are. [...] I say to my colleagues: they should have no fear. We in Britain are not going to turn our backs on the mainland of Europe or the countries of the Community'[68].

In 1968, Powell explained to C. Michael-Titus that, since the end of the Second World War, Britain had not been very pro-European for three main reasons, stemming from Churchill's three-circles theory: the concern to keep India in its bosom, the defence of its Empire, and its relationship with the United States. In his view, until the British were cured of the 'imperial myth', they would not be able to face up to the challenges of Europe. Powell defended European defence integration and a free trade area, which he called '*une Europe des patries*' (A Europe of nations), but made no mention of his refusal to see continued political integration[69].

> 'A Europe of Nations', of sovereign nations, is the only Europe to which Britain, so long as she herself remains a nation, could belong. [...] There is indeed a point at which the development of supra-national, not to say federal, institutions and authority, in the EEC is likely to be arrested. 'The Europe of Nations' is much the most probable form of the future face of Europe, as well as that in which Britain could most easily enter into the close relations that she ought to have with all the various nations of the adjacent continent.[70]

---

67 Enoch Powell, 'Untilted Document' (21 July 1966), 1–2, POLL 4/1/27, File 2, Powell Papers.

68 Heath, *Course of my Life*, 235.

69 Enoch Powell, 'L'Angleterre et ses problèmes européens', *Bulletin européen* (June 1968), 8, POLL 12/1/12, Powell Papers.

70 Powell, 'Speech to Conservative Women's Rally', 12–3.

He said that 'he was what is called "a European"'[71], but for him the word 'united' in 'United Europe' should not have the same meaning as in 'United Kingdom' or 'United States', 'such a thing is a chimera: undesirable and inconceivable for British people'[72]. Powell's view foreshadowed Thatcher's speech in 1988 when she put forward the idea of 'a family of nations'. The year 1969 subsequently was a turning point in his political thinking[73], for Powell started to develop his Eurosceptic stance by focusing on the political dimension of the EEC: 'One cannot pretend that the European Community is an economic, not a political community, [...] for the Community is political by its nature and from the start'[74]. De Gaulle was gone, and so was Powell's claim for a Europe of nations.

Heath's Europeanism vs Powell's 'Hard Euroscepticism'

Following his 1968 'Rivers of Blood' speech calling for a halt on immigration and voluntary repatriation in a racist and populist vein, which led Heath to dismiss him from the Shadow Cabinet, 'Powell had positioned himself as a prophet-in-exile'. As Robert Saunders puts it, 'Powell's contempt for Heath was not the cause of his opposition to the EEC, but he made no secret of his desire for revenge on a man whom he viewed as a traitor to his country'[75]. In the early 1970s, 'two national strategies' developed within the Conservative Party[76]. On the one hand, the centrepiece of Edward Heath's national strategy hinged on EEC membership, seen as a means of boosting the British economy, reversing Britain's decline, and rethinking Britain's role in an interdependent world. As Philip Lynch has pointed out, 'Heath's European convictions were a blend of idealism and realism', and his approach 'accepted an incremental pooling of national sovereignty' as well

71 Powell, 'Speech to Conservative Women's Rally', 3.

72 Powell, 'Speech to Conservative Women's Rally', 12.

73 Powell, *Common Market*, 9.

74 Powell, *Common Market*, 42.

75 Saunders, *Yes to Europe!*, 53. Nicholas True also supports this view. Nicholas True, 'European Union', in Lord Howard of Rising, ed., *Enoch at 100: A Re-Evaluation of the Life, Politics and Philosophy of Enoch Powell* (London: Biteback, 2012), 5.

76 Philip Lynch, *The Politics of Nationhood* (London: Macmillan, 1999), 22.

as 'a pragmatic intergovernmentalist vision of European integration'[77]. On the other, what fuelled Powell's opposition to joining the EEC after 1969 was not economic considerations but the loss of national sovereignty, seen as the end of political independence, self-government, and the legislative supremacy of the Westminster Parliament. The same author argues that:

> Powellism constructed an alternative post-imperialist nationalist strategy which redefined the conservative nation and constructed a political strategy built around monetarist economics, repatriation, and an end to New Commonwealth immigration, plus the defence of the nation-state and parliamentary sovereignty through opposition to membership of the EC and support for the Union with Northern Ireland.[78]

His approach embraced 'populist nationalism'[79], as Powell felt he had 'to articulate the feelings of ordinary people'[80], given that he believed the British people were largely against joining the EEC in the early 1970s[81].

In the preface to the 1966 Conservative Manifesto, Heath gave his vision of Britain's future: 'our country taking its place in the European Economic Community'[82]. In March 1967, Heath gave a series of lectures at Harvard University entitled *Old World, New Horizons*, in which he extolled the industrial and economic dynamism of the European Community[83]. In terms of foreign policy, he abandoned Churchill's three-circles theory in favour of Europe, which he saw as the only relevant sphere of influence for the UK. He believed that a strong and united Europe would be built with the UK's membership[84]. Heath was a lifelong Europeanist who proposed not only a change in foreign policy, but also a radical one in the identity and future of his party and nation. In the 1970 Conservative Manifesto, he pledged to

---

77 Lynch, *The Politics of Nationhood*, 29.

78 Lynch, *The Politics of Nationhood*, 38.

79 Corthorn, *Enoch Powell*, 104; Ben Wellings, *English Nationalism and Euroscepticism: Losing the Peace* (Oxford: Peter Lang, 2011), 107.

80 Heffer, *Like the Roman*, 586.

81 Powell, *Still to Decide*, 214.

82 'Action Not Words: The New Conservative Programme', 1966, <http://www.conservativemanifesto.com/1966/1966-conservative-manifesto.shtml>, accessed 17 November 2024.

83 Edward Heath, *Old World, New Horizons: Britain, Europe and the Atlantic Alliance* (Cambridge: Harvard University Press 1970).

84 Heath, *Old World*, 2.

'negotiate the right terms for Britain to join the EEC in the long-term interest of the British people, […] no more, no less'. This 'fair and equal settlement should be approved by Parliament' as MPs would listen to their constituents[85].

Following the Conservative victory in the 1970 general election, Prime Minister Edward Heath decided to set Britain on a fast track to European integration, as 'British membership of the EEC had long been [his] overriding political ambition and the cornerstone of his government's policy'[86]. While Geoffrey Rippon was leading the official negotiations for British entry in Brussels, Heath and Christopher Soames (the British Ambassador to Paris) tried to secure the support of French President Georges Pompidou, who was much more congenial to Britain than De Gaulle. What happened in Paris in the spring of 1971 was a turning point for Heath's objective, leading to the successful summit between Pompidou and the British Prime Minister in Paris on 20–21 May, as revealed by the archives in the Heath papers[87]. To gain Pompidou's support, the British government had to determine the French vision for the EEC, so as not to undermine it. In Soames's view, 'Pompidou is no European visionary panting for political unification. He is a cautious hard-bargaining, reticent Auvergnat with limited imagination and no talent for grandeur […] [who] has reached agreement on the beginnings of an economic and monetary union'[88]. Soames analysed the issue of sovereignty, and did not consider it a big issue, as 'Pompidou wants a European Europe with greater cohesion (though not integration)'[89]. He advised Heath to reassure Pompidou that the British government 'shared his view of the essential role of the nation state – that is to move pragmatically in the creation of new institutions': 'The Prime Minister will wish to stress that joining the Economic Community is for us the beginning of a road which must lead to closer political – and eventually defence – collaboration for Europe'[90]. ONG members had already underscored in *One Europe* that 'in a sense the loss of sovereignty

---

85 'A Better Tomorrow: Conservative Manifesto', 1970, <http://www.conservativemanifesto.com/1970/1970-conservative-manifesto.shtml>, accessed 17 November 2024.
86 Shepherd, *Enoch Powell*, 413.
87 EH 4/2/14E, Heath Papers.
88 'Communiqué from Christopher Soames to Sir Denis Greenhill, UK-EEC negotiations' (21 April 1971), 1, EH 4/2/14E, Heath Papers.
89 Ibid., 6.
90 Ibid., 3.

was qualified', for EEC member states would retain their veto power[91]. Soames put forward the idea that Heath should propose a personal meeting with Pompidou in Paris[92]. To ensure its success, Soames advised Heath to limit the primary negotiating points to Community finance, the principle of full Community preference, the future of sterling, sugar, and trade with New Zealand[93]. The list of issues was then reduced to those of an economic nature, excluding national sovereignty. The British ambassador in France argued that Heath would certainly manage to strike a deal with Pompidou, since the French president viewed British presence within the Community 'as offering a healthy counterweight to increasing German dominance'[94]. But there were two major problems to overcome: Pompidou was not prepared to see 'the disappearance of the French language in what would become an English-speaking Community'[95]. Although French public opinion was overwhelmingly in favour of British membership, Pompidou also had to deal with 'his Enoch Powells (the Gaullist ultras and the Communists)'[96], while Heath had to contend with Powell's staunch EEC opposition in Britain, as well as convince British public opinion. When Heath finally met Pompidou in May, he negotiated on economic issues, defended British interests, agreed to keep French as an official language in Brussels, and reassured the French president of 'the sincerity of Britain's intentions and Communautaire approach'[97], as Pompidou had previously questioned it in front of Heath when he 'opened a copy of *Le Figaro* to a full-page ad for British Overseas Airways Corporation proclaiming: L'AMÉRIQUE COMMENCE À LONDRES – America begins in London'[98].

In April 1971, Powell accused Heath of misleading the electorate over entry into the EEC, as he had the Conservative Manifesto torn up. The British Parliament needed the 'full-hearted consent of the country' to take Britain

---

91 Ridley, ed., *One Europe*, 5.

92 'Communiqué from Christopher Soames to Sir Denis Greenhill, UK-EEC negotiations', 2.

93 Ibid., 3.

94 Ibid., 5.

95 Ibid., 6.

96 Ibid.

97 'Record of Conversation between the Prime Minister and the President of the French President in the Elysée Palace' (Paris, 20 May 1971), 1–2, EH 4/2/14E, Heath Papers.

98 *Time*, 'The World: Europe: The British are Coming'.

into Europe, which was not the case in his eyes. Powell would repeat that charge against Heath many times. He considered Heath the 'tricker' and the trick was to present the negotiations as 'a fait accompli'[99]. He ironically said that he was sure Heath would be absolutely honest with Pompidou, telling the French president that public opinion in Britain was growing more and more hostile to British membership in the EEC[100]. Powell's attack on Heath prompted Rippon to discredit Powell as being inconsistent, by recalling his earlier support for the EEC[101].

Powell had decided to pursue a two-pronged strategy against Heath's European goal. The first involved giving major speeches in the House of Commons during debates on the European question (1970–1972) to voice his staunch opposition to British membership – which would strike a fatal blow against the sovereignty of Parliament – as well as in the six member countries during the first half of 1971, sometimes addressing audiences in their native language (Powell was fluent in French, German and Italian). Secondly, he published three books between 1971 and 1973[102], which collected all of his speeches against the Common Market. As Robert Saunders has indicated, 'Powell stumped the country like an itinerant preacher. His speeches were a call of faith, often couched in the language of national awakening'[103].

In his election address on 15 June 1970, Powell had already raised a key question: 'the question of joining the Common Market is the most fundamental of all. It is the question not merely what *sort* of a nation are we to be, but *what* nation are we to be?'[104] Laetitia Langlois has argued that Powell's anti-Europeanism was part of a wider reflection on British national identity, the roots of Britishness and the future of the nation. With the issue of Europe, he harnessed fears of the dissolution of Britain's historical heritage and national identity[105]. For Powell, Europe represented a threat like that of

---

99 Lewis, *Enoch Powell*, 153.
100 Heffer, *Like the Roman*, 594.
101 Robert Shepherd, *Enoch Powell: A Biography*, 412.
102 Powell, *The Common Market: The Case Against*; Powell, *Still to Decide*; Powell, *Common Market: Renegotiate or Come Out.*
103 Saunders, *Yes to Europe*, 54.
104 Rex Collings, ed., *Reflections of a Statesman: The Writings and Speeches of Enoch Powell* (London: Bellew Publishing, 1991), 467.
105 Langlois, 'Le Parti conservateur', 188.

immigration, because in both cases it was the very essence of Britishness that risked disappearing. As Simon Heffer explained in his biography of Powell, it was as a patriot that Powell opposed the loss of sovereignty, which he saw as inevitable with membership of Europe[106].

Powell's 'Hard Eurosceptic' stance was also fuelled by his defence of British parliamentary sovereignty. Using Michael Spicer's 1992 typology of the various trends of Euroscepticism, Powell could also be depicted as 'a Constitutionalist' and an 'anti-Common Marketeer'[107]: 'a nation has ceased to be sovereign when its sovereignty is shared or pooled in a larger political unit'[108]. Powell stuck to the constitutional settlement that sovereignty was one and indivisible – it could not be shared. Advancing the notion of British exceptionalism, which no other EEC members had, Powell referred to the superiority of British institutions throughout the course of British history:

> The sovereign independence of Britain and her parliament is so rooted in our circumstances and history[109]. [...] There is nothing abstract or theoretical about the sovereignty which would be surrendered. Parliament, in particular the House of Commons, would no longer be the body which took the principle decisions which govern the economic and social life of the people of this country and which determine its safety and existence.[110]

Powell thought that the sovereignty of the British Parliament was thus different from that of European member states[111]. Nor did he believe that the EEC would be fully parliamentary in the British sense in the future: 'an elected parliament cannot exist unless those who do the electing see themselves as a single whole'[112]. An elected European assembly would be heterogeneous. Powell went so far as to compare Britain within the ECC to Scotland in the UK: if administrative unity were

106 Heffer, *Like the Roman*, 339.
107 Michael Spicer, *A Treaty Too Far. A New Policy for Europe* (London: Fourth Estate, 1992), 166–85, cited by Alexandre-Collier, 'Le Phénomène eurosceptique', 57.
108 Enoch Powell, 'Speech at the Public Hall (Beckenham, 17 September 1971), 8, POLL 4/1/7, Powell Papers.
109 Powell, *Common Market: Renegotiate or Come Out*, 44.
110 Powell, 'Speech at the Public Hall' in Beckenham, 7.
111 Nicholas. J. Crowson, *Britain in Europe: A Political History since 1918* (London and New York: Routledge, 2011), 10.
112 Lewis, *Enoch Powell*, 149.

achieved, Britain would become a mere province, incapable of secession or vetoes on anything. In response to a remark by Jean Rey (President of the EEC Commission) in January 1970, which implied that by 1980 the Community would in fact have a common currency and just such a parliament elected by universal suffrage[113], Powell forecast a quasi-federal transformation of the EEC, making Westminster subordinate to a federal parliament, court, and laws.

Powell's opposition to Heath thus appeared to mirror that between Peel and Disraeli, which had caused the split of the Conservative Party. Although this did not occur, Powell eventually left the Conservative Party in 1974. As Robert Shepherd has suggested, Powell's defence of sovereignty in a Disraelian vein 'reflected his own passionate attachment to the House of Commons as the embodiment of the British nation, its history and traditions'[114]. Powell's brand of Toryism was reminiscent of Edmund Burke's gradual approach to change[115]: he did not anticipate that his party would implement such a radical political change in the British constitutional settlement by embracing European supranationalism. While he had first opposed the idea of a referendum, as he thought decisions should be made in the House of Commons, 'in his conversion to supporting [it] [in 1973], Powell pinned his hopes for reversing British entry into the EEC on the people'.[116] It failed in 1975, but his wish was eventually fulfilled in June 2016 with the Brexit referendum.

Conclusion

In addition to the legacy of his Rivers of Blood speech on immigration, Powell is remembered as a staunch Eurosceptic who fiercely opposed Heath on UK membership in the EEC during the 1970s, when two Conservative

113 Enoch Powell, 'Speech in Kingston-on-Thames' (12 January 1970), 1., POLL 4/1/6, Powell Papers.

114 Shepherd, *Enoch Powell*, 417.

115 Stéphane Porion, 'Non, non, non ! Le Combat tory d'Enoch Powell contre les réformes ou tentatives de réformes de la Chambre des Lords [1958 et 1969]', *Revue Française de Civilisation Britannique* 24/4 (2019), 6–8, <https://journals.openedition.org/rfcb/pdf/5114>.

116 Shepherd, *Enoch Powell*, 421.

nationalist visions clashed. The spectre of Powell resurfaced during the Brexit referendum, when his Eurosceptic arguments were reused. This chapter has put Heath's Europeanism into perspective and shown how he managed to persuade Pompidou to support the UK's entry into the EEC, and defined Powell's fluctuating stance on European integration, with a conceptual analysis of Euroscepticism and Europragmatism. Powell never forgave Heath for what he managed to do with Pompidou, namely changing the UK's future by imprisoning it within an increasingly political construction of Europe, and eroding the sovereignty of the British Parliament: 'Powell warned Heath that if he took Britain into Europe, he would go down in history bearing with him the indelible brand of broken faith and trust betrayed'[117]. Yet, Powell had not always been Eurosceptic, as before 1969 he minimised the question of sovereignty.

In his crusade against the UK's entry into the EEC in the early 1970s, Powell made a major mistake: he failed to perceive that the British were more sensitive to economic arguments (such as lower prices) than to an overly intellectual defence of British sovereignty[118]. Although he said, in Lyon in 1971, that 'there was no need to resort to theory to ascertain whether membership of the Community means the loss of national sovereignty'[119], he continued to defend it in too abstract a manner, as demonstrated by his 1976 analysis entitled 'Sovereignty'[120]. In 1977, Schoen described Powell in 1972 as 'defeated but not vanquished'[121], words that proved prophetic as Alfred Sherman (Thatcher's mentor) asked for Powell's view on the European question in the late 1970s and early 1980s, even though Powell was no longer a member of the Conservative Party. As shown elsewhere[122], it was Powell who convinced Sherman – who in turn gradually convinced Thatcher – that the loss of national sovereignty was the paramount issue. Thatcher had to look

[117] Shepherd, *Enoch Powell*, 419.
[118] Ibid., 414–5; Schoen, *Enoch Powell and the Powellites*, 80.
[119] Powell, *Still to Decide*, 221.
[120] Collings, ed., *Reflections of a Statesman*, 474–80.
[121] Schoen, *Enoch Powell and the Powellites*, 86.
[122] Stéphane Porion, 'The End of an Intellectual Journey: How Alfred Sherman's ideas on Immigration and the British Nation were Framed by Powellism (1968–1979)', in Olivier Esteves and Stéphane Porion, eds., *The Lives and Afterlives of Enoch Powell: The Undying Political Animal* (Abingdon: Routledge, 2019), 135–41.

beyond the economic dimension, and not just to renegotiate British terms to secure a lower British contribution to the European budget. Thatcher's Bruges speech in 1988 can thus be seen as Eurosceptic Powellism with a vengeance: a return to the idea of a Europe of nations[123] – 'a family of nations', to use Thatcher's own words.

Bibliography

Primary sources

Archives

'Communiqué from Christopher Soames to Sir Denis Greenhill, UK-EEC negotiations' (21 April 1971), EH 4/2/14E, Heath Papers.

Heath, Edward, 'Maiden Speech in the House of Commons' (Political Speech Archive, 1950), <https://www.ukpol.co.uk/edward-heath-1950-maiden-speech-in-the-house-of-commons/>, accessed 6 November 2024.

Longbottom, Charles, 'Correspondence with One Nation members' (8 February 1965), LONGDEN 4/1, Longden Papers.

Maudling, Reginald, 'The Conservative Party in Europe' (LCC (65) 24, 25 March 1965), POLL 3/2/1/7, Powell Papers.

'"One Nation" Tories Regroup for Europeanism', 1965, LONGDEN 4/1, Longden Papers.

Powell, Enoch, 'Indian Memorandum' (16 May 1946 & 3 December 1946), POLL 3/1/4, Powell Papers.

———, Enoch, 'Speech at Annual Meeting of Divisional Young Conservatives' (29 November 1949), D3123/223, Staffordshire Record Office.

———, Enoch, 'Speech at Graiseley School in Fellows Street' (14 December 1949), D3123/223, Staffordshire Record Office.

———, Enoch, 'Speech at the Annual General Meeting of the Penn Ward Branch at the Rose and Crowns' (between 26th October and 5th November 1950), D3123/223, Staffordshire Record Office.

———, Enoch, 'Untitled Document' (21 July 1966), 1–2, POLL 4/1/27, File 2, Powell Papers.

———, Enoch, 'L'Angleterre et ses problèmes européens', *Bulletin européen* (June 1968), 8, POLL 12/1/12, Powell Papers.

---

[123] Ben Wellings, *English Nationalism and Euroscepticism*, 165.

———, Enoch, 'Speech to Conservative Women's Rally' (Clacton, 21 March 1969), 3, POLL 4/1/5, Powell Papers.
———, Enoch, 'Speech in Kingston-on-Thames' (12 January 1970), 1, POLL 4/1/6, Powell Papers.
———, Enoch, 'Speech at the Public Hall (Beckenham, 17 September 1971), 8, POLL 4/1/7, Powell Papers.
———, Enoch, 'Speech to the Liechtenstein Press Club' (15 January 1972), POLL 4/1/8 File 4, Powell Papers.
'Record of Conversation between the Prime Minister and the President of the French President in the Elysée Palace' (Paris, 20 May 1971), 1–2, EH 4/2/14E, Heath Papers.
Ridley, Nicholas, ed., *One Europe* (London: CPC, 1965), 1–27, POLL 6/2/2, Powell Papers.
Sandys, Duncan, 'Britain and Europe' (LCC (65) 25, 25 March 1965), 3, POLL 3/2/1/7, Powell Papers.
South European Service, 5 April 1965, POLL 4/1/27, Powell Papers.

Published works

'A Better Tomorrow: Conservative Manifesto', 1970, <http://www.conservativemanifesto.com/1970/1970-conservative-manifesto.shtml>, accessed 17 November 2024.
'Action Not Words: The New Conservative Programme', 1966, <http://www.conservativemanifesto.com/1966/1966-conservative-manifesto.shtml>, accessed 17 November 2024.
Butler, Rab, *The Art of the Possible: The Memoirs of Lord Butler* (London: Purnell Book, 1971).
Collings, Rex, ed., *Reflections of a Statesman: The Writings and Speeches of Enoch Powell* (London: Bellew Publishing, 1991).
Heath, Edward, *Old World, New Horizons: Britain, Europe and the Atlantic Alliance* (Cambridge: Harvard University Press 1970).
———, Edward, *Course of My Life: The Autobiography of Edward Heath* (London: Hodder and Stoughton, 1998).
Powell, Enoch, *The Common Market: The Case Against* (Kingswood: Elliott Rightway, 1971).
———, Enoch, *Still to Decide* (Kingswood: Elliot Right Way Books, 1972).
———, Enoch, *Common Market: Renegotiate or Come Out* (Tadworth: Elliot Right Way Books, 1973).

Secondary sources

Alexandre-Collier, Agnès, 'Le Phénomène eurosceptique au sein du Parti conservateur britannique', *Politique Européenne* 6 (2002), 53–76.

———, Agnès, *La Grande-Bretagne eurosceptique ? L'Europe dans le débat politique britannique* (Paris : Éditions du Temps, 2002).

Corthorn, Paul, *Enoch Powell: Politics and Ideas in Modern Britain* (Oxford: OUP, 2019).

———, Paul, 'Enoch Powell, the Original Anti-immigrant, Anti-Europe, Pro-unionist Tory', *The Irish Times* (27 August 2019), <https://www.irishtimes.com/culture/books/enoch-powell-theoriginal-anti-immigrant-anti-europe-pro-unionist-tory-1.3997786>, accessed 10 December 2024.

Crowson, Nicholas, J., *Britain and Europe: A Political History since 1918* (London and New York: Routledge, 2011).

Davis, Richard, 'Euroscepticism and Opposition to British Entry into the EEC, 1955–1975', *Revue française de civilisation britannique*, 22/2 (2017), <https://journals.openedition.org/rfcb/1364>, accessed 2 April 2024.

'Enoch Powell – Judas?', YouTube (27 January/2017), <https://www.youtube.com/watch?v=GYy8ORPz1nE>, accessed 3 January 2025.

Foster, Anthony, *Euroscepticism in Contemporary British Politics: Opposition to Europe in the British Conservative and Labour Parties* (London: Routledge 2002).

Green, Ewen H. H., *Ideologies of Conservatism: Conservative Political Ideas in the Twentieth Century* (Oxford: OUP, 2002).

Harmsen, Robert, 'Is British Euroscepticism still Unique', in Justine Lacroix and Ramona Coman, *Les Résistances à l'Europe: Cultures nationales, idéologies et stratégies d'acteurs* (Brussels: Éditions de l'Université de Bruxelles, 2007), 69–92.

Heffer, Simon, *Like the Roman: The Life and Times of Enoch Powell* (London: Weidenfield, 1998).

Holmes, Martin, *The Eurosceptic Reader* (Houndmills and New York: Palgrave, 1996).

Langlois, Laetitia, 'Le Parti conservateur et l'adhésion à la Communauté européenne : coulisses d'un vote historique', *Outre-Terre* 49 (2016), 179–190.

Leconte, Cécile, *Understanding Euroscepticism* (Basingstoke: Palgrave Macmillan, 2010).

Leruth, Benjamin, Nicholas Startin, and Simon Usherwood, eds, *The Routledge Handbook of Euroscepticism* (London and New York: Routledge, 2018).

Lewis, Roy, *Enoch Powell: Principle in Politics* (London: Cassell, 1979).

Lord Howard of Rising, ed., *Enoch at 100: A Re-Evaluation of the Life, Politics and Philosophy of Enoch Powell* (London: Biteback, 2012).

Lynch, Philip, *The Politics of Nationhood* (London: Macmillan, 1999).

Pearce, Nick, Michael Kenny, and Lindsay Aqui, 'The Empire of England: Enoch Powell, Sovereignty and the Constitution of the Nation', *Twentieth Century British History*, 32/2 (2021), 1–30, <https://purehost.bath.ac.uk/ws/portalfiles/portal/210524969/The_Empire_of_England_final_version_with_copyediting_changes.pdf>, accessed 28 November 2024.

Porion, Stéphane, 'Enoch Powell et le powellisme : entre tradition disraélienne et anticipation néo-libérale, 1946–1968' (unpublished Phd thesis, Université Sorbonne-Nouvelle Paris 3, 2011).

———, Stéphane, 'Non, non, non ! Le Combat tory d'Enoch Powell contre les réformes ou tentatives de réformes de la Chambre des Lords [1958 et 1969]', *Revue Française de Civilisation Britannique* (2019), <https://journals.openedition.org/rfcb/pdf/5114>.

———, Stéphane, 'The End of an Intellectual Journey: How Alfred Sherman's Ideas on Immigration and the British Nation were Framed by Powellism (1968–1979)', in Olivier Esteves and Stéphane Porion, eds., *The Lives and Afterlives of Enoch Powell: The Undying Political Animal* (Abingdon: Routledge, 2019), 126–44.

———, Stéphane, 'Disraeli's Significant Influence on Enoch Powell's Tory Conception of Nationhood', *Cahiers victoriens et édouardiens*, 101, (Spring 2025), <https://journals.openedition.org/cve/15721>.

Roth, Andrew, *Enoch Powell: Tory Tribune* (London: Macdonald & Co, 1970).

Saunders, Robert, *Yes to Europe: The 1975 Referendum and Seventies Britain* (Cambridge: Cambridge University Press, 2018).

Shiels, David, 'How Enoch Powell Helped to Shape Modern Tory Euroscepticism', LSE blogs (3 June 2016), <https://blogs.lse.ac.uk/brexit/2016/06/03/how-enoch-powell-helped-to-shape-modern-tory-euroscepticism/>, accessed 10 December 2024.

Schoen, Douglas E., *Enoch Powell and the Powellites* (London: Macmillan, 1977).

Shepherd, Robert, *Enoch Powell: A Biography* (London: Pimlico, 1997).

Spiering, Menno, 'British Euroscepticism', in Robert Harmsen and Menno Spiering, eds, *Euroscepticism: Party Politics, National Identity and European Integration* (Amsterdam: Rodopi, 2004), 127–149.

Taggart, Paul, and Aleks Szczerbiak, eds, *Opposing Europe?: The Comparative Party Politics of Euroscepticism* (Oxford: OUP, 2008).
'The World: Europe: The British are Coming', *Time* (31 May 1971), <https://time.com/archive/6877510/the-world-europe-the-british-are-coming/>, accessed 30 December 2024.
Young, Hugo, *This Blessed Plot: Britain and Europe from Churchill to Blair* (London: Macmillan, 1998).
Young, John W., *Britain and European Unity (1845–1992)* (London: Macmillan, 1993).
Wellings, Ben, *English Nationalism and Euroscepticism: Losing the Peace* (Oxford: Peter Lang, 2011).

Rivalling the French? The Impact and Effectiveness of British European Policymaking, 1973–1990

N. Piers Ludlow

Throughout the formative years of the European Community, the French were widely seen as the most ruthless operators in Brussels, able to shape many of the EC's early policies in a fashion that suited their interests, and equally willing to block policies and developments that were seen as less advantageous to France. The Community which Britain joined in the early 1970s was to a very large extent fashioned by the French, much to the advantage of France. It is therefore unsurprising that the incoming British quite explicitly looked to the French example to learn how best to play the politics of European integration. The core aim of this chapter is to assess how well the British succeeded in rivalling the French in the course of their first two decades of EEC membership. Did London succeed in matching or even surpassing Paris in the degree of influence it exerted over policymaking in Brussels? Or did British achievements in this area fall well short of the country's initial aims? To begin answering these questions, this chapter will start by identifying the three crucial methods France used to exercise so much influence within the early Community: the direct impact of its national representatives in all of the various European negotiating fora where ministerial and official negotiators gather; the influence and weight of its European *fonctionnaires*, highly effective in steering European developments in directions congenial to France; and finally the country's ability to back up policymaking in Brussels with direct pressure on its partners away from the Community capital. The chapter will then ask how far Britain was able to rival France in each of these three aspects of Community policymaking. The central conclusion is that the British did achieve some very real success in emulating the French, becoming major players within the Brussels environment in the process. Such success was nevertheless systematically undermined by a number of flaws in the wider British approach to cooperation with its European partners. The effectiveness of Britain's representatives in

Brussels, its Eurocrats, and its bilateral diplomacy in support of its European goals were all diminished by the more general hesitancy of the country's approach to European integration.

French Success

French influence in Brussels sprang from three main sources[1]. The first was the direct impact of the country's representatives, whether it was mid-level civil servants outlining the French position to a Council working group, the French permanent representative presenting the French point of view to one of the most vital internal EC organs, the *Comité de Représentants Permanents* (COREPER), or a French government minister speaking for France in one of the many formations of the Council of Ministers. To some extent this impact derived from France's position not simply as a large member state – and in a system like the European Community size does matter, despite the ostensible equality of each member state – but also as the country that had initiated the building of an integrated Europe with the 1950 Schuman Plan, and which was generally seen as its leader during the early phases of the integration process[2]. Also crucial was the calibre and forcefulness of its representatives. French civil servants and ministers, often formed in the prestigious *Grandes Écoles* and having succeeded in a highly competitive civil service environment or the rough and tumble of French domestic politics, were seldom shy about advancing their position, clearly and with some determination. Jean-Marc Boegner, for instance, was widely regarded as the most formidable of the early permanent representatives; Maurice Couve de Murville, the French foreign minister for much of the 1960s, was similarly seen as a bruising, ruthless and highly effective advocate of often

---

1 On French European policy, see Laurent Warlouzet, *Le choix de la CEE par la France: l'Europe économique en débat de Mendès-France à de Gaulle (1955–1969)* (Paris: Comité pour l'histoire économique et financière de la France : IGPDE, 2011); Michael Sutton, *France and the Construction of Europe, 1944–2007: The Geopolitical Imperative* (New York: Berghahn Books, 2007).

2 Gérard Bossuat, *L'Europe des Français, 1943–1959: La IVe République aux sources de l'Europe Communautaire* (Paris: Publications de la Sorbonne, 1996).

controversial viewpoints[3]. Those representing France were also normally convinced of their right to steer the early EEC in one direction or another. Nor did they eschew the harder-edged aspects of international diplomacy. Within a Community context it was the French who, together with the Dutch, pioneered the use of cross-issue linkages – blocking advance in one field if not allowed to have their way in another – forceful threats about the possible consequences of delay, and infamously boycotts, notably the 1965–6 Empty Chair crisis[4]. Crucially, the French representatives were extremely well-coordinated amongst themselves, advancing the same arguments and adopting the same stance at every level of EC negotiations. This reflected the highly effective domestic coordination mechanism for European policy which had emerged in the form of the SGCI and contrasted strongly with the position of the Germans in Brussels, which was often seriously undermined by all too obvious internal divisions and interministerial disagreements[5]. Those speaking for France by contrast knew exactly what they wanted to achieve and could forcefully outline their stance, confident that their counterparts elsewhere in the Community system were putting forward the same arguments and lending their weight to a well-coordinated common effort[6].

A second major source of French influence in Brussels was the role of the French *fonctionnaires* who had joined the emerging Community institutions. Although officially independent, and indeed sworn to put aside national considerations in the exercise of their duties, such Eurocrats still served as

---

3 Couve's effectiveness was acknowledged by his longtime sparring partner, the Belgian foreign minister, Paul-Henri Spaak: *Combats inachevées* (Paris: Fayard, 1969), vol. 2, 365–6.

4 Andrew Moravcsik, 'De Gaulle Between Grain and Grandeur: The Political Economy of French EC Policy, 1958–1970 (Part 1)', *Journal of Cold War Studies* 2/2 (2000), 3–43.

5 Anne de Castelnau, 'Le SGCI : Une réponse administrative aux défis Européens de l'après-Guerre', in Laurence Badel, Stanislas Jeannesson, and N. Piers Ludlow, eds, *Les Administrations Nationales et la Construction Européenne. Une Approche Historique (1919–1975)* (Brussels: Presses interuniversitaires européennes-Peter Lang, 2006), 307–36.

6 For my own assessment of French European successes during the Gaullist era, see N. Piers Ludlow, 'From Words to Actions: Reinterpreting de Gaulle's European Policy', in Christian Nünlist, Anna Locher, and Garret Martin, eds, *Globalizing de Gaulle: International Perspectives on French Foreign Policies, 1958–1969* (Lanham, MD: Lexington Books, 2010), 74–6.

an important channel for French views and influence. In certain cases, this might mean they were actually responding to instructions or direct promptings from Paris. More often it simply reflected the fact that their instincts and assumptions were grounded in the country of their birth and education, and their behaviour was still shaped by their ongoing contacts and links with France. Furthermore, the geographical proximity of Brussels to France meant that a good number of French civil servants working within Community institutions – famously including Emile Noël, the executive secretary (later secretary-general) of the European Commission from 1958 to 1987 – returned to France virtually every weekend. An EEC joke of the era held that if one asked a French Eurocrat what aspect of Brussels they most appreciated, their reply would be 'the 17:30 Trans European Express (TEE) back to Paris each Friday'. Their main source of wider news and information, moreover, was almost certainly the French press, whether *Le Monde* or *Le Figaro*. So it was little wonder that French civil servants working within Community structures consciously and unconsciously nudged European policy in directions that reflected their national predilections and preferences[7]. And Noël quite systematically built up an extensive internal network of trusted lieutenants within all crucial parts of the Commission machinery. This was *his* personal resource rather than one directly at the service of the French government, but given that he and most of its members were French, it still served to amplify French influence within the early European Community[8].

A third source of French influence was the bilateral pressure that Paris exerted on its European partners away from Brussels. Here too size was a crucial part of the equation. France simply had more diplomats and diplomatic clout than any other early member states, with the very partial exception of Germany. It therefore had more leverage over its partners than any other of the Six. Furthermore, unlike the Federal Republic, France was not constrained by the shadow of the recent past and had few hesitations about throwing

---

7 The most detailed study of the first Eurocrats is Katja Seidel, *The Process of Politics in Europe: The Rise of European Elites and Supranational Institutions* (London: Palgrave Macmillan, 2010). See also Michel Dumoulin and Marie-Thérèse Bitsch, eds, *The European Commission, 1958–1972: History and Memories* (Luxembourg: Office for Official Publications of the European Communities, 2007), 241–72.

8 Gérard Bossuat, *Émile Noël, premier secrétaire général de la Commission Européenne* (Brussels: Bruylant, 2011).

its weight around. It had also demonstrated during the European Defence Community episode that it could ultimately walk away from the integration process, thereby stopping it in its tracks – a lesson that still resonated during the 1960s and into the 1970s, and again differentiated France strongly from Germany[9]. And the French president, especially Charles de Gaulle, but also his successors to a lesser degree, had a prestige and media prominence well above that of any other politician within the early EEC. As a result, when de Gaulle and subsequent French presidents spoke, Europe listened and reacted in a way that did not apply to even the German chancellors of this early era, let alone the leading politicians of Italy or the smaller member states[10].

Equally important was the emergence of a pattern of Franco-German cooperation, especially on European matters, institutionalised and routinised by the procedures of the 1963 Elysée Treaty[11]. It was true of course that neither the existence of this treaty, nor of the regular bilateral encounters that it put in place, guaranteed total accord between Paris and Bonn on European priorities. On the contrary, deep differences of opinion persisted between the two capitals, and several of the bilateral rapports between German leaders and their French counterparts, notably that between Ludwig Erhard and Charles de Gaulle, were very poor indeed[12]. Yet despite the fluctuating effectiveness of day-to-day Franco-German cooperation on European matters, it still mattered greatly that the French and German governments had created the expectation – in their own minds, that of their wider publics, and indeed their Community partners – that they would strive to coordinate their position, and that when they succeeded this was beneficial not just to France and Germany, but also to the wider fortunes of the integration process. France had thus supplemented its own pre-existing assets in terms of diplomatic clout and *savoir-faire* with an organised and sanctioned double act with the other leading Community member state.

---

9 For a fuller development of this argument see Ludlow, 'From Words to Actions', 71.

10 Lois Pattison De Ménil, *Who Speaks for Europe?: The Vision of Charles de Gaulle* (London: Weidenfeld and Nicolson, 1977).

11 Hélène Miard-Delacroix, *Im Zeichen der europäischen Einigung 1963 bis heute* (Darmstadt: Wiss. Buchges., 2010); Benedikt Schoenborn, *La mésentente apprivoisée: De Gaulle et les Allemands, 1963–1969* (Paris: Presses Univ. de France, 2007).

12 Benedikt Schoenborn, 'Les réticences du chancelier Erhard à l'égard de la France (1963–1966)', *Relations Internationales* 126/2 (2006), 3–14.

All of this made it very natural for the British to look to the French example when planning their own approach to European policy making. Like France, Britain was a former Great Power, still accustomed to exercising its influence, whatever the organisation or international setting. In common with France, it boasted the status symbols of permanent UN Security Council membership and a nuclear deterrent. Like France, its global reach and aspirations were strongly connected with its recent imperial past. And again, similarly to France, the UK's debate about the merits of European integration had included a strong strand of thought about how Community membership would lessen, or even reverse, the country's post-Second World War loss of global power and influence. The British hence approached Community membership determined not just to take part, but to lead[13]. If this was to happen, they would have to match, if not surpass, French influence in Brussels.

Partial Success

To a considerable extent, the British did succeed in emulating the French in terms of the efficacy of their representatives. The vast majority of those despatched to Brussels to outline and defend the British position were forceful, well-briefed and persuasive, whether at official or ministerial level. Most also adapted quickly to the conventions and patterns of Community diplomacy that had developed in the decade and a half of EEC development preceding the UK's arrival. The domestic coordination methods adopted in Whitehall helped ensure that the British position was normally as coherent and consistent as that of France, irrespective of which ministries were involved. The use of the Cabinet Office as the principal British mechanism for crafting a common position and strategy from the disparate ministerial viewpoints proved as efficacious as the French SGCI-centred approach[14].

13 The celebrated outburst of George Brown, the British foreign secretary, to his German counterpart Willy Brandt ('Come on Willy, you must get us in so that we can take the lead in the EEC') captured an opinion that spread well beyond the Labour front bench. Cited in John W. Young, *Britain and European Unity, 1945–1999* (Basingstoke: Macmillan, 2000), 95.

14 There is a brief discussion of the origins of the British arrangements in Stephen Wall, *The Official History of Britain and the European Community. Volume II: From Rejection to Referendum, 1963–1975* (Abingdon: Routledge, 2012), 431–2. For a more detailed look

There was, it is true, the occasional aberration. A few Labour ministers in Harold Wilson's government of 1974–76 were handicapped in their ability to perform effectively in the Council of Ministers by their opposition to Britain's membership of the EEC, and their corresponding refusal to adapt to the rules or manner of operation of a club they did not want to be part of – Tony Benn as Secretary of State for Industry from March 1974 to June 1975 would be an obvious case in point[15]. Even here, though, some Labour anti-Marketeers proved surprisingly successful in a Brussels context. Judith Hart, the Minister of Overseas Development in the Wilson government, is generally regarded, for instance, as having played a constructive role in renegotiating the Lomé Convention linking the Community to multiple states in the developing world, despite being passionate in her hostility to British membership[16]. Some British civil servants had less of an impact than they might have because of their failure to convince their counterparts that they were truly committed to the project under discussion. Possibly the clearest example of this is Ken Couzens's ineffectiveness in the context of the trilateral Anglo-French-German discussions that would ultimately lead to the birth of EMS, but not before the British had been left out of what became a Franco-German tête-à-tête[17]. But such exceptions serve mainly to cast into sharper relief the genuine impact that most British representatives had. Revealingly, the self-confidence and self-belief shown by many of them could and did lead to frequent confrontations with the previous leader of the pack in the form of their French counterparts. The titanic rows between Michael Butler, the British permanent representative in the late 1970s and early 1980s, and his French counterpart Luc de Nanteuil, became the stuff of Brussels legend[18].

---

at how they functioned in practice, see Lindsay Aqui, *The First Referendum: Reassessing Britain's Entry to Europe, 1973–1975* (Manchester: Manchester University Press, 2020).

15 Aoife Collins, 'The Cabinet Office, Tony Benn and the Renegotiation of Britain's Terms of Entry into the European Community, 1974–1975', *Contemporary British History* 24/4 (2010), 71–91.

16 This emerges strongly from Richard Johnson's chapter on Hart in Matthew Broad and William King, eds, *Labour and European Integration: A Biographical Approach* (Bristol: Bristol University Press, 2015), 138–155.

17 Peter Ludlow, *The Making of the European Monetary System: A Case Study of the Politics of the European Community* (London: Butterworths, 1982), 104–114.

18 Roy Jenkins refers to their tempestuous relationship in Jenkins, *European Diary, 1977–1981* (London: Collins, 1989), 583.

Britain's Achilles heel in terms of direct representation, however, turned out to be the newly established European Council. This had not existed in the 1960s and so was not mentioned above in the analysis of how France had established itself as the most influential founder member. But the regular gatherings of Europe's most senior political leaders were not simply something that the French suggested, but also that they proved masters of using to their advantage[19]. Both Valéry Giscard d'Estaing and François Mitterrand seemed in their element when Europe's leaders met to talk amongst themselves – employing to the full both their expertise on foreign policy matters in general and European Community business in particular, and their ability to provide their counterparts and the waiting media alike with suitably magisterial overviews of the European Community's position and prospects. Also crucial was the manner in which the French president and the German chancellor had normally carefully coordinated their positions on most of the key issues before the meeting began[20]. The European Council thus further accentuated French power and influence within a Community context and underscored the importance of the Franco-German axis. But it was to be a rather less congenial environment for British Prime Ministers. Wilson, the British leader when the European Council was invented in 1974–5, never seemed particularly interested in the new forum, his mind probably already half on the way he was planning to step back from active politics. His successor as prime minister and Labour leader, James Callaghan, was a little better, with a good rapport with the German Chancellor Helmut Schmidt in particular[21]. But he was never able fully to match the Giscard-Schmidt double act and was marginalised in the most important European Council development of this era, namely the launch of the European Monetary System[22].

Margaret Thatcher, while certainly making her mark, also struggled at this level. There was, it is true, a middle phase of Thatcher's European engagement,

---

19 Emmanuel Mourlon-Druol, 'Filling the EEC Leadership Vacuum? The Creation of the European Council in 1974', *Cold War History* 10/3 (2010), 315–39.

20 Michèle Weinachter, *Valéry Giscard d'Estaing et l'Allemagne: le double rêve inachevé* (Paris: L'Harmattan, 2004).

21 Mathias Haeussler, *Helmut Schmidt and British-German Relations: A European Misunderstanding* (Cambridge: Cambridge University Press, 2019).

22 Edmund Dell, 'Britain and the Origins of the European Monetary System', *Contemporary European History* 3/1 (1994): 1–60.

after the early ructions over the British Budgetary Question, but before the breakdown of relations with Helmut Kohl and Jacques Delors, where she could and did perform highly effectively. The row over Britain's budgetary contribution had broken her rapport with Giscard and Schmidt, but their departures from office in 1981 and 1982 respectively, allowed her to limit the lasting implications of her bruising confrontations with them[23]. The degree to which both the Italian and French governments seem to have worried, in the mid-1980s, about the seeming emergence of an Anglo-German alliance, built on shared opposition to any form of Community policy advance liable to cost more money, accurately reflects a period when Thatcher was not perpetually isolated or out of step with her most powerful fellow leaders[24]. Her successful advocacy for the Single Market programme during the 1984–7 period tells much the same story, as does the seemingly effective working partnership she developed with the Delors' Commission[25]. But all too often, her bravery and forcefulness were not accompanied by an instinct for seeking allies, nor by an eye for when a deal was there to be done. Instead, she often pushed too far, losing the support of those initially inclined to support her, and so alienating those who she was arguing against that resentments festered, rather than fading immediately the discussion moved onto another issue. Also important was the fact that prior to 1983 and after 1988, disagreement between Britain and its partners was spread over too many different fronts: instead of the pattern of ever-shifting alliances that usually characterises Community diplomacy, accompanied by a constant fluctuation between battles won, drawn and lost, the British all too often slipped into a pattern of recurrent isolation, defiant opposition and frequent defeat[26]. That such heroic but ill-starred opposition seemed to play quite well in the British press

[23] See N. Piers Ludlow, 'A Double-Edged Victory: Fontainebleau and the Resolution of the British Budgetary Problem, 1983–1984', in Michael Gehler and Wilfried Loth, eds, *Reshaping Europe towards a Political, Economic and Monetary Union, 1984–1989* (Baden-Baden: Nomos Verlagsgesellschaft, 2020), 45–71.

[24] Giovanni Lella, *La Francia di Mitterrand, l'Italia e il Rilancio della Costruzione Europea (1981–1986)*, PhD diss., Rome/Paris, La Sapienza/Université Sorbonne Nouvelle, 2022.

[25] Stephen Wall, *The Official History of Britain and the European Community, Volume III, The Tiger Unleashed, 1975–1985* (Abingdon: Routledge, 2019), 289–334.

[26] This is the thrust of Geoffrey Howe's critique of Thatcher, one that would ultimately lead to her resignation. See Geoffrey Howe, *Conflict of Loyalty* (London: Macmillan, 1994).

and to British public opinion only made matters worse, since it encouraged Thatcher and her successors to revel in their rows with their European counterparts, rather than trying to minimise their disagreements[27]. From 1986–7 onwards, Thatcher also suffered from both an increasingly tense personal rapport with the single most important figure in the European Council, namely Chancellor Kohl, and the Conservative Party's exclusion from the intra-Christian Democrat discussions that preceded most European Council meetings. These two trends came together to accentuate the likelihood of British isolation, since Kohl had often also succeeded in coordinating positions in advance with non-Christian Democrat allies like Mitterrand, Delors or Felipe Gonzalez before each summit began, meaning that Thatcher was confronted with a meeting most members of which had already mapped out a path to agreement with the German chancellor before formal discussions had even begun, but where she had very different views[28]. The effectiveness of British diplomacy in most European Community discussions was thus undermined (and overshadowed) by recurrent disagreement and defeat at the level that mattered most and attracted the lion's share of media attention – the European Council. These high-profile rows only cemented Britain's reputation as the perpetual malcontent, the awkward partner, or just simply the 'bad European'.

The pattern was equally mixed at the level of British fonctionnaires. Here too there were clear successes. Britain appointed a string of good to excellent European Commissioners – Roy Jenkins and Arthur Cockfield were the standout figures in the period under review, but Christopher Soames and Leon Brittan were also impressive – elected a number of successful and effective MEPs, and managed to secure senior official positions within the Commission and other key European institutions for a number of very able civil servants. Unsurprisingly, this led, within the European institutions, to a degree of movement away from the primarily French and German template of

[27] Thatcher's embattled position on the European front, but also the way in which she seemed to enjoy her defiant stance, comes through in Charles Moore, *Margaret Thatcher: The Authorized Biography. Volume Three, Herself Alone* (London: Allen Lane, 2019).

[28] This would be at its clearest in discussions over the path to EMU, the issue over which the gap between Britain and its partners would become most intractable. See Kenneth H. F Dyson and Kevin Featherstone, *The Road to Maastricht: Negotiating Economic and Monetary Union* (Oxford, New York: Oxford University Press, 1999), 534–600.

operation that had characterised the early Community bureaucracies, towards a new, somewhat more informal, British-inflected way of doing things[29]. The Irish and the Danes were particularly open to these changes – and the Dutch also – which made these alterations that much more acceptable and likely to last. The British did thus manage to make some change, largely for the better, to the ways in which Brussels and Strasbourg worked. And they also succeeded in striking a good balance between resisting the urge too nakedly and obviously to lean upon 'their' men (and a few women) within the Community institutions and yet ensuring that most British *fonctionnaires* in Brussels retained strong cultural, career and personal ties with the UK. Geographical proximity clearly helped, although travel back to England from Brussels in this time before the Channel Tunnel and low-cost airlines was both harder and more expensive than it has subsequently become; the continuing lure of subsequent British careers or universities for their offspring also made it more likely that close links would continue.

Against these positives, however, need to be placed the recruitment struggles of the early years – which had knock-on effects deep into the 1980s, since the failure to appoint enough younger Eurocrats in the 1970s meant that there were fewer strong internal candidates from the UK for more senior vacancies in the subsequent decade – and the way in which even high quality British figures within the Commission could be placed in awkward positions by the stances adopted by 'their' government[30]. Both Jenkins and his fellow British member of the Commission, Christopher Tugendhat, found their influence adversely affected by the aggressive line taken by Thatcher on the British budgetary question[31]. Cockfield, meanwhile, was not reappointed, largely because of his deteriorating rapport with Thatcher, despite his huge success during his four-year stint in Brussels. It was also the case that it took quite a while for the British to gain a major voice within one of the strongholds of French power within the Commission, namely Noël's Secretariat General. Christopher Audland, deputy secretary-general from 1973 to 1981, was not without influence, but he was not there long enough to begin matching

[29] Éric Bussière et al., *The European Commission 1973–86: History and Memories of an Institution* (Luxembourg: Publications Office of the European Union, 2014), 151–65.

[30] Virginia Willis, *Britons in Brussels: Officials in the European Commission and Council Secretariat* (London: Policy Studies Institute, 1982).

[31] Jenkins, *European Diary*, 601.

Noël's centrality. This helps explain Jenkins' decision that he would have to work with Noël, rather than against[32]. All of this makes David Williamson's 1988 appointment as Noël's successor really important – although he proved much less long-lasting in the post than Noël had been, and was too loyal to Delors as Commission President to attempt to counter the new French internal network being constructed by Delors and his formidable *chef de cabinet* Pascal Lamy.

The British were also reasonably successful in terms of deploying their wider diplomatic resources in support of their European agenda, although they struggled to fully equal the French. Like the French, the British were determined and resourceful and had a high-quality network of diplomats to fall back upon in their attempt to persuade countries to take their side in Community disputes. Also like France, British leaders were good at attracting media attention and ensuring that many beyond their borders listened to what they said – although in the case of European policy, this could be counter-productive, since cheap jibes made for home consumption could undermine Britain's wider stance towards the integration process. But also like the French, they countered some of these positives with a tendency to be overbearing and arrogant, therefore repelling potential allies, in addition to a degree of myopia towards the potential influence of smaller member states within a Community context. Building alliances with the small was never the *forte* of either the French or the British. Where Britain really lost out vis-à-vis France, however, was in two further areas. The first was that the French already had the single biggest ally within the EC system, namely Germany. The Franco-German relationship did not always work smoothly of course. And the British did periodically try to either insinuate themselves within the double act, or to build their own bilateral special relationship with either Paris or Bonn[33]. But throughout the 1970s and 1980s (and indeed beyond), the British could do little but watch with frustration as at many crucial moments the Paris-Bonn link reasserted itself and proved more decisive than either Anglo-German or Anglo-French ties. The collaboration between Giscard and Schmidt was

---

32 N. Piers Ludlow, *Roy Jenkins and the European Commission Presidency 1976–1980: At the Heart of Europe* (Basingstoke: Palgrave Macmillan, 2016), 176.

33 Haeussler, *Helmut Schmidt and British-German Relations*; Laurence Baratier-Negri, *Valéry Giscard d'Estaing & le Royaume-Uni: le couple Franco-Britannique sur la scène internationale de 1974 à 1981* (Paris: Sorbonnes université presses, 2018).

absolutely central to the successes of the integration process of the 1970s, notably the creation of the European Council and the birth of the EMS; that between Mitterrand and Kohl fundamental to many of the highpoints of the 1980s and early 1990s, from the Stuttgart Declaration through to the convening of Intergovernmental Conferences to discuss both Economic and Monetary Union (EMU) and Political Union[34]. And when Franco-German collaboration flowered, the British were inevitably marginalised to some extent. Underpinning both the success of the Franco-German partnership and Britain's lack of success in breaking into or emulating it was a further factor that the British struggled to match, namely the way in which both the French and West Germans were highly adept at talking the talk about the importance of European unity, whereas the British struggled to do so[35]. No British Prime Minister in this era – or indeed ever, with the partial exceptions of Edward Heath and Tony Blair – could match the rhetorical enthusiasm for the European cause of Mitterrand or Kohl in full flight. Indeed, Thatcher in particular was clearly alienated and repelled by what she regarded as empty verbiage. Her own most celebrated attempt to outline her European vision – the Bruges Speech of 1988 – appalled many of her continental counterparts, while galvanising domestic Euroscepticism within Britain[36]. Joining France and Germany as the clear leaders of the Community would be hard when the British found it so impossible to speak inspirationally and idealistically about what the integration process was meant to be about. This left the British either on their own, resisting a process that others sought to push forward, or more occasionally flirting with a link up with Italy, which they never wholly believed in, and which lacked credibility given the yawning gap between Italy's own idealistically inflected rhetoric about Europe and Britain's very different manner of presenting its views[37].

---

34 Miard-Delacroix, *Im Zeichen der europäischen Einigung 1963 bis heute.*

35 Oliver Daddow, 'Interpreting the Outsider Tradition in British European Policy Speeches from Thatcher to Cameron', *JCMS: Journal of Common Market Studies* 53/1 (2015), 71–88.

36 Cary Fontana and Craig Parsons, '"One Woman's Prejudice": Did Margaret Thatcher Cause Britain's Anti-Europeanism?', *JCMS: Journal of Common Market Studies* 53/1 (2015), 89–105.

37 N. Piers Ludlow, 'In Search of Balance: Italy, Britain and the "dream" of Another European Axis', in Piero Craveri and Antonio Varsori, eds, *L'Italia nella costruzione Europea. Un bilancio storico (1957–2007)* (Milan: FrancoAngeli, 2009).

Overall, therefore, the British did manage to construct a strong position for themselves in the course of the 1970s and 1980s. This could periodically translate into significant policy achievements, like that of pushing the Single Market agenda. But they fell someway short of their self-proclaimed goal of matching the French. In part this reflected the failure of British officials in Brussels to build the type of influence network that first Noël and then Delors successfully created amongst French *fonctionnaires*. It also reflected the failure of the British to either break into the *couple Franco-Allemande*, or to replace it with an alternative bilateral axis. But most fundamentally, it reflected the way in which Britain's own ambivalence about European integration cut across its bid to exert strong influence. This hamstrung Wilson, Callaghan and Thatcher at European Council level. It all but removed any chance of seducing either Paris or Bonn away from their bilateral embrace. And by the end of the decade, it was ensuring that the British were often much too systematically isolated on the bigger questions of the day to exercise the power and influence of which they might otherwise have been capable. Ironically, in the late 1980s, the British probably got closest to imitating the French in the manner in which they replicated the isolation in Brussels into which the French had fallen at the tail end of the Gaullist period[38]. This was most certainly not the model of 'matching the French' that Edward Heath had had in mind in 1973.

Bibliography

Aqui, Lindsay, *The First Referendum: Reassessing Britain's Entry to Europe, 1973–1975* (Manchester: Manchester University Press, 2020).

Baratier-Negri, Laurence, *Valéry Giscard d'Estaing & le Royaume-Uni: le couple Franco-Britannique sur la scène internationale de 1974 à 1981* (Paris: Sorbonnes université presses, 2018).

Bossuat, Gérard, *Émile Noël, premier secrétaire général de la Commission Européenne* (Brussels: Bruylant, 2011).

——, Gérard, *L'Europe des Français, 1943–1959: La IVe République aux sources de l'Europe Communautaire* (Paris: Publications de la Sorbonne, 1996).

38 N. Piers Ludlow, *The European Community and the Crises of the 1960s: Negotiating the Gaullist Challenge* (London: Routledge, 2006), esp. Chapter 6.

Bussière, Éric, et al., *The European Commission 1973–1986: History and Memories of an Institution* (Luxembourg: Publications Office of the European Union, 2014).

Castelnau, Anne de, 'Le SGCI : Une réponse administrative aux défis Européens de l'après-Guerre', in Laurence Badel, Stanislas Jeannesson, and N. Piers Ludlow, eds, *Les Administrations Nationales et la Construction Européenne. Une Approche Historique (1919–1975)* (Brussels: Presses interuniversitaires européennes-Peter Lang, 2006), 307–36.

Collins, Aoife, 'The Cabinet Office, Tony Benn and the Renegotiation of Britain's Terms of Entry into the European Community, 1974–1975', *Contemporary British History* 24/4 (2010): 471–91.

Daddow, Oliver, 'Interpreting the Outsider Tradition in British European Policy Speeches from Thatcher to Cameron', *JCMS: Journal of Common Market Studies* 53/1 (2015), 71–88.

De Ménil, Lois Pattison, *Who Speaks for Europe?: The Vision of Charles de Gaulle* (London: Weidenfeld and Nicolson, 1977).

Dell, Edmund, 'Britain and the Origins of the European Monetary System', *Contemporary European History* 3/1 (1994): 1–60.

Dumoulin, Michel, and Marie-Thérèse Bitsch, eds, *The European Commission, 1958–1972: History and Memories* (Luxembourg: Office for Official Publications of the European Communities, 2007).

Dyson, Kenneth H. F., and Kevin Featherstone, *The Road to Maastricht: Negotiating Economic and Monetary Union* (Oxford, New York: Oxford University Press, 1999).

Fontana, Cary, and Craig Parsons, '"One Woman's Prejudice": Did Margaret Thatcher Cause Britain's Anti-Europeanism?', *JCMS: Journal of Common Market Studies* 53/1 (2015): 89–105.

Haeussler, Mathias, *Helmut Schmidt and British-German Relations: A European Misunderstanding* (Cambridge: Cambridge University Press, 2019).

Howe, Geoffrey, *Conflict of Loyalty* (London: Macmillan, 1994).

Jenkins, Roy, *European Diary, 1977–1981* (London: Collins, 1989).

Johnson, Richard, chapter on Judith Hart in Matthew Broad and William King, eds, *Labour and European Integration: A Biographical Approach* (Bristol: Bristol University Press, forthcoming).

Lella, Giovanni, *La Francia Di Mitterrand, l'Italia e Il Rilancio Della Costruzione Europea (1981–1986)*, PhD diss., Rome/Paris, La Sapienza/Université Sorbonne Nouvelle, 2022.

Ludlow, N. Piers 'A Double-Edged Victory: Fontainebleau and the Resolution of the British Budgetary Problem, 1983–1984', in Michael

Gehler and Wilfried Loth, eds, *Reshaping Europe towards a Political, Economic and Monetary Union, 1984–1989* (Baden-Baden: Nomos Verlagsgesellschaft, 2020), 45–71.
———, N. Piers, 'From Words to Actions: Reinterpreting de Gaulle's European Policy', in Christian Nünlist, Anna Locher, and Garret Martin, eds, *Globalizing de Gaulle: International Perspectives on French Foreign Policies, 1958–1969* (Lanham, MD: Lexington Books, 2010), 74–6.
———, N. Piers, 'In Search of Balance: Italy, Britain and the "dream" of Another European Axis', in Piero Craveri and Antonio Varsori, eds, *L'Italia nella costruzione Europea. Un bilancio storico (1957–2007)* (Milan: FrancoAngeli, 2009).
———, N. Piers, *Roy Jenkins and the European Commission Presidency 1976–1980: At the Heart of Europe* (Basingstoke: Palgrave Macmillan, 2016).
———, N. Piers, *The European Community and the Crises of the 1960s: Negotiating the Gaullist Challenge* (London: Routledge, 2006).
Ludlow, Peter, *The Making of the European Monetary System: A Case Study of the Politics of the European Community* (London: Butterworths, 1982).
Miard-Delacroix, Hélène, *Im Zeichen der europäischen Einigung 1963 bis heute* (Darmstadt: Wiss. Buchges., 2010).
Moore, Charles, *Margaret Thatcher: The Authorized Biography. Volume Three, Herself Alone* (London: Allen Lane, 2019).
Mourlon-Druol, Emmanuel, 'Filling the EEC Leadership Vacuum? The Creation of the European Council in 1974', *Cold War History* 10/3 (2010): 315–39.
Moravcsik, Andrew, 'De Gaulle Between Grain and Grandeur: The Political Economy of French EC Policy, 1958–1970 (Part 1)', *Journal of Cold War Studies* 2/2 (2000), 3–43.
Schoenborn, Benedikt, 'Les réticences du chancelier Erhard à l'égard de la France (1963–1966)', *Relations Internationales* 126/2 (2006), 3–14.
———, Benedikt, *La mésentente apprivoisée: De Gaulle et les Allemands, 1963–1969* (Paris: Presses Univ. de France, 2007).
Seidel, Katja, *The Process of Politics in Europe: The Rise of European Elites and Supranational Institutions* (London: Palgrave Macmillan, 2010).
Spaak, Paul-Henri, *Combats inachevées* (Paris: Fayard, 1969).
Sutton, Michael, *France and the Construction of Europe, 1944–2007: The Geopolitical Imperative* (New York: Berghahn Books, 2007).

Wall, Stephen, *The Official History of Britain and the European Community. Volume II: From Rejection to Referendum, 1963–1975* (Abingdon: Routledge, 2012).
———, Stephen, *The Official History of Britain and the European Community, Volume III, The Tiger Unleashed, 1975–1985* (Abingdon: Routledge, 2019).
Warlouzet, Laurent, *Le choix de la CEE par la France: l'Europe économique en débat de Mendès-France à de Gaulle (1955–1969)* (Paris: Comité pour l'histoire économique et financière de la France : IGPDE, 2011)
Weinachter, Michèle, *Valéry Giscard d'Estaing et l'Allemagne: le double rêve inachevé* (Paris: L'Harmattan, 2004).
Willis, Virginia, *Britons in Brussels: Officials in the European Commission and Council Secretariat* (London: Policy Studies Institute, 1982).
Young, John W., *Britain and European Unity, 1945–1999* (Basingstoke: Macmillan, 2000).

Georges Pompidou and the Anglo-American Plot Behind the Creation of a 'Monument' for the Modernisation of France

Boris Hamzeian

Pompidou and the American Skyscraper as a Symbol of Modernising the 'Vieilles Pierres' of Paris

Almost fifty years after its inauguration, the Centre national d'art et de culture Georges Pompidou stands as one of the most iconic works of the past century. With a design philosophy that dissolves the boundaries between architecture, engineering, metallurgy, electronics, emerging technologies, and museology, this landmark embodies the synthesis of a collective effort. The project brought together the architectural workshop led by Renzo Piano and Richard Rogers, the engineering expertise of Ove Arup & Partners, influential figures in curatorial discourse such as Pontus Hulten, and industrial giants like Krupp Industrie und Stahlbau.

To fully grasp what might be considered the first genuinely European public work of the French Fifth Republic, it is necessary to place the Centre within the philosophical and political vision of its key advocate, President Georges Pompidou. By delving into archival records scattered across France, the UK, and Italy, it is possible to piece together the fragments of a political and cultural network that intertwined political action, international diplomacy, a shared passion for contemporary art with his wife Claude, and a profound fascination with foreign avant-gardes[1].

---

1 See the collection preserved by the Renzo Piano Foundation, now part of the archives of the Politecnico di Milano (FRP); the private collection of Richard Rogers, held at the RSHP agency; the private collection housed in the archives of the engineers at Ove Arup & Partners (AA); the construction archive of the Centre Pompidou (20100307); and the presidential archives of Georges Pompidou (5AG2), Sébastien Loste (640AP), Henri Domerg (574AP), and the Bibliothèque Publique d'Information (19950353), all preserved at the Archives Nationales in Paris (AN). Additionally, the documentary and audiovisual collections held at the Institut Georges Pompidou (IGP).

The first clear signs of these ambitions merging with the modernisation of the *vieilles pierres* (old stones) of Paris emerged during the late 1960s, with a major real estate initiative in the Les Halles district. This area, historically home to the city's central markets and situated between the Louvre Museum and the Marais neighbourhood, was slated for a transformative redevelopment. The project involved demolishing the nineteenth-century iron-and-glass pavilions designed by the architect Victor Baltard at the behest of Napoleon III to host the central city markets. In their place, plans called for a multifunctional complex consisting of residential apartments, offices, hotels, and cultural institutions, all integrated around the new underground station of the regional RER rail network.

As part of the review of six French architectural proposals submitted for the competition to redesign the district, Pompidou, then serving as prime minister, persuaded President De Gaulle to reject all of the submitted designs[2]. Instead, he advocated refocusing the project around a tower-like structure to house the Ministry of Finance, which at the time was still located in one of the wings of the Louvre Palace[3]. Beyond its symbolic significance – associating De Gaulle's presidency with the economic power of the French state – this proposal reveals the prime minister's fascination with American skyscrapers, which he admired during his former official visits to the United States.

Although the events of May 1968 and de Gaulle's departure from power ultimately led to the skyscraper project being excluded from the transformation of Les Halles, the image of a vertical architectural piece to be placed in the heart of the old city became firmly etched in Pompidou's mind. It stood as an evocative symbol of the type of modernity he envisioned for France[4].

---

2 The leaders of the teams invited to submit their projects for the renovation of the Halles district were Claude Charpentier, Louis Arretche, Atelier d'Urbanisme et d'Architecture-A.U.A., Louis de Hoÿm de Marien, Michel Marot and Jean Faugeron. For an analysis of the projects, see: Hamzeian, 'Centre national d'art et de culture Georges Pompidou : Monument national e Live Centre of Information. Cronache di idea, progetto e fabbricazione, 1968–1977', PhD diss., Ecole Polytechnique Fédérale de Lausanne-EPFL, 46–47.

3 See Boris Hamzeian, *Live Centre of Information, From Pompidou to Beaubourg, 1968–1971* (New York-Barcelona: Actar Publishers, 2022), 16–25.

4 Jacques Michel, 'Interview with Georges Pompidou (Le président de la République définit ses conceptions dans les domaines de l'art et de l'architecture', *Le Monde*, 17 October 1972, 1 and 12.

The Fascination With the Anglo-American Architectural Debate and Efforts Toward Organising the International Competition to Build the Centre Du Plateau Beaubourg

In the autumn of 1969, just weeks after his inauguration as president of the French Republic, Pompidou revisited his vision for the tower project. Seeking to align it closely with his presidency, he reimagined its purpose as a 'monument' dedicated to 'contemporary art and thought'[5]. Within a few months, the project's vision became clearer, evolving into a centre intended to house the historical collections of the Musée national d'art moderne (MNAM) (still located in the outdated Palais de Tokyo); the Centre national d'art contemporain (CNAC) and the Centre de Création industrielle (CCI), two newly established venues dedicated, respectively, to contemporary art and architecture, and to urbanism and product design; the first public access library of France, Bibliothèque publique d'information (BPI); and ultimately the Institut de Recherche et Coordination Acoustique/Musique (IRCAM), a research centre for acoustics and music conceived to facilitate the return to France of composer and conductor Pierre Boulez, following his voluntary exile abroad during the first half of the 1960s.

Pompidou's conviction that the models and designers for his 'monument' were not to be found within France, but instead abroad, was confirmed through a series of actions linked to preparations for the architectural competition that would soon lead to what became known as the Centre du plateau Beaubourg. Some of these initiatives were directed by the ministerial body responsible for overseeing the project, the Délégation pour la réalisation du Centre Beaubourg, while others were directly initiated by Pompidou, often through the involvement of his son-in-law Henri Domerg, who served as the presidential secretary for cultural and artistic affairs.

The first concrete steps demonstrating the organisers' admiration for American architecture are demonstrated by the research trips taken by two key figures from the Centre's leadership: Jean-Pierre Seguin, the initiator and first director of the BPI, and Germain Viatte, curator at the CNAC. In 1968, Seguin

---

5 Georges Pompidou, Letter to Edmond Michelet [unsent first draft], 30 November 1969, AN, 574AP, folder 10; Georges Pompidou, Letter to Edmond Michelet, 15 December 1969, AN, 574AP, folder 10.

travelled to the United States and Canada to explore a new breed of library designed to encourage democratic and popular access to reading. Similarly, in 1971, Viatte embarked on a study tour of England, the United States, and Canada to examine a series of museums built in the post-war period[6].

At this stage, the president's focus was on the various actors involved in creating his 'monument', and the panel members tasked with evaluating them. Regarding the participants, as early as December 1969 Pompidou expressed his intention to extend the competition to foreign architects. Eager to engage with the currents of contemporary avant-garde movements, he instructed the Délégation to facilitate participation by teams of architecture students and emerging young professionals. 'We must', Pompidou wrote, 'also make sure that the competition is accessible to all talented architects, even if they are young and lack the financial means [to participate]'[7].

When it came to the panel, Pompidou sought to identify figures capable of engaging with the most 'modern' architectural languages. He urged the Délégation to include internationally renowned architects, as well as specialists from fields that would reflect the Centre's content, such as museum curators and orchestra conductors[8].

In the spring of 1970, Pompidou entrusted Sébastien Loste, a key member of the Délégation with a former career as an employee of the Minister of Culture, and François Mathey, the director of the CCI, with compiling lists of potential panellists for his approval. His interest in American architecture was evident in the consultation he sought from Arthur Drexler, the director of the Department of Architecture and Design at New York's Museum of Modern Art (MoMA). Drexler recommended including Louis Kahn, one of the foremost figures in post-war American and international architectural discourse, on the panel[9]. However, for reasons that remain unclear, Kahn's

---

6 Jean-Pierre Seguin, Bibliothèque Nationale – Bibliothèque des Halles. Voyage d'études au Canada et aux États-Unis [compte-rendu du voyage], October 1969, AN, 19950353, folder 3; Germain Viatte, Voyage en Irlande, au Canada et aux États-Unis, 1971, AN, 574AP, folder 88.

7 Georges Pompidou, Letter to Edmond Michelet, 15 December 1969, *op. cit*, p. 1–2.

8 Ibid.

9 François Mathey, Liste d'architectes américains proposé par Dreixler[sic], Conservateur du département architecture au Museum of Modern Art de New York, undated [spring 1970], AN, 20100307, folder 17.

name was replaced with that of another internationally recognised American architect, Philip Johnson, known for his artistic and cultural projects, including the Lincoln Center for Performing Arts in New York[10].

Seeking to create a jury that would reflect a broader international dialogue and include non-architects, Loste and Mathey revised the panel composition, proposing configurations of seven, nine, or ten members, each consisting of an equal number of architects and 'users'. The proposals presented in the summer of 1970 maintained a strong American presence while introducing British representation. The names under consideration included several prominent figures of post-war British modernism: the architects Leslie Martin, Denys Lasdun, and Colin St John Wilson, as well as the former director of the British Museum, Sir Frank Francis[11].

In July, Pompidou revisited these proposals, noting both the advanced age of some of the jury members, and the absence of representatives from countries such as Japan, Brazil, and the Scandinavian nations, which he considered to embody the new frontiers of the international avant-garde[12]. 'This jury is a bit "classical"', wrote Pompidou. 'There are no architects from Brazil, [...] no Japanese ... I would prefer a list of architects chosen from among these "moderns"'. Pompidou's feedback prompted Loste and Mathey to rework the panel composition. In the final version, the Anglo-American representation was reduced to Johnson for architects, and Francis for 'users'. The president's openness to the new boundaries of the avant-garde was reflected in the appointments of the Brazilian architect Oscar Niemeyer and the Danish

---

10 For the various versions of the panel composition for the Centre Pompidou, see the drafts preserved in folder 17 of file 20100307 at the collection 20100307 in the Archives nationales.

11 Sébastien Loste, Proposition pour le jury du concours international du plateau Beaubourg, 27 July 1970, AN, 574AP, folder 10. It is possible that Jean-Pierre Seguin played a role in the choice of Philip Johnson in the panel. As he mentions in his *memoire* dedicated to the history of the BPI, Seguin had met Johnson during his travels to discover American libraries. During the meeting, Johnson introduced Seguin to his project for the Boston Public Library and drew a sketch for the library Seguin was attempting to realise in Paris. Jean-Pierre Seguin, *Comment est née la BPI : invention de la médiathèque* (Paris: Centre Georges Pompidou, 1987), 60.

12 Henri Domerg, Note to the attention of the president of the Republic. État présent de la préparation du projet du Plateau Beaubourg, 15 July 1970, AN, 574AP, folder 10, p. 3.

architect Jørn Utzon, who had already gained an internation reputation, respectively, for designing some of the finest building of modernist Parisian architecture, such as the headquarters of the Communist Party in Paris, and winning the international competition to build the Sydney Opera House, accomplished with the essential collaboration of Ove Arup engineering[13].

In compiling the list of participants for the competition, Mathey and Loste initially focused on inviting a range of notable figures. Among the French architects competing for Parisian competition, the most prominent invitations were extended to representatives from the United States, the United Kingdom, and Italy[14]. The American list featured leading figures from post-war modernist discourse, such as Louis Kahn, Marcel Breuer, Ieoh Ming Pei, Paul Rudolph, James Spayer, John Dinkeloo, and Kevin Roche, along with the renowned firm Skidmore, Owings and Merrill (SOM). The list also included younger avant-garde representatives from the 1960s, including Robert Venturi, Charles Moore, and Richard Whitacker. In the British camp, Leslie Martin was part of the first category, while the second included Theo Crosby, James Gowan, James Stirling, and the Archigram group. The prominent role of American architects in the competition was further underscored by Drexler's input. The MoMA director recommended inviting established figures such as Breuer, Rudolph, and Bunshaft (from Skidmore, Owings and Merrill), as well as Johnson, Cesar Pelli, and younger members of the so-called Whites and Grays groups, including Michael Graves, Robert Venturi, Richard Meier, and Aldo Giurgola.

Between the summer of 1970 and spring of 1971, the Délégation embarked on an extensive promotional campaign, sending its members on a whirlwind tour of numerous capitals to garner as many participants as possible, and make the Paris competition the most significant event for post-war international architectural competition. The first stops on Bordaz's tour were notably

---

[13] Sébastien Loste, Proposition pour le jury du concours international du plateau Beaubourg, 27 July 1970, AN, 574AP, folder 10.

[14] German Viatte, François Mathey, Blaise Gautier, Propositions pour invitations, undated [spring 1970], AN, 20100307, folder 156; François Mathey, Architectes étrangers à inviter (Mathey) en dehors de ceux qui ne seraient pas retenus pour le jury, undated [spring 1970], AN, 20100307, folder 17.

dedicated to the Anglosphere, with events scheduled in London, New York, Philadelphia, Washington, Chicago, Toronto, and Montreal[15].

Thanks to the coordination between the Ministries of Culture and Foreign Affairs, along with French embassies, this promotional tour resulted in 682 competition entries, including 191 from France, and a notable 138 from the United States[16]. This number underscores the effective promotional campaign on the American architectural scene, as well as the efforts of the Délégation and Johnson to secure the highest number of American participants in the competition.

What is surprising, however, is that none of the prominent figures Drexler and Mathey mentioned were among the competitors. Instead, the core of American submissions came from young architects, many of whom were collaborators or students of the well-known figures sought by the competition organisers[17].

A similar pattern emerged in other countries in the Anglosphere, such as Canada and the United Kingdom, where the names initially suggested by the organisers were also absent. Aside from Moshe Safdie, Michael Charles Pearson, Arthur Erickson, and Geoffrey Massey, most of the entries from Canada and the UK came from universities. A particularly significant case was the Architectural Association School of Architecture in London, which produced submissions from Nora Kohen, Will Alsop, and Julius Tabacek, in collaboration with Dennis Crompton of the Archigram group; Rem Koolhaas and Aristides Romanos, along with Elia Zenghelis; and Wolf Wolfgang Pearlman and Robert Stones[18].

Amidst the extensive promotional efforts for the competition, Pompidou focused on inviting a single figure, the American architect Marcel Breuer, one of the most distinguished figures of the modern movement in the post-war US. On 15 December 1970, just a few weeks before the competition

---

15 Ph. B., 'La croisade de M. Bordaz pour le concours d'architecture du centre d'art contemporain', *Le Monde*, 13 January 1971.

16 Délégation pour la réalisation du Centre Beaubourg, Concours International pour la réalisation du Centre Beaubourg, Rapport du Jury. Liste des participants au concours pour la creation du Centre Beaubourg a Paris, par nationalité, July 1971, AN, 20100307, folder 2.

17 Ibid.

18 Ibid.

opened, Pompidou and his wife Claude hosted a dinner with the painter Hans Hartung and his wife Anna-Eva Bergman, both internationally renowned for their abstract art. During the dinner, the Hartungs and Pompidous discussed Breuer, to whom the Hartungs had entrusted the design of a house-studio in Antibes. Pompidou's interest in Hartung's recommendation is further confirmed by the monograph *Marcel Breuer. Projets et réalisations récents*, which Hartung sent to Pompidou shortly after the dinner[19]. Among the projects featured in the book is the Whitney Museum, which Pompidou had previously discussed with Loste, who praised its interiors while criticising its exterior design. Following Hartung's suggestion, on 20 December Pompidou asked Bordaz to make all of the necessary arrangements to convince Breuer to participate in the competition of the Centre Beaubourg[20]. Despite Bordaz's efforts to reach out to Breuer and arrange a meeting during his January 1971 trip to the United States, Breuer ultimately chose not to enter the competition.

The Competition Selection Process and the Problematic Emergence of the 'British' Proposal

Between June and July 1971, the jury met behind closed doors at the Grand Palais to present Pompidou with one of the 682 anonymous proposals submitted to the organisers. The importance placed on Johnson's judgement suggested he played a pivotal role in the selection process. Archival records show that the organisers were specifically anticipating the victory of an American project. How else can one explain Bordaz's request to Johnson, just weeks into the selection process, to send images of the 'major libraries and museums of the United States' (which Johnson would later clarify as 'recent' in his response) to be showcased during the exhibition of the winning projects[21]?

---

19 Hans Hartung, Letter to Georges Pompidou, 16 December 1970, AN, 555AP, folder Hartung.

20 Michel Jobert, Note pour monsieur Domerg, 19 December 1970, AN, 574AP, folder 10; Henri Domerg, Letter to Robert Bordaz, 21 December 1970, AN, 574AP, folder 10.

21 Philip Johnson, Letter to Robert Bordaz, 22 June 1971, AN, 20100307, folder 78; Robert Bordaz, Letter to Philip Johnson, 8 June 1971, AN, 20100307, folder 78.

The favourable atmosphere surrounding Johnson and Anglo-American architectural trends is evident in the choice of the three finalist projects from the first round. The French duo of Michel Duplay and François-Noël Deffontaines envisioned the Centre Beaubourg as an urban matrix of courtyards and viaducts. The American team led by Jorge Ambrosini, Tadeusz Berezowski, David Soffer, and Macario Aguirre showcased a colossal suspended slab covering the entire Plateau Beaubourg, thus transforming the construction site into a covered piazza. The Anglo-Italian team led by the engineers of Ove Arup & Partners, and architects Renzo Piano, Richard Rogers, and Gianfranco Franchini also portrayed the Centre Beaubourg as a public metropolitan platform intended for the public. They nonetheless made more than half of this surface an open-air piazza, reducing the future building to a lightweight sequence of flexible and empty platform to be suspended via a three-dimensional wall featuring informational audiovisual screens for the public[22].

The Anglo-American angle was reaffirmed in the second selection round. With the French entry eliminated, the competition was now reduced to a contest between the Piano, Rogers, Franchini, and Arup proposal, and a Venturian-inspired project by an American team led by Giovanni Cosco, a collaborator of Denise Scott Brown. Interestingly, despite the strict anonymity mandated by the competition rules, as the final decision neared, the jurors began to speculate about the affiliations and nationalities of the two projects, attributing one to an American protégé of Venturi, and the other to a British firm.

The importance of the nationality of the favoured Anglo-American project became so pronounced that Bordaz disregarded the rules and presented the project's main elements to Pompidou between 12 and 13 July, even as the jury's deliberations were still underway. 'The author of the project would be British', read a note prepared by Domerg for the president on 12 July[23]. 'Bordaz proposes inviting a few ambassadors, particularly the British one

[22] Deuxième passage du jury, décision du 8 juillet 1971, projets retenus, 8 July 1971, AN, 20100307, folder 18. On the selection process see Hamzeian, *Live Centre of Information*, 228–305.

[23] Henri Domerg, Note to the attention of the president of the Republic, 12 July 1971, AN, 574AP, folder 10.

if the chosen project is British', another note from Domerg, written the following day, confirmed[24].

Through Domerg's notes, Pompidou became aware of the project and prepared for the political ramifications implicit in selecting a British design. The fact that Pompidou chose to secretly visit the Grand Palais galleries displaying the projects on the night of 13 July, accompanied by Claude, and that the decision was made during the decisive meeting on 14 July, suggests that despite what some politicians entrusted to the French press in the aftermath of the publication of the competition results, the French president consciously entrusted his 'monument' to Piano, Rogers, Franchini, and Ove Arup & Partners.

Despite the jurors' emphasis on the British origins of the project through Ove Arup & Partners[25] – one of the most prestigious engineering firms of the time – the press response was scathing. The public presentation of the project, held in July in the presence of the British ambassador and the competition winners, was interrupted by protests from several French architects, led by Georges Candilis.

Although no publication explicitly attacked the Italian-English composition of the winning team, the project was quickly perceived as disrespectful to the historical centre of Paris. It was soon associated with a range of disparaging labels that would characterise its complex relationship with public opinion. Terms such as 'factory', 'art supermarket', 'cultural department store', 'glass carcass', 'plexiglass box', 'lost packaging', 'drive-in', 'garage', 'suitcase', 'storage cabinet', 'soapbox', 'cultural silo', and 'utilitarian building' flooded the press in July 1971 to describe the presidential 'monument'[26].

A few days after the press conference, and despite the advice of his collaborators, in an attempt to send a strong signal to the media, Pompidou invited the winners to the Élysée. There he encouraged them to pay special attention to the project's appearance and aesthetic nature. What Pompidou

---

[24] Henri Domerg, Note to the attention of the president of the Republic, 13 July 1971, AN, 574AP, folder 10.

[25] A testament to the recognition of Ove Arup & Partners is the preparation of a detailed profile dedicated to this firm, to be placed alongside that of Piano+Rogers Architects. *Untitled [sketch for a Curriculum Vitae of Ove Arup & Partners]*, AN, 20100307, folder 19.

[26] For a comprehensive list of the epithets found in magazines and newspapers published between July and August 1971, see: Boris Hamzeian, 'Centre national d'art', 597–616.

explicitly shared with the winners of the competition was the desire of a monument meant to endure for centuries[27]. How to find a common ground between what Piano called an impermanent, lightweight, constantly flexible 'anti-monument', and the presidential need for a monumental symbol of the brand new, post-war French modern era? This was one of the fundamental questions present throughout the process.

The conversation between Pompidou and the winners was quickly exploited by Pierre-Charles Krieg, a deputy from Pompidou's own party and president of the Permanent Commission of Les Halles at the Paris Council. In an article published in *La Nation*, Krieg reinterpreted Pompidou's remarks as a 'disappointment'. He suggested the president's disillusionment with a project that seemed far removed from the monumental vision he had originally intended, and which, in what Krieg considered being Pompidou's view, lacked even basic architectural merit[28].

Krieg's interpretation contradicts the efforts Pompidou made to broaden the competition's scope by inviting foreign architects and young architects with limited financial resources. Pompidou sought to include those he considered to be emerging figurers in contemporary discourse, and to identify panellists capable of recognising this new form of avant-garde architecture. Despite the critical success the project would enjoy in the following decades, the supposed hostility Pompidou felt towards the winning design can be interpreted as reflecting a nationalist surge from the French establishment in response to a non-French proposal. The fact that Pompidou did not react to the multiple attempts to involve him in the debate should be understood as the eloquent silence of a president who, while perhaps not fully aligned with the architecture envisioned in the proposal, recognised its avant-garde nature, and decided to embrace it in order to renew the French architectural debate, as well as the image of Paris and all of France.

---

27 Henri Domerg, Note to the attention of the president of the Republic, 15 July 1971, AN, 574AP, folder 10.

28 'Les lauréats du Concours pour le Plateau Beaubourg reçus par M. Pompidou', *L'Aurore*, 21 July 1971; 'Les projets pour le Centre Beaubourg seront exposés au Grand Palais', *Le Monde*', 23 July 1971. See also: Philippe Aubert, 'Plateau Beaubourg : M. Krieg mécontent', *Combat*, 21 July 1971; 'Le projet correspond – il à l'idée que s'en faisait M. Pompidou? Demande M. Krieg', *Le Monde*, 21 July 1971; Aubert, 'Le projet retenu pour le Plateau Beaubourg : une architecture qui ne fera pas date', *Combat*, 20 July 1971.

The British Engineering Firm Faces Public Opinion and the French Steel Industry

The harsh debate, and the strong opposition of French public opinion toward the winning proposal of the Centre Beaubourg competition, was not the only challenge for Piano+Rogers Architects and Ove Arup & Partners following the competition victory. Throughout the fine-tuning of the project, running from the fall of 1971 to 1973, the foreign English-Italian team needed to overcome the resistance of key stakeholders involved in the project. These included officials at the Délégation, municipal and state commissions tasked with overseeing compliance in various aspects and stages of the project, and French construction firms responsible for providing the labour and technical expertise required.

One of the most emblematic aspects of this complex acceptance process was the steel firm Arup engineers, which was founded in 1972 and led by Ted Happold, Peter Rice and Lennart Grut. The aim was to establish the Centre project as a statement of the steel casting technique, which was gaining prominence at the time for its use in North Sea oil platforms, and in components for next-generation nuclear reactors. The technical solution envisioned by Arup consisted in a main truss beam resting on two symmetrical cantilevered beams articulated according to the system invented in the nineteenth century by the German engineer Heinrich Gerber for large span bridges. Following an idea that had originated with Ted Happold, and that was to be developed by Peter Rice, Arup intended to design the beam joints and even the entire cantilever beam (later known as the *garberette*) from cast steel. In doing so, he sought to make the Centre the manifesto of a new kind of avant-garde structure.

In order to produce pieces of colossal dimensions that were unequalled across the globe, the challenge facing Arup's engineers was not only technical but also political and diplomatic, and involved gaining the confidence of both the client and the actor from the French steel industry.

To understand the intricate technical and political context in which Ove Arup's engineers found themselves, it suffices to note that despite their crucial role as the primary promoters of the project, after the competition win the French state refused to entrust them with the responsibility of building the Centre alongside the Piano+Rogers Architects team. The approach, which sought to blur the boundaries between architecture and engineering – a philosophy Ove Arup defined as 'Total Design' – was entirely foreign to the French tradition. This tradition was still firmly rooted in the Beaux-Arts distinction between the professions of architect and engineer. Under these circumstances, the Délégation forced the engineers to act as consultants for Piano+Rogers Architects, leading to tensions that the project team would carry with them until the Centre's inauguration.

The process of gaining the Délégation's trust involved multiple complex steps. It was not until a private meeting at Arup's headquarters in London in January 1973, nearly a year and a half after the project began, that Bordaz, who attended along with Ove Arup, was finally convinced of the engineers' technical expertise to build the cast steel structure for Beaubourg. Bordaz was persuaded by Ove Arup that the key to the success of the presidential 'monument' laid in the shapes and lines of cast steel joints[29]. 'The structure is the architecture' was the firm directive Ove Arup gave to Bordaz during the meeting[30].

Gaining the trust of the French steel industry proved even more complex. Throughout the consultations, the steel companies repeatedly expressed doubts about the feasibility of Arup's structural solution. They coordinated efforts to influence the outcome of the bidding process, which ultimately ended in failure on 15 March 1973. The timing of this event, coming just months after the expansion of the European Community to include the United Kingdom, suggests that France was not yet ready to embrace the realisation of a monument to the Fifth Republic grounded in the British engineering avant-garde[31].

Amid this mutual distrust between English engineers and French steel manufacturers, Bordaz was persuaded to look once again beyond national borders, revisiting the international landscape that had played a role in the Centre's origins. Within weeks, Arup's engineers laid the groundwork for the involvement of foreign companies, many of which had previously only served as consultants. These included major players such as US Steel

29 Povl Ahm, Notes of a meeting with monsieur Bordaz in Ove Arup office on Friday, 5 January 1973, 12 January 1973, AA, 4123, folder 32.
30 Ibid.
31 Robert Bordaz, Letter to Voyer, Sotracomet, Secometal, CFEM-Creusot-Loire and Ruchard-Ducros, 15 March 1973, AN, 20100307, folder 308.

and British Steel, in addition to companies such as Pohlig Heinz Bleichert (PHB) and Nippon Steel, which, by the late 1970s would become pioneers in manufacturing cast steel pieces for civil construction.

When PHB, in collaboration with the renowned steel company Krupp Industrie und Stahlbau, declared its ability to implement Arup's structural design while adhering to the Délégation's budget and timeline, Bordaz found himself faced with an impasse that transcended the Centre project and escalated into a state matter.

Entrusting Krupp with producing the Centre's steel as designed by Arup – which could be manufactured by PHB and Krupp – would transform the Centre into an international project, emblematic of the new French-British alliance and the European Community market. However, this decision came with a triple dilemma: first, the potential fallout with the French steel industry, which was on the brink of a systemic crisis at the time; second, the contradiction to the nationalist economic policies initiated by Pompidou himself; and finally, the moral quandary of assigning the steel production for the 'monument' to the same company that had, only a few decades earlier, forged armaments for the Nazi military.

To resolve the impasse, Bordaz turned to Pompidou, who on 13 April 1973 removed any remaining reservations, and gave the go-ahead for signing the German contract[32].

The president's decision would not be revisited, even in the face of an appeal from Philippe Boulin, the general director of Creusot-Loire, France's main competitor in the bidding process for the Centre's steel. In May Boulin sought the support of Bernard Ésambert, the chief engineer of Mines and technical adviser at the Élysée, in an attempt to persuade the president to reconsider[33]. 'The assignment to Italian and English architects and to a British engineering firm', Boulin wrote, 'has already demonstrated France's broad-mindedness. Will French industry now be excluded from the realization [of this project] after being denied its design?' In the same document, Boulin emphasised 'the painful memories' associated with the name Krupp, warned of a potential

---

32 Henri Domerg, Note to the attention of the president of the Republic, 13 April 1973, AN, 5AG2, folder 1065.

33 Philippe Bourdin Letter to Bernard Ésambert, 18 may 1973, AN, 20100307, folder 310; Philippe Boulin, *E.P.C.B.* Établissement Public du Centre Beaubourg lot n 6 charpente métallique, 18 May 1973, AN, 20100307, folder 310.

'crisis' and the 'serious social repercussions' the presidency could face from this decision, and even expressed a willingness to lower his bid as a 'sacrifice' he was ready to endure for France.

Pompidou's unwavering stance in the face of such pressure was likely the final act related to his 'monument' before his untimely death in April 1974, in the midst of the construction process. To understand this decision, it can be interpreted in connection with the diagnosis of illness that the French president must have known would prevent him from seeing the project's completion[34]. As a result, his willingness to proceed with producing the Italian-British design of the Centre Pompidou thanks to Krupp's German steel could be seen as a deeply personal desire to ensure the legacy of his 'monument', and to associate it with the idea of an international and above all European venture. However, Pompidou's steadfastness can also be understood through comments he made, specifically in a note to Domerg, in which he wrote: 'Oh well, Krupp. It will be a lesson for the French, and if we are attacked, we must say so'. In this blend of provocation and challenge, one can detect the same resolve that had driven the origins of Beaubourg, and motivated Pompidou to look beyond French borders from the very beginning of this project. As the final act to protect and ensure the realisation of his 'monument', Pompidou thus confirmed a firm and genuine intention to lead France into an unprecedented modernity.

Archives

Archives Nationales in Paris (AN).

- President Georges Pompidou (5AG2)
- Sébastien Loste (640AP)
- Henri Domerg (574AP)
- Bibliothèque Publique d'Information (19950353)
- Centre Pompidou construction archive (20100307).

Institut Georges Pompidou (IGP) documentary and audiovisual collections.
Ove Arup & Partners engineers private Archives (AA).
Politecnico di Milano Archives (FRP).
Richard Rogers private Archives, held at the RSHP agency, private archives.

---

34 On the early diagnosis of Pompidou's illness, see for instance: 'La Maladie du Président', *Le Monde*, 9 April 1974.

Bibliography

Aubert, Philippe, 'Plateau Beaubourg : M. Krieg mécontent', *Combat*, 21 July 1971.

———, Philippe, 'Le projet retenu pour le Plateau Beaubourg : une architecture qui ne fera pas date', *Combat*, 20 July 1971.

Boucher, Philippe, 'La croisade de M. Bordaz pour le concours d'architecture du centre d'art contemporain', *Le Monde*, 13 January 1971.

Hamzeian, Boris, 'Centre national d'art et de culture Georges Pompidou : Monument national e Live Centre of Information. Cronache di idea, progetto e fabbricazione, 1968–1977', PhD dissertation, Ecole Polytechnique Fédérale de Lausanne-EPFL.

____, Boris, *Live Centre of Information, From Pompidou to Beaubourg, 1968–1971* (New York-Barcelona: Actar Publishers, 2022).

____, Boris, *Le Centre Pompidou et le défi du Total Design* (Paris-Saint-Etienne: Presses universitaires de Saint-Etienne, 2024)

'La Maladie du Président', *Le Monde*, 9 April 1974.

'Le projet correspond – il a l'idée que s'en faisait M. Pompidou? Demande M. Krieg', *Le Monde*, 21 July 1971.

'Les lauréats du Concours pour le Plateau Beaubourg reçus par M. Pompidou', *L'Aurore*, 21 July 1971.

'Les projets pour le Centre Beaubourg seront exposés au Grand Palais', *Le Monde*', 23 July 1971.

Michel, Jacques, Interview with Georges Pompidou 'Le président de la République définit ses conceptions dans les domaines de l'art et de l'architecture', *Le Monde*, 17 October 1972.

Seguin, Jean-Pierre, *Comment est née la BPI : invention de la médiathèque* (Paris: Centre Georges Pompidou, 1987).

Preserving the Archives of the Presidents of the French Republic: The Example of Georges Pompidou

Bénédicte Fichet

Introduction

When he submitted a report on archives to the French prime minister in 1996, Guy Braibant said that 'Without archives, there can be no State, no History, no Republic'[1]. This phrase concisely sums up the powerful link between archives and political power.

Georges Pompidou's presidency is particularly interesting in this respect, as it proved to be a pivotal period. There is also the legacy of the public archives inherited from the revolutionary period. Most importantly, political life has refocused since the start of the Fifth Republic around the presidency, which necessarily led to changes in how presidential archives are handled. Paradoxically, the premature death of Georges Pompidou (and the difficulty of finding his papers) helped to change practices, with the aim of improving the collection of archives.

The purpose of this contribution is threefold: (i) to look back at the history of the French National Archives, and especially at how they were set up to preserve state papers; (ii) to take a closer look at the very special status of presidential archives; and (iii) to present the types of documents held in presidential archives, with a particular focus on the bilateral relations between Georges Pompidou and Sir Edward Heath.

The National Archives of France: A Two-hundred-year-old Institution Created to Preserve the Papers of the State

The creation of the French National Archives dates back to the French Revolution. In medieval and early modern France, ecclesiastical, communal,

[1] G. Braibant, *Les Archives en France*, Rapport remis au Premier ministre, La documentation française, 1996, 303 p.

seigneurial, and later royal institutions endeavoured to preserve their archives. During the seventeenth century, the French monarchy attempted to centralise the papers of its main ministries but proved unable due to the lack of an administration specifically dedicated to this task[2]. It was not until the French Revolution that the notion of 'public archives' truly came into being, and that the centralisation of these archives became a reality with the creation of the French National Archives.

The French Revolution created profound upheaval in France, which logically led to new methods of managing archives. Between 1789 and 1793, the royal and ecclesiastical institutions of the *Ancien Régime* were abolished. At the same time, new institutions were created, either continuing or breaking with those of the *Ancien Régime*.

On 29 July 1789, the Constituent Assembly declared that it would 'choose a safe place to deposit all original documents relating to the operations of the *Assemblée* [Constituent Assembly]'[3]. The deputies appointed a deputy from the Third Estate to head this new repository, Armand-Gaston Camus, who would bear the title of 'archivist of the National Assembly'[4].

The organisation of the archives was clarified on 12 September 1790 with the law relating to the National Archives[5], which created a service whose mission was defined in Article 1 as follows: 'The National Archives are the repository of all acts establishing the constitution of the kingdom, its public law, its laws and its distribution into departments'.

The aim of the National Archives was to demonstrate the transparency of the Assembly's decisions, in contrast to the state secret practice of absolutism. Initially, only the archives of the Assembly were concerned, but a series of laws gradually directed the papers of defunct institutions (seigniorial and

2 V. Duclert, 'République et archives', *Revue française d'administration publique* 102, 'La mémoire de l'administration', (2002), 270.

3 The National Constituent Assembly was the first of its kind in French history. It was instituted by the deputies of the Third Estate at the Estates General of 1789, who swore the oath of the Jeu de Paume, and with the support of a few deputies from the nobility and clergy established themselves as the National Assembly on 17 June 1789, and then as the National Constituent Assembly on 9 July 1789.

4 Duclert, 'République et archives', 271.

5 In French, '*loi relative aux Archives nationales*'. See M. Cornu, Ch. Nougaret, Y. Potin, B. Ricard, and N. Wagener, eds, *1979, Genèse d'une loi sur les archives*, (La documentation française, 2019), 59.

local courts, provincial administrations, religious orders, judicial bodies, trade guilds) to the National Archives. The private archives of *émigrés* were also transferred[6], as were those of the Crown after 10 August 1792 (the fall of the constitutional monarchy).

Four years later, the *Convention Nationale* (National Convention) clarified the role of the National Archives with the law of 25 June 1794 concerning the organisation of the archives established at the National Representation (according to the revolutionary calendar: 7 Messidor year II)[7,8]. This fundamental text, which remained in effect until the Archives Act of 3 January 1979, governed the organisation of French archives for almost two centuries.

Several key ideas underpin this republican project. The first is the obligation for the National Archives to have a central repository: 'the archives established at the National Representation are a central repository for the entire Republic' (article 1). This notion of a 'single repository' was already mentioned in the 1790 law. The second article describes what must be preserved and clearly states that 'It is the sole responsibility of the Legislative Body to order the deposit of archives'.

Another idea is particularly important in this law of 1794, namely access to archives. As opposed to the earlier practice of state secrecy, the principle of free consultation of archives and free access to documents became a civic right: 'Any citizen may request communication of the documents contained in all repositories, on the days and times that are set: this will be given to them free of charge and without travel, and with the appropriate precautions for oversight. The copies or extracts requested will be delivered at the rate of fifteen pennies per roll' (article 37).

6 Emigrants during the French Revolution.

7 The National Convention was a constituent assembly elected in September 1792 during the French Revolution, following the fall of Louis XVI on 10 August 1792, and the failure of the constitutional monarchy. This assembly, which succeeded the Legislative Assembly, was elected for the first time in France by universal male suffrage and was tasked with drawing up a new Constitution. It remained in office from 21 September 1792, the date of the proclamation of the Republic, until 26 October 1795, the promulgation of the Constitution of Year III, which established the Directoire regime.

8 In French 'loi concernant l'organisation des archives établies auprès de la Représentation nationale'. Ibid., 60.

The concept of free access to public archives is a particularly important one. Article 15 of the Declaration of the Rights of Man and of the Citizen from 26 August 1789 states that: 'Society has the right to demand an account from a public official of his administration'. The Constitution of 3 September 1791, which established a constitutional monarchy and was the first experiment in a liberal regime, included the text of the Declaration of the Rights of Man and of the Citizen in its preamble, further broadening its scope.

Another principle was also present in the 1794 law: the need for a national archival network consisting of multiple archival services functioning as the repositories for the nation's memory. The desire for centralisation did not mean that all archives were kept in a single building, but rather in a number of premises that had to be coordinated in order to prevent them from operating independently.

The law of 26 October 1796 (5 Brumaire An V) completed the system by establishing an archival service in each departmental capital[9].

The French historian Vincent Duclert has analysed the organisation of archives in France as follows: 'The French Revolution [...] made archives and their policy a key element in the construction of a modern State and the development of democratic citizenship. By creating the National Archives in 1790, the National Assembly established the institution's political dimension: at the service of civil servants and citizens, it is as much about individual freedoms as it is about national memory and the modernity of the State. It is at the heart of the new sovereignty born of the Revolution of Rights'[10].

On 28 May 1800 (Consul decree of 8 Prairial, An VIII), the National Archives ceased to fall under the legislative and came under the authority of the Ministry of the Interior. At the same time, the departmental archives were placed under the authority of the prefects created a few months earlier[11].

---

9 In French 'loi qui ordonne la réunion dans les chefs-lieux de départements, de tous les titres et papiers acquis à la République'. Ibid., 61.

10 Duclert, 'République et archives', 270.

11 The office of prefect and sub-prefect were created by Napoleon Bonaparte on 17 February 1800 when he was First Consul, via the law of 28 Pluviôse An VIII, thereby deconcentrating the department-based state established by the National Assembly on 26 February 1790. The prefect became the central and sole authority within the territorial jurisdiction of the department.

In 1806, the organisation and mission of the Archives, which was no longer national but imperial (since 1804), were defined by the decree of 15 March, which provided for the regular growth of collections by ordering the transfer of any administrative papers over fifty years old[12].

In 1808, Napoleon also decided to bring together all of the existing archives in Paris in a single place under one authority[13]. This was located in the former Palais de Soubise (in central Paris, in the Marais district), a temporary location that became definitive after the Archives Palace project on the île aux Cygnes was abandoned[14].

Confiscated during the French Revolution, the Hôtel de Soubise was sold for the benefit of the creditors of the Soubise family, which was also true for the adjacent building, the Hôtel de Rohan. On 6 March 1808, the Hôtel de Soubise was acquired by the state and allocated to the Imperial Archives by Napoleon I. At the same time, the Hôtel de Rohan became the Imprimerie impériale.

Nearly twenty years after the founding of the National Archives, a single location finally came to embody this centralisation of state papers: the Hôtel de Soubise.

In December 1804, Pierre Daunou succeeded Armand-Gaston Camus. He also endeavoured to improve the conservation of archives; in 1811 he laid the foundations for what was to become the filing system of the Archives nationales (and later that of the Archives départementales in 1841).

This is an organic system in which documents are classified according to the institution that produced them (the *fonds*) and then assigned to archival offices (the *section*), and grouped according to administrative, legal or

12 C. Béchu, ed., *Les Archives nationales, des lieux pour l'histoire de France* (Paris: Somogy, 2008), 64.

13 Before moving to the Hôtel de Soubise in 1808, the National Archives were first housed in one of the rooms of the Constituent Assembly in Versailles, before moving to various locations in Paris (Bibliothèque des Feuillants, rue Saint-Honoré, the former Capuchin convent, the Tuileries Palace and the Bourbon Palace). Some of the archives were also kept at the Palais de Justice and the Sainte-Chapelle in Paris.

14 J.-P. Babelon, *Les archives, mémoire de la France* (Paris: Gallimard, 2008), 16 and 27. The need for space had increased, as it included the archives of Napoleon's great Empire, whose papers had been transported to Paris: the Italian principalities and the Vatican, the German states, Austria, Spain, the Netherlands, etc. The first stone was laid on 15 August 1812, and the project was definitively abandoned on 1 February 1815.

political powers (the series, identified by letters). Within this framework, the symbolic and political significance is clearly visible: series A is dedicated to 'laws and decrees', series B to the Assembly, series C to the Revolutionary Committees, and so on.

In order to keep pace with the steady growth in its holdings, the Archives nationales built a series of repositories over the course of the nineteenth and twentieth centuries, extending beyond the Hôtel de Soubise to occupy the entire area between the rue des Francs-Bourgeois, the rue des Archives, the rue des Quatre-Fils and the rue Vieille-du-Temple, now known as the '*quadrilatère des Archives nationales de France*'[15].

Historical archive repositories, known in French as *grands dépôts*, were built in two stages: between 1838 and 1848 (Louis-Philippe repositories), and between 1859 and 1880 (Napoleon III repositories).

The major repositories were designed to celebrate the foundational nature of the archives. Preserving evidence of the construction of the state dating back a millennium, they are also the raw material of history, which Jules Michelet, the Director of the Historical Section of the National Archives from 1830 to 1852, continued to magnify with his writing. At the centre of the row of storerooms is the *trésor des Chartes* (Chartes treasure room)[16]. Including all of the titles relating to the domanial and diplomatic interests of the Crown, this original collection was kept from the reign of Saint-Louis until the eve of the Revolution in the sacristy of the Sainte-Chapelle. By virtue of its location at the very heart of the National Archives, the repository perpetuates the sanctity of its contents.

In 1866, the symbolic character of the site was further enhanced by the inclusion of the famous *armoire de fer* (iron cabinet) in the woodwork[17]. The construction of this safe was planned by the National Assembly on 29 July 1789 to protect its most precious documents from fire and theft. Camus had the safe built in 1790. It consists of two enormous metal boxes protected by three locks; one of the keys is engraved with the words 'Dedicated to the

---

15 These four streets form a quadrilateral, hence the term: the quadrilateral of the French National Archives.

16 O. Guyotjeannin and Y. Potin, 'La fabrique de la perpétuité : le trésor des chartes et les archives du royaume, XIIIe-XIXe s.', *Revue de synthèse. Fabrique des archives, fabrique de l'histoire*, 5th series (2004), 15–44.

17 Béchu, *Les Archives nationales*, 138–9.

Nation, 14 December 1790'. Over the years, this *armoire* has always been used to store documents deemed the most important in the history of the nation.

The contents of the *armoire* have varied over the years, reflecting what each generation considers important to the nation's history. Since 1996, it has revived its revolutionary heritage by containing all of France's constitutional texts. It also contains the Declaration of the Rights of Man and of the Citizen. The most important documents to be included are the French Constitution, the 1799 metre and kilogram, the Jeu de Paume oath, and the will of Napoleon I. The last document entered date dates back to 8 March 2024: a sealed constitutional law of 8 March 2024 on the freedom to have recourse to voluntary interruption of pregnancy.

After the Second World War, amid a boom in administrative production, the number of linear metres to be conserved increased sharply, with the buildings located in the heart of Paris approaching saturation point. The government began to look for new premises and chose the former NATO buildings located near Paris in Fontainebleau[18], not far from the famous Renaissance château. These buildings were allocated to the archives with the founding of the *cité interministérielle des archives.*

Three decades later, the problem of overcrowding is still being present. The French government chose the site of Pierrefitte-sur-Seine (north of Paris) for the construction of a new building specially built for archives. It was designed by the architect Massimiliano Fuksas and inaugurated by French President François Hollande in 2013.

Today, the National Archives are spread over two sites[19]: the Hôtel de Soubise: for *Ancien Régime* archives and notaries; and Pierrefitte-sur-Seine for post French Revolution.

---

18 The Cité Interministérielle des Archives was created in 1969 to receive a large number of deposits from central government departments. In 1962, the results of a survey carried out by the Direction des Archives de France estimated that there were 800 linear kilometres of documents in the archives produced by the administration, both existing and future. After a number of studies, the Fontainebleau site was chosen in the interest of developing the Paris region, and because the land used by NATO's European headquarters was returning to French control. On 21 December 1967, Prime Minister Georges Pompidou allocated 9 hectares of Camp Guynemer, which had been released following Charles de Gaulle's decision in 1966 to withdraw French armed forces from NATO's integrated command.

19 The Fontainebleau site was definitively closed in 2016.

The oldest documents are Merovingian papyri from the seventh century. The most recent documents are from this year (paper and digital). The archives represent approximately 380 linear kilometres and 70 terabytes of data[20].

The National Archives preserve and make accessible the archives of the central government administrations (with the exception of the Ministry of Defence and the Ministry of Foreign Affairs), in addition to original documents produced by Paris notaries, and private archives of national interest.

The internal organisation is based on three divisions:

- The Public Management Division, which oversees all matters relating to receiving and orienting the public.
- The Archives Management Division, which is responsible for collecting, sorting, studying, classifying and organising archives: this division is divided according to the organisation of French ministries.
- The digital and conservation Division, responsible for interdisciplinary and forward-looking professional research projects.

The state exists through its archives from both a historical and contemporary perspective. Not only do archives make it possible to write the history of the state but they also form the structure of the current administration and, as such, play a part in its very functioning: they are the instruments of 'living administration'[21]. Charles Braibant, the former Director of the Archives de France, highlighted this dual function, adding that 'archives are the attic of history and the arsenal of administration'[22]. The architect of the Pierrefitte-sur-Seine building, Massimiliano Fuksas, described his work as a 'precious chest of memory' that is part of this continuity[23].

The distinctive feature of the National Archives is that they are consubstantial with the context in which they were created, which is to say they are revolutionary in origin, the foundation of a new regime. They are also

20 The law on the freedom of creation, architecture and heritage (CAP law), enacted on 7 July 2016, defines archives as 'all documents, including data, regardless of their date, place of storage, form or medium, produced or received by any natural or legal person, and by any public or private service or body in the course of their activity'.

21 S. Monnier, 'Les archives, une affaire d'État', *Revue du droit public* 6 (2020), 1500.

22 E. Taillemite, 'Quelques souvenirs de trente-sept ans aux Archives', *Hommage à Jean Favier* (Paris: Fayard, 1986), 651.

23 D. Bétard, 'Les archives sous tension', *Le Journal des Arts*, 2 October 2012.

the reflection of a centralising state, not just a place of the past, but linked to the powers of the time.

How are the Archives of the Presidents of the Republic kept in France?

For two centuries, the centralisation of public archives has been central to the workings of the National Archives. This logic therefore applies to presidential archives, but not without difficulties.

On 21 July 1936, a decree made it compulsory for documents from ministries and government departments that were no longer needed to be deposited in the National Archives. This decree, entitled 'Deposit in state archival repositories of papers from the ministries and administrations dependent upon them', was issued by the National Archives[24], and co-signed by the Council President Léon Blum, and Minister of Education Jean Zay. This text goes into great detail about the history of the National Archives and the difficulties encountered since their creation. A strong desire on the part of the authors is evident: 'the purpose of this decree is to definitively establish order in this area for the present and the future, by supplementing the previous decrees with the provisions that are missing, whose absence explains their partial ineffectiveness, and by giving the appropriate prescriptions the force of a regulation approved by the Council of State'.

Despite this determination, under the Third and Fourth Republics, this law was not applied to the presidential archives: the custom was to clear them out before the arrival of a successor. Furthermore, it was customary for presidents to manage their papers as they saw fit after leaving the Élysée Palace, and some advisers kept their files in order to follow the progress of certain matters of particular interest to them[25].

---

[24] 'Versements dans les dépôts d'archives d'État des papiers des ministères et des administrations qui en dépendent'. See M. Cornu et al., 1979, 79.

[25] S. Bula, J. Irigoin and C. Obert, eds., *Archives de la présidence de la République, Ve République : Georges Pompidou (19 juin 1969–2 avril 1974)*, (La documentation française, 1996), 13.

Since 1958, the presidency has dominated the political life of the Fifth Republic; this political refocusing has led to a new and different approach to the conservation of archives produced by the head of state[26].

The first question that arises is what is meant by 'archives of the Presidency of the Republic'. The reality is more complex than it appears and also explains why the organisation of archival collection was not as straightforward as it was for ministries or other governmental department.

The archivist Pascal Geneste has offered the following analysis:

> Constitutionalists know that the Presidency of the Republic is not an administration as such, but rather a cabinet, a staff of an original kind, linked above all to the status of the Head of State, a status that cannot be ignored since it confers eminent prerogatives in the diplomatic and military fields – what is referred to as the 'reserved domain' of the Head of State – and above all prerogatives in the regular functioning of public powers. This is why these archives have for a long time been wrongly confused with the person of the President, and why they have long been seen as more private than public archives, and consequently experienced different fates.[27]

De Gaulle, who was very attached to the written word, and especially concerned about preserving the documents that would give history an account of his activities as head of state, organised the various stages of handing over his archives to the National Archives himself. In 1961, he asked Alice Garrigoux, a curator at the Bibliothèque nationale (French National Library), to be seconded on a part-time basis to carry out the necessary conservation and classification work. She was soon assisted by Alix Chevallier, also a curator at the Bibliothèque nationale, who was in turn assisted by a Republican guard[28].

This was the beginning of an archival service at the Élysée Palace. However, the failure of the referendum on 27 April 1969 led to de Gaulle's departure the following day. He had the archives moved to 5, rue de Solférino[29]; the

---

26 N. Even, ed., *Archives de la présidence de la République, Ve République : Général de Gaulle (1959–1969)*, (Archives nationales, 2012), 8: 'the Élysée Palace was henceforth the centre of power, since, in the words of the General himself, for power to be exercised, "there still had to be a leader and a State"'.

27 Béchu, *Les Archives nationales*, 302.

28 Even, *Archives de la présidence*, 7. Private secretary to de Gaulle from 1945 to 1970.

29 The current headquarters of the Charles de Gaulle Foundation.

files still held at the presidency were transferred to his office, and dated back to the days of the *Rassemblement du peuple français*[30].

Other documents found their way to his offices on Avenue de Breteuil. On 21 April 1970, de Gaulle wrote to André Chamson, the Director of the Archives de France: 'I think it would be appropriate for my archives currently at 37, avenue de Breteuil to be sorted, listed, and inventoried. I also think that this work should be done by a specialist appointed by you [...]. Monsieur de Beaulaincourt could contact you with regard to this subject[31]. My intention is to one day hand over to the National Archives everything that has the character of State documents, as I did with my war archives'. From 1971 to 1985, these documents were transferred to the National Archives by his son, Admiral Philippe de Gaulle.

Following the death of Admiral Philippe de Gaulle on 13 March 2024, his family wished to offer for sale a number of writings and personal memorabilia relating to de Gaulle. The auction was held at Artcurial in December 2024. Of the 372 lots offered for sale, more than a third (140) were pre-empted. The family still kept public documents, which were handed over to the National Archives. This is notably the case for the handwritten text of the appeal of 18 June 1940[32].

During his lifetime, Pompidou was concerned about the posterity of his papers, products, and receipts as head of state and, in this sense followed in his predecessor's footsteps. In the margin of a note on the Élysée Palace archives written in 1971 by Henri Domerg, his adviser on cultural affairs and brother-in-law, Pompidou mentioned that 'it is indeed necessary to collect the documents annotated by [his] hand, and to have them classified by a

---

30 The Rassemblement du peuple français (RPF) is a French political party founded by Charles de Gaulle in 1947 and dormant since 1955. Although it is often classified as right-wing, it refuses to see itself as part of the right-left divide and is the only party in the history of Gaullism launched by de Gaulle.

31 Private secretary to de Gaulle from 1945 to 1970.

32 Patrimoine du général de Gaulle : l'État préempte 140 lots sur 372 dans le cadre de la vente chez Artcurial : <https://www.culture.gouv.fr/fr/presse/communiques-de-presse/patrimoine-du-general-de-gaulle-l-etat-preempte-140-lots-sur-372-dans-le-cadre-de-la-vente-chez-artcurial> (accessed July 2025).

qualified person, submitting to him those for which he would have doubts about the advisability of giving archival status'.[33]

This note, written in March 1971, specifies that the documents fall into two categories: files from the Élysée Palace, and files from the General Secretariat of the Presidency of the Republic, defined as 'archives of the Presidency'. These are in fact political files relating to Pompidou's actions as head of state.

Measures were taken by the two successive *secrétaires généraux de la présidence de la République*, Michel Jobert[34] and Édouard Balladur[35], to set up this organisation, but at the time of Pompidou's death, they had not yet been fully implemented. With the help of former close associates such as François-Xavier Ortoli and Michel Jobert, Édouard Balladur organised the centralisation of files that had previously been kept by various individuals. An initial classification was carried out over several weeks. Balladur asked 'everyone to sort their files so that they could be handed over to the National Archives, and to write a note summarising Georges Pompidou's actions in the sector for which they were responsible'[36]. As Pompidou's death was sudden, only part of the archives was transferred to the National Archives. Given the urgency of the situation, some archives were left *in situ*, while others were taken away by the president's close associates.

Paradoxically, this chaotic situation had a beneficial effect on archives, not for those of Pompidou, but for those of his successors: in order to prevent this dispersal of public papers from happening again, the next president, Valéry Giscard d'Estaing, quickly created the post of archivist within the walls of the Élysée Palace. The role of the Élysée archivist is to manage the day-to-day

---

33 Archives nationales de France, AG/5(2)/1060. See also B. Fichet, N. Latte and V. Richard, 'Un matériau pour saisir l'histoire : le récit des archives de Georges Pompidou', in *Dans l'intimité du pouvoir de la présidence de Georges Pompidou* (Paris: Nouveau monde éditions, 2019), 265–71.

34 Michel Jobert was *directeur adjoint* (deputy chief of staff) then *directeur de cabinet* (chief of staff) for the prime minister (1963–1968), in addition to *secrétaire général de la présidence de la République* (1969–1973, secretary-general of the presidency of the French republic).

35 Édouard Balladur was *chargé de mission* then *conseiller technique* (technical adviser) in the cabinet of the prime minister (1963–1968), in addition to *secrétaire général adjoint* and then *secrétaire général de la présidence de la République* (1969–1974).

36 É. Balladur, *La Tragédie du pouvoir : le courage de Georges Pompidou* (Paris: Fayard, 2013), 276.

organisation of archives, and to prepare for their transfer to the National Archives, a sort of 'records management' before its time[37]! The Élysée archivist is in daily contact with the various departments at the Élysée, but also with the archivist in charge of the presidential archives at the National Archives (who is more concerned with long-term conservation)[38].

For Georges Pompidou, the problem resided in the incomplete nature of what had been collected by the National Archives in 1974, and in the dispersal of some of the files.

In 1989, two of Pompidou's former colleagues, Édouard Balladur and Pierre Messmer[39], decided to found the Association Georges Pompidou[40], with the support of Claude Pompidou[41]. This Association, recognised as being of public utility in 1993, preserves the memory of the political, economic, cultural and social actions of the former president[42].

From the very first months of the foundation's creation, one of its major missions was to encourage Pompidou's former colleagues who still had archives at home to hand them over to the National Archives. A collaboration between the National Archives and the Georges Pompidou Institute was established and has proven very fruitful.

Gradually, other former colleagues also handed over their papers to the National Archives, including Olivier Philip, Simonne Servais and Michel Woimant. Personal archives were also created for colleagues after Jean Daney de Marcillac[43], Édouard Balladur[44], and Henri Domerg[45] handed over their files[46].

---

37 The English term of 'records management' is used without translation by French archivists. It describes all measures designed to rationalise the production, sorting, conservation, and use of current and intermediate archives.

38 D. Farcis, 'La collecte des archives ministérielles : les «missions » des Archives nationales', *La Gazette des archives*, 119, (1982). 188–209.

39 Prime minister (1972–1974).

40 The Association became the Georges Pompidou Institute in 2014.

41 Claude Pompidou (1912–2007) was Georges Pompidou's widow.

42 <https://www.georges-pompidou.org/> (accessed July 2025).

43 Archives nationales de France : fonds 540 AP Jean Daney de Marcillac.

44 Archives nationales de France : fonds 543 AP Édouard Balladur.

45 Archives nationales de France : fonds 574 AP Henri Domerg.

46 For further information about the papers of colleagues, see B. Fichet et al., 'Un matériau', 270. All of the inventories for the archives of his colleagues are available online on the National Archives website.

In 1994, the Association launched an oral history programme on Pompidou and the changes in France in the 1960s and early 1970s[47]. The aim was to gather the testimonies of all colleagues, actors and witnesses, both French and foreign, who were contemporaries of Pompidou (1911–1974), and who played a decisive role during this period.

These interviews provide information on his youth and education, social circles, networks, convictions, and actions as a statesman. They also allow us to study the decision-making process, the workings of institutions, and French political life. The interviews cover various aspects of economic policy and social change, as well as international and defence issues. A final objective is to understand how contemporaries perceived Georges Pompidou and his actions[48].

An inventory of this work was published by the Archives nationales in 1996[49], describing 1,250 boxes. For Claude Pompidou, these documents reflect her husband's great capacity for work: 'He always wanted to know everything, to understand everything. The files he was given never seemed to contain enough information for him. He would annotate them in the margins, demand more details, and address words to that effect to his collaborators'[50].

For Jacques Chirac 'the archive of documents from his presidency, which was tragically interrupted in 1974, is an irreplaceable tool, and all the more precious because Georges Pompidou himself wrote a great deal, and annotated the documents submitted to him. Through the arid wording of archived documents, it is a working method, a vision of things, a certain idea of France that came to maturity with General de Gaulle, that is being expressed'.[51]

However, this inventory is far from marking the end of Pompidou's archive collections, for two main reasons. Firstly, because several former advisers close

---

47 There are over 170 recorded testimonies.

48 The interviews were digitised since 2010. They can be consulted at the Georges Pompidou Institute and the National Archives. For further information visit: <https://www.georges-pompidou.org/archives-orales-linstitut-pompidou> (accessed July 2025).

49 Bula and Obert, eds, *Archives*. This inventory has been updated since 1996. See the online inventory on the National Archives website : <https://www.siv.archives-nationales.culture.gouv.fr/siv/rechercheconsultation/consultation/ir/consultationIR.action?consIr=&frontIr=&optionFullText=&fullText=&defaultResultPerPage=&irId=FRAN_IR_005069&formCaller=GENERALISTE&gotoArchivesNums=false&auSeinIR=false&details=false&page=&udId=> (accessed July 2025).

50 Claude Pompidou, *L'Élan du cœur* (Paris: Tempus Perrin, 2018), 135.

51 Bula, Irigoin and Obert, eds, *Archives*.

to the president (or their families) have continued to hand over documents to the National Archives. Michel Jobert's archives were added very recently[52].

In addition, Claude Pompidou and her son, Professor Alain Pompidou, wished to entrust documents previously kept at their home, which led to the creation of a 'personal' collection (555 AP) distinguished from the 'presidential' collection (AG/5(2)).

The personal collection has grown steadily over the years[53], and complements the presidential collection. Although not very voluminous, it is of great historical value. It especially contains a diary, in the form of a notebook, covering the period from 1949 to 1953. It provides a wealth of information on the relationship between de Gaulle and Pompidou.

There is also abundant correspondence – maintained until his death – with his childhood friend Robert Pujol. Several literary manuscripts, both published and unpublished, are also worth mentioning. More unusually, the archives include objects with a strong symbolic charge, such as Pompidou's briefcase when he was prime minister, French and foreign decorations he received throughout his life, a stamp bearing his signature, and a pendant-medallion containing the code for nuclear weapons, which he wore until his death. The same complementarity exists in the field of photography. There are photographic reports produced by the services of the presidency, as well as boxes of family photographs, and frames containing prints of particular value, such as these two autographed portraits of de Gaulle, each containing a few personal words addressed to Pompidou in 1946 and 1954.

Fifty years after Pompidou's death, it would be tempting to consider that knowledge of his archives is a closed subject. On the contrary, the additional collections made in recent months show that this corpus has continued to grow over time.

The collection of presidential archives has evolved since the presidency of Valéry Giscard d'Estaing. In addition to the appointment of an archivist at

---

[52] Archives nationales de France : Fonds 89 AJ Michel Jobert.

[53] Archives nationales de France, fonds 555 AP Georges Pompidou : <https://www.siv.archives-nationales.culture.gouv.fr/siv/rechercheconsultation/consultation/ir/consultationIR.action?consIr=&frontIr=&optionFullText=&fullText=&defaultResultPerPage=&irId=FRAN_IR_057928&formCaller=GENERALISTE&gotoArchivesNums=false&auSeinIR=false&details=false&page=&udId=> (accessed July 2025).

the Élysée Palace, the president was the first to sign a 'deposit contract', on 25 October 1979[54]. Although the term had no legal basis, it was extended to ministerial cabinets in the 1980s[55].

It represents a new method that encourages the release of public documents: the *protocoles de remise* (also known as *protocoles de versement*) recognise the public nature of the documents produced, putting an end to the system of private deposit that had prevailed since the 1960s. However, the signatory retains a right of access to the documents deposited. In addition, any access by a third party is subject to the agreement of the signatory, for a period that generally varies from 30 to 60 years. The aim of the protocol is to ensure the collection of funds of major interest for the history of the Fifth, namely by establishing a relationship of trust with their producers. To achieve this, the archivists working in the ministries raise awareness as soon as the members of government take office.

Paradoxically, the trauma of Pompidou's sudden death led to the adoption of new measures to ensure the better collection of archives from subsequent presidents: the appointment of an archivist at the Élysée and the signing of a protocol are two major tools that have enabled the National Archives to preserve many important documents for the political history of the Fifth Republic.

How are the Archives of the Presidents of the French Republic Organised?

The organisation of presidential archives is itself a result of how the presidency operates.

During the Third and Fourth Republics, a dozen or so people formed the president's 'House' and were responsible for providing him with information on domestic and foreign policy, and for the presidency's relations with the government, Parliament, the press, and the French people.

---

54 P. Canavaggio, 'Apparition d'une pratique *contra legem* : le cas des protocoles', in Cornu et al., eds, *1979*, 457–76.

55 The law on archives of 15 July 2008 retroactively recognises the validity of previous protocols. Beginning with Valéry Giscard d'Estaing and up through the present, all French presidents, prime ministers and ministers have signed a protocol.

Under the Fifth Republic, de Gaulle reorganised the presidency[56], setting the number of staff at around forty, and establishing a hierarchical distribution of their functions. The Élysée henceforth consisted of a Secrétariat Général (General Secretariat), a cabinet, an État-major particulier (military staff of the president), and a Secrétariat général pour la Communauté et les Affaires africaines et malgaches (General Secretariat for the Community and African and Malagasy Affairs)[57].

The Secrétariat Général was created in January 1959. Its main function was to inform the president and make his point of view known to members of the government. Under the authority of the Secrétariat Général, it consisted of four *conseillers techniques*, each responsible for a major sector of government activity (foreign affairs, legal affairs, the economy, social affairs and national education), and a dozen *chargés de mission*. The role of the cabinet was to regulate the day-to-day activities of the Élysée Palace, organise the president's schedule, and attend to his letters. In the military sphere, the État-major particulier assumed the functions of the Secrétariat Général. As for the Secrétariat général pour la Communauté et les Affaires africaines et malgaches[58], it acted as a specialised office and handled the president's personal relations with African and Malagasy heads of state.

Georges Pompidou adopted a different structure, set out in the decree of 20 June 1969 on appointments to the office of president[59]. The Secrétariat Général formed a single unit consisting of the *secrétaire général* (secretary-general) and *secrétaire général adjoint* (deputy secretary-general)[60], the head of the État-major particulier, the *chef de cabinet*, the head of the Secrétariat particulier, the *conseillers techniques* and *chargés de mission*, members of the État-major particulier, and *aides de camp*.

The division of the Secrétariat Général into four main sectors disappeared, and the *chargés de mission* reported either to *conseillers techniques* or directly

56 Bula, Irigoin, and Obert, eds, *Archives*, 11.

57 It was abolished by decree on 21 June 1974.

58 This service has been the subject of a specific inventory: *Archives du Secrétariat général des Affaires africaines et malgaches et de la Communauté (1958–1974)*, P. Geneste and J.-P. Bat, eds., Archives nationales, 2015.

59 Ibid., 12. In French : 'arrêté portant nominations à la présidence de la République'. Published in the *Journal officiel* on 21 June 1969.

60 These positions had not existed during the previous seven-year term.

to the *secrétaire général*. Only the *conseillers techniques* responsible for economic and financial affairs, foreign affairs, social affairs, and administrative affairs had a *chargé de mission* reporting to them. For example, Jean Daney de Marcillac, who was a *chargé de mission*, worked closely with Jean-René-Bernard, *conseiller technique* for financial affairs. Michel Freyche, *conseiller technique* for financial affairs, the economy and planning, worked with Charles Wiener de Croisset, *chargé de mission*. The *chargés de mission* for diplomatic matters were Jean-Bernard Raimond until May 1970, Jean-Louis Lucet until April 1974, and Alfred Siefer-Gaillardin from July 1973 to May 1974. They reported to *conseiller technique* Georges Gaucher from June 1969 to April 1970, Jean-Bernard Raimond from May 1970 to December 1973, and Gabriel Robin from December 1973 to April 1974. François Lavondès, *conseiller technique* for social and administrative affairs, had Gilbert Carrère, Gilbert Masson and Jean-Marie Robert reporting to him in succession.

The activities of the presidency have been carried out up to the present day at the Élysée Palace, the residence of presidents since Louis-Napoléon Bonaparte[61]. The mansions at 2 and 14 rue de l'Élysée, acquired by de Gaulle to house the État-major particulier and the Secrétariat général pour la Communauté et les Affaires africaines et malgaches. The hotel at 23 rue de Marigny was acquired under Georges Pompidou to accommodate distinguished foreign guests. The Alma palace at 11 quai Branly housed the Conseil Supérieur de la Magistrature. In addition to the Élysée Palace, the presidential residences include the Rambouillet castle, used for international meetings, the Pavillon de Marly, used for presidential hunting, and the Fort de Brégançon, the head of state's holiday destination.[62]

The presidency is still a special institution; it does not have its own budget and staff like a ministry[63]. The appropriations for the presidency are included in the Finance Act, in the common charges section of the budget of the

---

61 The Élysée Palace has been the official Parisian residence of presidents since the law of 12 December 1848. Built in the eighteenth century for the Count of Évreux, this private mansion, set between courtyard and garden, is characteristic of the architecture of its period. It has undergone modifications and name changes with each successive owner. Now a presidential residence, it has continually been refurbished.

62 For more information on French presidential residences: F. Oppermann, *Dans les châteaux de la République. Le pouvoir à l'abri des regards* (Paris: Tallandier, 2019).

63 Bula, Irigoin, and Obert, eds., *Archives*, 13.

Ministry of Finance; the *directeur de cabinet* is the authorising officer for expenditure, which is carried out directly by the chief financial officer of the presidency, who reports to him. These appropriations were set at a very low level by de Gaulle and, despite adjustments, still covered less than 10 % of the actual expenditure of the Élysée under Pompidou. Most of the expenditure is covered by other government departments: for example, the acquisition of the buildings allocated to the presidency is the responsibility of the Domaines[64], while maintenance and works are the responsibility of the Ministry of Culture. Similarly, almost all of the staff – several hundred people – are *mis à disposition* (made available) to the presidency by their original administration, which continues to pay their salaries and manage their careers.

The archives transferred by the presidency are organised according to a filing plan that broadly follows the hierarchical order set out in the decree of 20 June 1969 organising the departments of the presidency. I will not present all of the services but will focus primarily on the archives that are useful for understanding the bilateral relationship between France and the United Kingdom[65].

The Secrétariat Général of the Pompidou presidency included a team of collaborators, most of whom had already assisted him at Matignon. The Secrétariat Général set up by President Pompidou included the *secrétaire général* – Michel Jobert from 1969 to April 1973, then Édouard Balladur – in addition to approximately ten *conseillers techniques* and *chargés de mission*. A *secrétaire général adjoint* was also appointed: Édouard Balladur from 1969 to April 1973, and Jean-René Bernard from May 1973. The number of *conseillers techniques* increased from five in 1969 to nine in 1974. The chargés de mission reported either to a *conseiller technique* or directly to the *secrétaire général*. The total number of staff, around twenty, remained stable over these five years.

Assisted by the *secrétaire général adjoint*, the *secrétaire général* is the president's privileged collaborator: this individual receives information addressed to the president from the *conseillers techniques* and *chargés de mission*, and

64 The *Domaines* or *Service des Domaines* is the former name for the *Direction de l'Immobilier de l'État*. It is a department of the Ministry of the Economy and Finance, under the supervisory authority of the *Direction Générale des Finances Publiques* (DGFiP). It defines and implements the state's policy for its real property and public establishments and is responsible for interministerial governance.

65 For a complete view of the classification plan, see ibid. 9–10.

coordinates their work, providing his opinion on the decisions that the president is required to take; the individual provides a link between the Élysée Palace and the prime minister by representing the head of state on interministerial committees, and by preparing the agenda for the Council of Ministers with the *secrétaire général du gouvernement*.

The practice of holding *conseils restreints* (restricted councils), which President Auriol used for foreign policy issues, was taken up by de Gaulle and extended by Pompidou. These councils, which were not provided for in the 1958 Constitution, were convened when the president wished to examine certain information in greater depth, prepare a summit meeting, or give impetus to certain sectors of activity; it was here that the bulk of presidential decisions were prepared, the Council of Ministers having lost its role under the Fifth Republic as the privileged body to which matters were submitted for discussion. The restricted councils under the chairmanship of the head of state were attended by the prime minister, the *secrétaire général de la présidence de la République*, the *secrétaire général du gouvernement*, very often the minister of finance, as well as ministers and senior civil servants chosen for the agenda. A *conseiller technique* or *chargé de mission* was responsible for drawing up the record of decisions signed by the president.

The files drawn up by the diplomatic advisers in place from 1969 to 1974 – Georges Gaucher, Jean-Louis Lucet, Jean-Bernard Raimond, and Gabriel Robin[66] – generally consist, for each country, of correspondence exchanged between the president and foreign heads of state or government, and reports of the president's meetings with political figures: this series also includes meetings with members of the government, mainly the prime minister and the minister of foreign affairs, along with senior civil servants.

---

66 Archives nationales de France, AG/5(2)/103–127. These documents are entirely complementary to those kept in AG/5(2)/1009–1039. For the relationship between Sir Edward Heath and Georges Pompidou, see AG/5(2)/107 dossier 5, AG/5(2)/108, AG/5(2)/1014, AG/5(2)/1015. We have the boxes containing the president's own documents, with the minutes of the various meetings between Heath and Pompidou. It is in these boxes that we find the original letters sent by Heath to Pompidou, and a copy of those sent by Pompidou. For example, on 29 October 1971 Pompidou wrote to congratulate the United Kingdom on its entry into the Common Market, and Heath sent a reply. We also have a letter from Heath to Pompidou after his visit to Paris in May 1971.

The Élysée did not have an independent protocol department[67], but a 'branch' of the Ministry of Foreign Affairs consisting of three foreign affairs officials responsible for organising the president's official trips to Paris and the provinces (scouting locations, accompanying the president). This department also prepared the receptions given by the head of state during official trips abroad, as well as official visits to France by foreign dignitaries. It was also responsible for receiving VIPs, organising official meals and receptions, and extending invitations to presidential hunting parties. As for the series for lunches, dinners, and receptions, they constitute a sort of 'diary' for the president, alternating between events of a purely ceremonial nature, and those of a more political nature: Pompidou's frequent lunches in the company of journalists and personalities representing different sectors of the country's activities were a means of information and maintaining contact with the French people, as well as an opportunity to signal his opinion or intentions on certain domestic policy issues.

Finally, mention should be made of the photographic coverage of the presidency. At first, photographic coverage was provided exclusively by the central photographic service of the Ministry of the Interior, and by the Central Service of Judicial Identity under the Third Republic and early Fourth Republic. From September 1952, the daily monitoring of the activities of the head of state was taken over, under the mandate of René Coty, by the photographic service of the presidency, which was created at the time.

Pompidou's presidency was marked by several particularities. The photographic service still used black and white film, as it had under previous presidencies, but there were the first tests using colour slides, with forty colour format negatives during Pompidou's trip to Togo (22–24 November 1972).

The volume of photographs is very large: the photographic department of the Élysée Palace took a total of 26,804 photographs, a very marked increase due primarily to advances in the media used. The collection includes 704 reports between 20 June 1969 and 2 April 1974.

[67] Archives nationales de France, AG/5(2)/644–779. For the relationship between Sir Edward Heath and Georges Pompidou, see AG/5(2)/672 dossier 1, AG/5(2)/691 dossier, AG/5(2)/722, AG/5(2)/738. These files contain many details on the organisation of meetings between Heath and Pompidou. For example, the constitution of the French delegation in November 1972 is annotated by Édouard Balladur. We also have the booklet detailing the programme.

Lastly, the main change in how the photographic service operated under Pompidou's presidency was that it followed the president on his travels abroad, and no longer just in France, whereas under René Coty and de Gaulle, the Elysée used private photographic agencies for these reports abroad, or received souvenir albums from the inviting powers.

The expanded scope of the department's activities under Pompidou also helps to explain the net increase in the number of photographs taken during his term of office. For example, according to this collection, there are only a few shots taken by the Chine nouvelle agency during talks with Mao Tse Tung in Peking, China on 12 September 1973.

We have photographic coverage of official presidential trips taken by the Elysée service itself. Of particular note are the photographs taken in Great Britain (Chequers Manor) for the signing of the Channel Tunnel Treaty on 17 November 1973[68].

There are also a great many photographs in the personal collection (fonds 555 AP), totalling approximately 10,000 images. This is the personal collection built up by Georges and Claude Pompidou. It includes a large number of diplomatic gifts as well.

The reports from the Pompidou presidency have all been digitised and are available on the National Archives website[69]. The same applies to other presidents.

The relationship between Sir Edward Heath and Georges Pompidou offers an instructive view of how presidential archives are organised, and how to search them[70].

---

68 For the relationship between Sir Edward Heath and Georges Pompidou, see AG/5(2)/979, AG/5(2)/982, AG/5(2)/983 (photographs online on the website of the National Archives).

69 Reportages photographiques de la présidence de Georges Pompidou (1969–1974): <https://www.siv.archives-nationales.culture.gouv.fr/siv/rechercheconsultation/consultation/ir/consultationIR.action?consIr=&frontIr=&optionFullText=&fullText=&defaultResultPerPage=&irId=FRAN_IR_055457&formCaller=GENERALISTE&gotoArchivesNums=false&auSeinIR=false&details=false&page=&udId=> (accessed July 2025).

70 See also Archives nationales de France AG/5(2)/1040 for the Militaries Affaires, fonds supprimer 86AJ/115, 86AJ/118–120, 86AJ/122 and fonds Édouard Balladur 543AP/32.

Conclusion

'Happy people do not have a history, so I hope historians have little to say about my mandate' Pompidou said to a journalist from *Paris Match* in June 1969. Fifty years after his death, it is clear that historians still have many questions to answer, not because the French were unhappy, but because the preserved archives allow us to say a lot!

If the premature death of the president raised fears of the definitive disappearance of his presidential papers, this was not the case thanks to the involvement of his colleagues and friends who worked on their collections – especially in collaboration with the Georges Pompidou Institute – and allowed their entry and conservation in the National Archives.

The Pompidolian period, as well as that of his successor Valéry Giscard d'Estaing, was one in which new methods for collecting archives were forged, the benefits of which we can still be appreciated today[71].

Bibliography

Babelon, Jean-Pierre, *Les archives, mémoire de la France* (Paris: Gallimard, 2008).

Balladur, Édouard, *La Tragédie du pouvoir : le courage de Georges Pompidou* (Paris: Fayard, 2013).

Bétard, Daphné, 'Les archives sous tension', *Le Journal des Arts*, 2 October 2012.

Béchu, Claire, ed., *Les Archives nationales, des lieux pour l'histoire de France* (Paris: Somogy, 2008).

Braibant, Guy, *Les Archives en France*, Rapport remis au Premier ministre, La documentation française, 1996.

Bula, Sandrine, Janine Irigoin and Caroline Obert, *Archives de la présidence de la République, Ve République : Georges Pompidou (19 juin 1969–2 avril 1974)*, (La documentation française, 1996).

Canavaggio, Perrine, 'Apparition d'une pratique *contra legem* : le cas des protocoles' in Cornu et al., eds, *1979*, 457–76.

71 My warmest thanks to Nicky Bernhard, Neil W. Malloy and Marie Ranquet for their advice in preparing this contribution.

Cornu, Marie, Christine Nougaret, Yann Potin, Bruno Ricard, and Noé Wagener, eds, *1979 Genèse d'une loi sur les archives*, (La documentation française, 2019).
Duclert, Vincent, 'République et archives', *Revue française d'administration publique* 102, 'La mémoire de l'administration', (2002).
Even, Nicole, ed., *Archives de la présidence de la République, Ve République : Général de Gaulle (1959–1969)*, Archives nationales, 2012.
Farcis, Daniel, 'La collecte des archives ministérielles : les «missions » des Archives nationales', *La Gazette des archives*, 119, (1982).
Fichet, Bénédicte, Noémie Latte and Vivien Richard, 'Un matériau pour saisir l'histoire : le récit des archives de Georges Pompidou', in *Dans l'intimité du pouvoir de la présidence de Georges Pompidou* (Paris: Nouveau monde éditions, 2019).
Guyotjeannin, Olivier and Yann Potin, 'La fabrique de la perpétuité : le trésor des chartes et les archives du royaume, XIIIe-XIXe s.', *Revue de synthèse. Fabrique des archives, fabrique de l'histoire*, 5th series (2004).
Monnier, Sophie, 'Les archives, une affaire d'État', *Revue du droit public* 6 (2020).
Oppermann, Fabien, *Dans les châteaux de la République. Le pouvoir à l'abri des regards* (Paris: Tallandier, 2019).
Taillemite, Étienne, 'Quelques souvenirs de trente-sept ans aux Archives', *Hommage à Jean Favier* (Paris: Fayard, 1986).

Appendix

The Edward Heath archives conserved at the Bodleian Libraries

The following information is taken from the Bodleian website[1].

The archive was purchased by the Bodleian Libraries in 2011 from the Sir Edward Heath Charitable Foundation, with help from the National Heritage Memorial Fund and Friends of the Bodleian.

Prior to its relocation to the Bodleian Libraries, the archive was physically stored at Sir Edward Heath's former residence, Arundells, Cathedral Close, Salisbury, Wiltshire, SP1 2EN.

Collection overview

The collection consists of approximately 4,500 boxes, and includes personal and family correspondence, diaries, scrapbooks, printed ephemera and photographs relating to most aspects of Heath's personal and family life, including wartime service, early post-War employment (with the exception of his period of employment with the Civil Service and banking), and political career.

---

1 <https://archives.bodleian.ox.ac.uk/repositories/2/resources/13043>, consulted July 2025.

Beginning in 1965 and spanning the period of Heath's premiership up through 2004, the majority of the material appears to have been collected and filed on Heath's behalf by his Private Office staff, and it is clear that all aspects of his life were administered to some degree by his Private Office. For instance, correspondence and meeting requests were routinely intercepted by the Private Office staff. Although Heath's personal opinions and commentary are still often evident, they are not always possible to disentangle from those of his Private Office.

Heath's political career makes up approximately 60 % of the collection, although much more survives from his period as a backbench MP after 1975 than for his periods as a Minister and Prime Minister, most likely because most of the material created in those roles was transferred to The National Archives. While the political papers component of the Heath Archive reflects the party-related and political aspects of his roles, there is also much to do with policymaking, including when he was in Government. A substantial portion (approximately 20 %) of the political papers consists of correspondence with members of the public, most of which was dealt with on Heath's behalf by his Private Office.

During the 1990s, when Heath was writing his memoirs, gaps in his own archive were often filled with photocopies from other relevant archives, including collections held by The National Archive, the Churchill Archives Centre, and the Bodleian Library.

A small portion (less than 1 %) of the Heath Archive consists of audio-visual and born-digital material.

These boxes contain a rich and diverse collection of papers from his time in office and the shadow cabinet, as well as personal papers from his early life as an undergraduate at Balliol College, along with his active role in student politics during the 1930s.

The archive has great research potential, as it offers a range of primary sources for scholars and students with an interest in twentieth-century history and politics. Biographers will also be able to reveal less-known aspects of Heath's private life, such as his distinguished war service, and his passion for music and sailing.

Arrangement

The arrangement of the archive essentially reflects the one imposed by staff at Heath's Private Office when the material was *in situ* at his residence,

Arundells, in Salisbury, Wiltshire, where it was reorganised and listed during the 1990s.

With minimal re-arrangement, the archive has been (or will be) catalogued into fifteen key series as detailed below, which aim to represent a thematic approach to Heath's career:

1. A: Personal and Family Papers
2. B: Political Papers: Pre-Parliament (to 1950)
3. C: Political Papers: Bexley and Sidcup constituency matters (1946–2001)
4. D: Political Papers: Ministerial and Shadow Ministerial (1951–1965)
5. E: Political Papers: Leader of the Opposition (1965–1970)
6. F: Political Papers: Prime Minister (1970–1974) and Leader of the Opposition (1974–1975)
7. G: Political Papers: Backbench MP (1975–2001) and Retirement (2001–2004)
8. H: Articles, Broadcasts, Speeches, Press releases and Press cuttings
9. J: Memoirs and Literary Works
10. K: Charitable Work; Music and the Arts
11. L: Photographs
12. M: Published/Printed Material
13. N: Business Interests
14. O: Audio-visual Material
15. P: Born-digital Material

Related materials

For Heath's periods as Leader of the Opposition between 1965 and 1970 and 1974 and 1975, there is much overlap with material held as part of the Conservative Party Archive, also at the Bodleian Library.

The National Archives also holds material relating to Sir Edward Heath as follows:

1. Minister of Labour (1959–1960): series LAB 77/4 and LAB 77/5
2. Lord Privy Seal (1960–1963): Series FO 800
3. Prime Minister (1970–1974): series PREM 15, PREM 5/510 and PREM 5/511

The catalogue of the Edward Heath Archive is available online. This is the second edition and further material will be added in subsequent editions as a result of ongoing cataloguing work. The original finding aid edited by Jeremy McIlwaine with contributions by Rachael Gardner (2016), Iram Sadar (2018), Carl Cooper (2018), Ben Peirson-Smith (2018), Alice McDonald (2018), Kelly Burchmore (2018) and Miten Mistry (2018).

A presentation of the Edward Heath archives was organised prior to the study day at the Bodleian Library, at which documents illustrating his relationship with Georges Pompidou were presented.

Testimony by Juliet Campbell

As a non-academic, I hesitate to intervene. But as a junior diplomat, I was in the room for most of the negotiations surrounding the UK's first application for entry into the European Communities in 1961–63, and I must be one of the few people still alive who was actually there.

I remember the final meeting, when Couve de Murville confirmed that what de Gaulle had said in his press conference meant the end of negotiations. I think it was the same day that Heath summoned a meeting of the British delegation to discuss what had happened. He ended his analysis by saying that in applying to join the EEC, the British Government had hoped membership would reinvigorate the British economy, but that we would now have to do so exclusively using our own resources. He also said that Britain would not be able to join until de Gaulle had died.

I remember the attitudes of the time more clearly than the details of the negotiation itself. Working in the Foreign Office in the late 1950s, I was struck by how quickly officials changed tack when Macmillan decided to pursue entry. The efforts to outflank the EEC using tactics such as the creation of EFTA were quickly replaced by genuine excitement about the entry negotiations. I think it was true that throughout much of my career, the French were regarded as our chief antagonist, enemy almost, within the Communities. Some of this had its roots in the first negotiations. The FO did not initially have a big pool of European specialists, and it was the people who bore the scars of 1963 who continued to be involved. They took special pleasure in scoring off the French.

There certainly was a widespread belief, on both sides of the Channel, that joining the EEC would help solve Britain's economic problems, just as the original Six had prospered after the Community was first established, in a kind of halo effect. But as we have just been reminded, Britain ran into strong economic headwinds, and the first years of membership were very difficult.

Notes on Contributors

Juliet Campbell CMG (1935) is a British diplomat and former university administrator. After studying at Oxford, she joined the Foreign and Commonwealth Office (FCO) in 1957, specialising in European affairs with postings in Brussels and Paris, as well as Bangkok, The Hague, and Jakarta. From 1988 to 1991, she served as the UK Ambassador to Luxembourg. In 1992, she became Mistress of Girton College, Cambridge, and later member of the University Council, retiring in 1998. In 2023, she published her memoirs on her diplomatic and academic career.

Anne Deighton is Emeritus Professor at the University of Oxford in the Department of Politics and International Relations and is also a member of the university's History Faculty. She currently holds a Leverhulme Emeritus Research grant (number EM-2021-060) and has published extensively on British foreign policy and European security. She has held a Jean Monnet *ad personam* chair, along with visiting professorships in France (Paris, I, III, IV, and Sciences Po), Germany, Switzerland, and Belgium. In addition, she has served on the Council and Executive Committee of Chatham House, London, and been a member of the European Union Liaison Committee of Historians.

Marie-Claude Esposito is Emeritus Professor at Sorbonne Nouvelle-Paris 3 and is a member of the research team 'Integration and Cooperation in the European Area (ICEA)'. She has published several books and many articles on the British economy, with particular emphasis on banking and financial topics. Her featured publications for the 'Franco-British relations and Europe, from membership of the EEC to Brexit' Conference (Maison Française d'Oxford, 17 May 2024) are: "La politique économique des gouvernements conservateurs d'Edward Heath, 1970–1974", in Stéphane Porion (dir.), *Le Royaume-Uni à l'épreuve de la crise 1970–1974*, (Atlande, 2017); and "Britain Joining the European Economic Community: The Pompidou-Heath Summit, 20–21 May 1971", in Stéphane Porion (dir.), *Fresh Perspertives on the UK in Crisis 1979–1979* (Atlande, 2017).

Bénédicte Fichet is a Heritage Curator at the National Archives of France (Paris), where she is in charge of the archives for prime ministers, in addition to the public and personal archives of Georges Pompidou. She contributed to the exhibition catalogue *68: Les archives du pouvoir. Chroniques inédites d'un État face à la crise* (Éditions de l'Iconoclaste, 2018), as well as the collective work *Dans l'intimité du pouvoir de la présidence de Georges Pompidou* (Nouveau Monde Éditions, 2019). She also contributed to the *Dictionnaire Pompidou* (Robert Laffont, 2024), and is a member of the Scientific Advisory Board of the Institut Georges Pompidou.

Daniel Furby is Lecturer at the European Law and Governance School, part of the European Public Law Organization in Athens. His research focuses on UK foreign policy since 1945, with a specific focus on UK policies towards European integration and international organisations. He completed his doctorate on the UK's accession to the European Community at Queen Mary University of London. He has also worked as a Brussels-based analyst of contemporary European affairs, including the euro crisis and Brexit.

Boris Hamzeian is an architect, the holder of a PhD (École Polytechnique Fédérale de Lausanne), and Associate Professor at the École Nationale Supérieure d'Architecture de Saint-Étienne (ENSASE). After completing his doctoral thesis on the history of the Centre Pompidou, he joined the institution as co-head for the conservation and promotion of one of its heritage collections, as an adviser to the 2025–2030 transformation project, and as the editor of a series of books on the Centre's history (published by Actar Publishers, Lettera Ventidue, Presses Universitaires de Saint-Étienne, and Éditions du Centre Pompidou). His research on technomorphic and neo-avant-garde architecture has led to publications on the work of Renzo

Piano, Richard Rogers, UFO, Aldo Rossi, Ugo La Pietra, and Rem Koolhaas. He curated the exhibition *UFO, Performer l'Architecture* (FRAC Centre-Val de Loire), and served as scientific adviser to Le Fil Rouge: Renzo Piano Building Workshop (Architecture Gallery, Columbia University). His research has been supported by the Swiss National Science Foundation and the Italian Council and has been recognised by awards from the Académie d'Architecture (France) and the Institut Georges Pompidou.

Beatrice Heuser is Distinguished Professor at the Free University of Brussels (VUB) and heads the Strategy Section at the Bundeswehr Command and Staff College in Hamburg. She has previously held professorships at the Department of War Studies, King's College London, and at the Universities of Reading and Glasgow. She holds degrees from the University of London (BA, MA) and the University of Oxford (DPhil), in addition to a Habilitation (professorial thesis) from the Philipps-University of Marburg. She has also taught at Sciences Po in Paris, as well as Sorbonne, Assas, Paris VI, and Reims Universities, along with two universities in Germany. From 1997–1998, she worked in the International Staff at NATO headquarters in Brussels. Between 2003 and 2007, she served as Director for Research at the Military History Research Office of the Bundeswehr in Potsdam. She has worked primarily on war – see her *WAR: A Genealogy of Western Ideas and Practices* (2022) – and on aspects of strategy, including her books *Reading Clausewitz* (2002), *Strategy before Clausewitz* (2017), and *The Evolution of Strategy* (2010), which covers the period from Antiquity to the Present. She has specifically focused on nuclear strategy, in addition to insurgency and counterinsurgency strategy. Her most recent book is *Flawed Strategy: Why Smart Leaders Make Bad Decisions* (Polity, 2025).

Guillaume Lacroix is a French diplomat. He has served in various capacities in Dar es Salaam, Washington, and Brussels. From 2017 to 2021, he served as Consul General in Chicago for the Midwest region. From 2021 to 2025, he was posted at the Embassy of France in London.

N. Piers Ludlow is Professor of International History at the London School of Economics, where he has taught since 1998. His main research interests are the history of European integration and Britain's problematic relationship with it. His next book will be a study of Britain's four and a half decades of Community membership, from 1973 to 2016.

Stéphane Porion is Senior Lecturer in British Studies at the University of Tours (France) and a researcher at ICD (EA 6297). He completed a PhD on Enoch Powell's political and economic ideas (1946–1968) at the University of Sorbonne-Nouvelle (Paris, France). His research focuses on Conservative political and economic thought from 1945 to the present. He co-edited a book in French with Louise Dalingwater on the British Conservative Party in the 2010s (Presses du Septentrion, 2023) and a special issue with Catherine Marshall on 'One nation conservatism from Disraeli to Johnson' (*Revue Française de Civilisation Britannique*, 2023).

Olivier Sibre is director of Studies and Research at the Institut Georges Pompidou and seminar lecturer in international relations (Modern Asia) at Sorbonne University. He is the holder of an *agrégation* and completed a PhD in modern history at Sorbonne University in 2008. In 2012, he published *Le Saint-Siège et l'Extrême-Orient (Chine, Corée, Japon) de Léon XIII à Pie XII* (Collection de l'École Française de Rome, Prix Jean Sainteny de l'Académie des sciences morales et politiques). His research focuses on international relations, religion, and politics, the Holy See as a global player in the international system (governance, formal and informal players, conflicts, peace, and mediation), Europe, Asia-Pacific, education, assistance, and humanitarian action. He is a member of the UMR SIRICE, the ArchivesPie12 program, and the ANR GlobalVat project at l'École Française de Rome. As the scientific secretary of the EHNE labex (Écrire une Histoire Nouvelle de l'Europe), and later as director of studies and research at the Institut Georges Pompidou, he published on Europe and the history of the Trente Glorieuses (Christine Manigand, Olivier Sibre, *Le dictionnaire Pompidou*, Robert Laffont, 2024). His two most recent publications are the chapters 'Rooting the Fifth Republic, Georges Pompidou (1969–1974)' and 'The Holy See and the New World: Asia-Pacific (1945–1953)', published by Palgrave Macmillan and Berghahn Books.

Agnès Tachin is Lecturer in Contemporary History at CY Cergy Paris Université and a member of the Héritages-Culture/, Patrimoine/s, Création/s research laboratory (UMR 9022). Her research focuses on international relations, the history of representations, and the Fifth Republic. She has published *Ami est rivale. La Grande-Bretagne dans l'imaginaire français à l'époque gaullienne.1958–1959* (P.I.E. Lang 2009), edited the book *Le temps du voyage. Les déplacements internationaux des chefs d'État et de gouvernement XXe–XXIe siècle contemporaine* (P.I.E. Lang

2022), and, more recently, a special feature entitled 'Chasse et représentations (XIX–XXIe siècle)' in *Les cahiers d'Agora : revue en Humanité* (no. 7, 2023).

Cesare Vagge (Genoa, 1995) completed his DPhil in Modern European History at Merton College, Oxford, in May 2024. His doctoral research, supervised by Professor Martin Conway, focused on the institutional and strategic evolution of French and Italian industrial policy from the late interwar period to the creation of the European Economic Community (EEC). From April 2024 to June 2025, he worked as Postdoctoral Research Assistant to Professor Andrew Thompson CBE at the University of Oxford. In this capacity, he contributed to drafting the final report of the Global Commission on Modern Slavery, led by former British Prime Minister Baroness Theresa May of Maidenhead. Beginning in October 2025, he will serve as a Postdoctoral Researcher at Nuffield College, Oxford.

Collection Georges Pompidou

Série Archives

La série Archives est consacrée à la publication de volumes thématiques représentatifs de l'action de Georges Pompidou. Les documents sont essentiellement issus des archives de la présidence de la République. Ils se composent de comptes rendus d'entretiens, de notes de collaborateurs, de correspondances, d'interventions dans la presse, etc. Pour l'essentiel, ces publications couvrent la période 1962-1968, où Georges Pompidou fut le Premier ministre du général de Gaulle, et la période 1969-1974, durant laquelle Georges Pompidou fut président de la République française. Chaque volume est mis en œuvre par un universitaire et un chargé de recherches de l'Institut Georges Pompidou, qui proposent des analyses inédites de chacun de ces documents. La série est placée sous le patronage conjoint de l'Institut Georges Pompidou, par l'intermédiaire de son conseil scientifique, et des Archives nationales.

Série Études

La série Études propose des monographies ainsi que des ouvrages collec- tifs issus de colloques scientifiques organisés par l'Institut Georges Pompidou consacrés à un domaine de l'action de ce dernier. Ces travaux de grande qualité rassemblent contributions scientifiques et interventions de témoins majeurs ayant été associés à l'action de l'ancien président de la République française.

Directrice de collection : *Christine Manigand,*
Présidente du Conseil scientifique de l'Institut Georges Pompidou

Dans la série Archives

N° 1 Gilles Le Béguec et Frédéric Turpin, *Georges Pompidou et les institutions de la Ve République*, 2006, 281 p, ISBN 978-90-5201-056-4

N° 2 Gilbert Noël et Émilie Willaert, *Georges Pompidou, une certaine idée de la modernité agricole et rurale*, 2007, 481 p, ISBN 978-90-5201-057-1

N° 3 Bernard Lachaise, Jean-Paul Cointet et Sabrina Tricaud, *Georges Pompidou et les élections (1962-1974)*, 2008, 342 p, ISBN 978-90-5201-336-7

N° 4 Éric Bussière et Émilie Willaert, *Un projet pour l'Europe. Georges Pompidou et la construction européenne*, 2010, 447 p, ISBN 978-90-5201- 596-5

N° 5 Élisa Capdevila et Jean-François Sirinelli, *Georges Pompidou et la culture*, 2011, 253 p, ISBN 978-90-5201-685-6

N° 6 Sylvain Schirmann et Sarah Mohamed-Gaillard, *Georges Pompidou et l'Allemagne*, 2012, 408 p, ISBN 978-90-5201-058-8

N° 7 Éric Bussière et Pauline Massis Desmarest, *François-Xavier Ortoli et l'Europe : réflexion et action*, 2016, 267 p, ISBN 978-2-8076-0007-2

Dans la série Études

N° 1 Bernard Lachaise, Gilles Le Béguec et Frédéric Turpin (dir), *Georges Pompidou, directeur de cabinet du général de Gaulle. Juin 1958 – Janvier 1959*, 2006 (2e tirage 2006), 183 p, ISBN 90-5201-316-0

N° 2 Pascal Griset (dir), *Georges Pompidou et la modernité. Les tensions de l' innovation, 1962-1974*, 2006, 315 p, ISBN 90-5201-329-2

N° 3 Gilbert Noël et Émilie Willaert (dir), *Georges Pompidou et le monde des campagnes, 1962-1974*, 2007, 347 p, ISBN 978-90-5201-357-2

N° 4 Bernard Lachaise et Sabrina Tricaud (dir), *Georges Pompidou et Mai 1968*, 2009, 201 p, ISBN 978-90-5201-468-5

N° 5 Éric Bussière, François Dubasque, Robert Frank et Nicolas Vaicbourdt (dir), *Georges Pompidou et les États-Unis. Une « relation spéciale » 1969- 1974*, 2013, 238 p, ISBN 978-90-5201-337-4

N° 6 Sabrina Tricaud, *L'entourage de Georges Pompidou (1962-1974). Institutions, Hommes et Pratiques*, 2014, 453 p, ISBN 978-2-87574-128-8

N° 7 Frédéric Fogacci, Cédric Francille, Gilles Le Béguec (dir.), *L'élection présidentielle de 1969*, 2016, 266 p, ISBN 978-2-87574-341-1

N° 8 Mathieu Flonneau, Christine Manigand (dir.), *Georges Pompidou et une certaine idée de la France heureuse*, 2018, ISBN 978-2-8076-0845-0

N° 9 Frédéric Tristram et Gilles Le Béguec (dir.), *Penser l'avenir au temps de Georges Pompidou*, 2018, ISBN 978-2-8076-0881-8

N° 10 Gilles Le Béguec, Émilia Robin, Nicolas Rousselier (dir.), *Léo Hamon (1908-1993)*, 2018, ISBN 978-2-8076-0948-8

N° 11 Christine Manigand et Olivier Sibre (dir.) avec la participation de Cédric Francille, *Jean-Bernard Raimond, un diplomate en politique*, 2020, ISBN 978-2-8076-1327-0

N° 12 Christine Manigand et Olivier Sibre (dir.), *Georges Pompidou, Robert Poujade et les défis de l'environnement. Le « ministère de l'impossible »*, 2023, ISBN 978-2-87574-736-5

N° 13 Christine Manigand et Pascal Griset (dir.), *La santé publique sous Georges Pompidou. Politique, recherche et société (1962-1974)*, 2024, ISBN 978-3-0343-4933-8

N° 14 Bruno Poucet et Philippe Nivet (dir.), *Georges Pompidou et l'éducation*, 2025, ISBN 978-3-0343-5501-8

N° 15 Olivier Sibre (ed.), *Franco-British relations and Europe, from EEC membership to Brexit. Georges Pompidou and Edward Heath*, 2026, 226p., ISBN 978-3-0343-6240-5

www.peterlang.com

www.ingramcontent.com/pod-product-compliance
Ingram Content Group UK Ltd.
Pitfield, Milton Keynes, MK11 3LW, UK
UKHW020710041026
15590UKWH00002B/588

9 783034 362405